The North-East Diaries

The North-East Diaries

A Funny Thing Happened in Blyth

J.R. Bates

Names may have been changed to conceal the identity
of certain characters in the book.

Copyright © 2022 by J.R. Bates

FIRST EDITION

ISBNs:
Paperback: 978-1-80227-861-3
eBook: 978-1-80227-862-0

http://www.jrbates-author.co.uk

Contents

Introduction

A Funny Thing Happened in Blyth - is part memoir and part fiction about childhood and growing up in a northern industrial community. It is a remembrance of the pit town of Blyth during the first three years of the 1960s, when children roamed the streets, and made their own entertainment. Christmas excitement, Guy Fawkes night, blackberry week, juvenile rivalries, football matches, running away from home and school life all feature in this entertaining tale of a 60s rite of passage.

Characters appear and reappear in many of the chapters and they are held together by the central character and narrator, Sidney (Hawky) Brown, a young lad going through his junior school and first grammar school years in the town. Hawky and his coterie of acquaintances are, or were, real people and the stories are predominantly real-life incidents but the dialogue, now poorly recalled, has for the main part been summoned-up as close to truth as memory permits, and is used as the springboard for many of the events.

The older members of Hawky's family and other adults in his life are viewed from the boy's perspective in passages shot through with misinterpretations and frustrated expectations. The odyssey from innocence to worldliness starts here. Hawky edges towards a yearned for maturity through revealing encounters, blunders and an eventual success (passing his eleven plus) that his peers try to turn into another kind of failure. We leave him in his second year of grammar school facing a new phase of his life with a trace of uncertainty and a thread of hope.

The narrator at times is a curious observer of the supposedly adult world. Several of the more public real-life events of the time (such as the lining up of the planets 1962, Tristan da Cunha, the Berlin Wall, the birth of the Beatles, and the smallpox outbreak) are perceived through the eyes of Hawky.

Names have been changed only for embarrassing incidents – or as they used to say in 'Dragnet' – 'and to protect the innocent'.

Local People in the Book

Sidney (Hawky) Brown - Alan (Titch) Irving - Ian (Ashy) Ash - Stan Fowler – Ronnie Armstrong – Charlie Chuck – John (Chinny) Nelson – PC Marnock – Buglass (farmer) – Marjorie (Mrs) Brown – Linda Brown – Kenny Brown – Ken Robinson – Mr Harrison (teacher at Forster School) – Billy the Baker – John Norris – Jim (Batesy) Bates – Bill Taggart – Charlie Chuck – His wife Martha – Helena (Martha's sister) – George (Willick) Wilkinson – Balmer twins – John Norris – Mona (dinner lady) – Bella Gang (and there were many of you) – Trude – Connors – Roly Forman – Doctor Campbell – Derek Raisbeck – Mr Hunter (teacher at Morpeth Road school) – Michael Lamb – Alan Lawton – Fred Douglas – Mr Tweddle (headmaster Morpeth Road) – Andy Reid – Mrs Bates (Batesy's mam) – Sylvia Connor – Bowman – Carol Thompson – Milly McClair – Olive McClair – Ray Lindores – Mickey Linney – Tilmouth – Jimmy Riddell – Mrs Winters (Hallside) – Linda Winters – Brian (Billy) Long – Bill Long – June Marshall – Linda Maddison – Jennifer Minter – Irene Smallman (Curry) – Davey Preston – Julie Harris – Harry Thompson – Mary-Jane Thompson – Tommy Forman – Lilla Forman - Lynn Forman – Scone (Laidlaw) – Jim White – Wally Anderson

– Mick Murphy – Jack Jennings – Irene Cummings – Bobby Cummings – Miss Brown (teacher) – John Charlton – Alan Potter – Tom McDougall – Keith McNeil – Wilf Rees – Danny McCluskey – Norman Hills – Malcolm Allsopp – Jim Bates (Batesy's dad) – Malcolm Gaskin – Marjorie Luke – Apologies to those I've missed or overlooked.

Various teachers with nicknames (BGS) have been named also – and the boys' first rollcall for 1 North form 1962 but only surnames. Allsopp, Atkinson, Bates, Brown, Brownbridge, Charlton, Curry, Godfrey, Harrison, Hurford, Lough, McCluskey, Morey, Polwarth, Preston, Walker...... and a lad called Wilkin, who had managed to attach himself to the wrong class.

Events in this Book

Most of the events/happenings in this book are real life events. Any which would be embarrassing to the person concerned have been name changed. Some are partly fictitious – the 'Who's Charlie Hurley' being the main one but based on a real event. The Easter Egg event also but once again name-changed. The others are as remembered with some, but very few name changes. If anyone has been named in one of the passages and they don't remember the same train of events, my apologies for a memory of 60 years ago now dimly recalled but written to the best of my ability. You won't be named in anything controversial in the book. Then there was The Bella Gang/Cowpen Gang... how silly were we? But no knives, or guns or grudges... I hope, otherwise you won't buy my book. This is a young lad's take on life as we lived it then... and hopefully our kids and grandkids can experience something similar... it was a good existence. Thank you for reading!

Many Thanks to –

Lorraine Bates – for pushing me to complete the book.

Sid (Hawky) Brown - for the original idea and collaboration (RIP Sid)

Brian Long – for the support and ideas (Who's Charlie Hurley), And for m/s critique.

Stephen Chicken - for the original BGS teachers photo.

Alan Dickson – for the original front cover artwork (much appreciated).

David (Doog) Harrison – for taking the time to read through the initial transcript.

Irene Curry – for taking the time to read through the initial transcript.

Scott (project manager) – for guidance and help throughout the publishing process.

And all the North-east folk, past and present who make that part of the country so unique.

Sid Brown's Tale

Here Comes Sid, The Cowpen Kid

His name was Charlie Chuck, and he was the best of men, and some say the worst of men. To paraphrase 'A Tale of Two Cities' seems the best way to describe the man who had such a profound influence on my life, albeit for such a short period of time. Truth be told he still influences the way I live my life now.

This is my story...and partly his.

My name is Sid Brown, or Sidney Hawky Brown as one of my newfound Cowpen Estate friends christened me on my arrival in Blyth in December 1960; the Hawky emerging because of my Scottish roots, and my friend's mispronunciation of 'Och aye the noo' which became 'Hawkeye the noo', and then rapidly just Hawky.

The circumstances surrounding our family's move from Scotland to Northumberland are all a bit of a blur. Born in June 1951 I lived my formative years in Kirkcaldy, which is in Fife, but my mother and father split up while my dad was involved with the new mine which was due to open in 1960. I didn't see him regularly anyway, as he was always working, or in the pub, or at the bookies, and those early memories are all of mam crying, or desperately trying to scrape together enough money to feed myself and my brother and sister... and afterwards, the shouts and arguments when we kids were in bed...the sudden silence, and the door slamming, and then the lonely sobbing from the front room.

Unfortunately, they are my memories of Kirkcaldy during those bleak years, but I wish they could have been more positive, because it's such a fantastic place, as I discovered many years later. Sadly, they're not, and I think subconsciously I must have blotted out such a lot. I know my brother and sister did.

One cold winter's day, unexpectedly and suddenly, with a flurry of activity involving a removal lorry, suitcases and carrier bags, my mother, my siblings, and I were transported from Fife to Cowpen Estate, Blyth, and a council house in Hallside. How this all transpired, and how we ended up there, is still a mystery today, but this was the beginning of my new journey...a journey with its ups and downs, but nevertheless a journey I would remember fondly for the rest of my life. I was a young lad, trying to make my mark in a strange environment, attempting to adapt to a strange, and unique Northumbrian culture, and trying with all my might to just be accepted as one of the lads in the Blyth that existed in those first few exciting years of the 1960s.

If you don't believe some of what follows, well...I don't blame you, I would be dubious too, and I lived through it, but, to the best of my recollection, the following story is how it all materialized.

CHAPTER 1

Red Rocks

There were four of us, exploring a wasteland known as Red Rocks and looking for the famed acid bath, a lake of viscid fluid, into which it was rumoured, a lad called Ronnie Armstrong had lost his welly when jumping over it. Reputedly, that pool of acid had dissolved every bit of the welly, apart from the heel. The quartet in the gathering were, myself, Titch Irving, Ian Ash, and a stocky dark-haired kid called Stan Fowler whom I'd never met before.

We searched far and wide for what seemed an age, hunting high and low for the fabled acid bath, exploring out almost as far as Horton, and all the areas in-between. We had little joy in our search, so we spent a pleasant half-hour on the return leg frog catching at the timber pond. Eventually, all four of us, now tired and thirsty, we decided to call it a day, and concluded that the acid bath was an urban myth. We headed for home.

Half an hour later though, we were hiding nervously behind a huge mound of crumbling rocks. The rocks were actually compressed coal waste, masquerading as boulders, and they absolutely stank of sulphur, or something equally noxious. Red Rocks was where the surrounding mines had deposited the spoil that was dug out from the ground and because it wasn't coal, it was dumped, and heaped, and left to blacken and disfigure the landscape.

From where we were hiding ourselves, we could see in the near distance the humped back of the monster that was the Bella Pit Heap, the largest of the local mountains of colliery detritus, and it loomed menacingly over Cowpen Estate and the Isabella Colliery houses. At that precise moment however, we were frightened, all four of us, for down below, in the strip of land that hunkered up against the rail line that ran from Newsham to Bebside, we'd spotted a shifty looking man, wearing a military combat jacket...and he was burying a dead dog.

"Titch, what should we do?" Stan whispered nervously.

Although by far the smallest of the group, Titch was nevertheless our leader, because he knew everything, and I mean absolutely everything; he was our oracle. Whatever you asked him, he knew, instantly...without a shadow of doubt, without any hesitation, and because of that vast storeroom of knowledge, he took his rightful place as head of this mini gang.

Titch had been the first to discover where bairns came from...which to be fair, we'd all heard rumours about. However, and this was the clincher, he also told us he knew how they were put there in the first place. Personally, I was dubious about the 'how they got there' information. It wasn't logical, it was rude, and, let's be honest, I couldn't imagine the Queen doing that, or mam and dad and all our neighbours, doing what Titch said...I just wasn't convinced.

The information didn't seem plausible, but I didn't dare question him about it.

But the reality was that he knew other impressive things, like how the Germans had lost the war. He told us it was because Hitler and his best friend Mr Himmler only had one testicle, and another German friend called Gerbils didn't have any at all. That's how they were beaten.... Titch declared, they ran out of testicles, and the British army even had a song about it. If any doubters existed, or, if proof be needed, Titch announced, the evidence was in the Albert Hall.

I didn't know what testicles were, and didn't want to show my ignorance, so, in the innocent acceptance of Titch's superior intellect, I just assumed they must have been tanks or fighter planes, maybe even aircraft carriers.

Subsequent developments convinced me that it must have been true, because my mam gave me a good telling off when I asked her about Hitler's testicle. She seemed shocked and wanted to know who had been filling my head with horrible stories like that. Her reaction confirmed the truth of it. It put me in a difficult situation. I couldn't incriminate Titch, so, reluctantly, fingers crossed behind my back, I told her that the culprit was someone called Chinny Nelson. I'd never even spoken to the lad, didn't know who he was or what he looked like, but I remembered Titch talking about him, and the name was so distinctive. Mam told me never to play with him again...no problem, I didn't.

Our immediate predicament, however, remained serious. Still on lookout, and with the rest of his gang eyeing him nervously, Titch pondered the situation for a moment, then, mind made up, crawled in red Indian fashion to the peak of the pile of rocks for a better look. After a few long moments, with Titch silently assessing our options, the difficult situation suddenly morphed into a crisis.

"Bliddy hell," was the cry, as he cursed, and then came slithering down the rubble stack, on his backside. "It's Charlie Chuck, aahmm not kiddin', and he just saw me," he said in a panicked voice. "He probably saw all of us, we'd better make a run for it...if he's killed a dog, he could kill us an' all, cos we're witnesses."

We were all frightened now, but Titch, in leadership mode, swiftly took command of the situation.

"We should split up just in case he comes up here and tries to surround us," he said. "Stan, you and Ashy go that way," he ordered, pointing in the general direction of Bebside, "run as fast as you can, and don't get caught".

They looked terrified but didn't need to be told twice. Ashy and Stan set off at a breakneck lick, both crouching down so as not to be seen from below. Within a few seconds they'd disappeared into one of the innumerable hollows and gullies which punctuated the mounds of waste, with just the occasional glimpse of a bobbing head as they ran away towards Bebside. I glanced uneasily at Titch. I was nervous myself and could have done with some reassurance, but none was forthcoming. I'd never seen him frightened before, but he was shaking.

"You're the fastest Sid...if he catches me go straight to the police, PC Marnock, and tell him everything that happened." He was scaring me now because he was serious. "Let's get moving, we'll run the opposite way, towards Newsham, he can't follow both ways at once and catch all of us, and if we escape, then we'll head over the railway line and make for the Bella."

We ran and ran, desperately, like antelopes evading danger, leaping over depressions in the ground, scrambling up inclines, fear pushing us on, as though our lives depended on it, until, after a few minutes that seemed like hours, both of us out of breath we slumped down, behind a mound, panting and sucking in air.

We lay on the black and grey slag of the coalmine waste, trying to get our breath back. Then, after a minute or two of silence and with my breathing back to normal I asked, almost apologetically.

"Who's this Charlie Chuck bloke then?"

Titch was still panting and took another few moments to sort his breathing out.

When he replied he had a look of disbelief on his face.

"You're kiddin', right?...Everybody knows who he is. He's the bloke that killed loads of people in the war, all with his bare hands...or a dagger..." Titch had become animated. "He even used a great big sword that he made himself in his workshop, and then, when it broke, and he had no weapons left, he killed someone with a pencil; stuck it right in his eye." he made a jabbing gesture like a diminutive Zorro. "Squidged it round and round, right into his brainbox." He paused and looked puzzled. "Surely your mam and dad must have told you to keep away from him?"

I didn't know what to say, being unacquainted with Blyth folklore. I just shrugged.

"Mam doesn't know much about Cowpen yet, you know. We've only been in Blyth since Christmas.

5

"Your dad must have heard about Charlie Chuck though, surely?"

I shrugged, "I haven't got a dad...well I mean I have got a dad," I elaborated, 'but he doesn't live here with us". The conversation had just become personal, and I wasn't comfortable.

"Why not?" Titch asked, like a dog with a bone. "Is he poorly or summat?"

It took me a few moments to respond. My brief hesitation wasn't due to ignorance, but to embarrassment. Everyone should have a dad, but I didn't, at least not a one to boast about. Some kids that I knew, had dads who were dead, and they talked about them with pride. I couldn't, because mine wasn't, and pride wasn't something I felt, so I was on the defensive.

"No, he isn't poorly, at least I don't think so." I paused for a few seconds; I was uncomfortable, to be in a conversation about my dad. Then it all came tumbling out - pent up anger, it wasn't anyone's fault, certainly not mine or Titch's.

"It's 'cos me mam says he's a total waste of space...okay!... he goes to the pub and drinks beer all the time and loses all his money on the horses or the dogs or playing cards. Sometimes he spends money on a fancy woman; that's why mam left him and came to Cowpen. He wasn't very nice to me mam...he was a fat pig, and he used to knock her about, and didn't care about me and my brother and sister, but don't you dare tell anyone Titch...or I'll bash you one."

There was no immediate reply. An uneasy silence. Titch kept his head down, deciding how to respond, and when he did, he sounded annoyed and disappointed.

"You're my pal Sid, I wouldn't say anything to anyone, but don't ever say you'll bash me again.... 'cos 'aahhmm' not yer dad, and aahh' didn't do any of that bad stuff, so I'll fight you if you want."

He would have, too...he was a gutsy kid.

That wasn't the exact moment we became friends, but it was a starter and I realised in that instant I needed to find an apology of some sort, without appearing feeble.

I said, "Sorry Titch, I don't want to fight you...I just don't want anybody to know about me dad and all that stuff. Me mam had a stinkin' time and so did me brother and sister, and me an' all. If anybody found out she'd go mental."

Titch gave me an elbow jab... "Naebody will ever find oot from me," he winked, and we both smiled at each other. "Aahvv nivvor heard anybody say sorry afore."

We laughed. Titch was concerned that I still had too much of my Fife accent, and he'd been trying to teach me how to speak Geordie...or Blyth, and to be honest he wasn't a great teacher, and I wasn't a fast learner.

"Worraboot Charlie Chuck? D'ya think he'll folly us?" I asked, with a speculative stab at Blyth speak.

Titch couldn't help but smile at my attempt, and grimace at the same time. "Not now, I don't think so...we can just wait here for a bit, listen for any noises...I hope he didn't recognise me."

"Anybody as ugly as you would be easy to recognise," I joked.

Tich laughed.... "Are you talking to me or to a mirror?"

I liked Titch...he was...different.

We sat for a while, not talking, just listening for sounds of pursuit, none came. Then Titch broke the silence.

"Who's your favourite singer?" asked Titch.

"Why?"

"Cos aah want to know what me mate likes."

It was a question to which I'd never given much thought. I didn't really have a favourite, but I quite liked being called a mate, so I pulled a name out of my head.

"Adam Faith."

"Ya kiddin', right?...Poor me, fell doon the lavatory... someone came and pulled the chain and aah went a shootin' doon the drain." Titch perfectly parodied the Adam Faith song 'Poor Me' and we both fell about laughing, giggling like little girls.

"So, who's yours?"

"My what?"

"Favourite singer." Titch seemed surprised, and hesitated.

"Don't laugh...right? Aah' like Lonnie Donegan..."

We both started singing... "Well in 1814 we took a little trip, along wi' Colonel Packin down the mighty Mississip, we took a little bacon, and we took a little beans, and we fought the bloomin' British at the town of New Orleans."

We knew all the words to the popular songs. It was good fun and Lonnie Donegan was the biggest name in skiffle at that time.

The song had always puzzled me though.

"Who do you reckon Colonel Packin was Titch?"

It was his turn to shrug, looking uncomfortable. "How do I know, I don't know everything...it's a song, it's probably just a made-up name, it's not proper history or stuff like that."

That comment came as a surprise because Titch was the smartest kid in Cowpen and usually would have trotted out an answer without hesitation.

I thought his response over for a few seconds, then said, "It could be though, couldn't it? 'Cos why else would Lonnie make up a name like that? He could just have made up a name like Colonel Smith or General Thompson or summat, and why was he singing about a battle at New Orleans with the bloomin' British if it isn't true?...so I think it probably is, Titch. It's probably something that happened in history that he's going on about."

"Aahh divvent' knaa' man, aahh divven't care if it's proper history or not, but knowin' you, you'll probably go to the library the morra' to find oot. You've always got your nose stuck in a book,...okay Sid. Don't be a smart arse it's just a song man, naebody cares if it's real or not?"

"Yeh, but Titch think about it. We'll be taking the eleven plus next year; we might need this history stuff to pass the exam and get to grammar school. What if there's a question in there about Colonel Packin?"

"Don't be daft," said Titch, "There won't be questions like that; they'll be about sums and spellin', and anyway, me and you won't go to grammar school - it isn't for us; it's for doctor's kids and suchlike."

I didn't like disagreeing with Titch, but this time I had to. He was wrong.

"No, it's not," I replied, feeling strongly about it. "Honest, Titch, me mam told me. It's for everybody now, man. Me mam says that the Labour party have made a law so that anybody can go to hospital for free, you know; you don't have to pay the doctor anymore, like used to happen before the war, when the Tories done it, and they've done another law that says anybody can go to grammar School even if you're poor, if you're clever enough Titch. It's not just for rich folks and their kids. You and me can go there if we try. You're good at school, at sums an' that."

"That won't happen, we'll be going to PLR...or Bebside, that's just the way it is." Titch turned away with a gesture of finality.

He turned back, "Don't try to be better than what we are man, doesn't matter what anybody says, we're still council house kids, and grammar school will always be for the rich kids in the big houses down Broadway or them people in the new houses on Leeches estate".

There was no more to be said.

"Anyway, I'm goin' in the army when I leave school... you don't need grammar school for that. You don't need to be good at sums and spellin' to fight Japs."

Titch seemed quite adamant, so I changed the subject.

"Which way should we go home?"

The question energized him; he was back in control.

An hour later I was back at my own kitchen door. During the trek home, Titch and I had traversed a mucky stream which Titch told me was called the Yeller Babby, crossed the railway line, ran across Buglass - the farmer's tatie field, climbed the Bella heap, and up over the top, slithered down the other side and then ducked into the cut that led into Hallside. Titch took leave of me then with a dig of his elbow and shot off at a pace towards his own house on Dene View

Drive, wishing to avoid going anywhere near Devonworth which was where Charlie Chuck lived.

It felt like I'd reached a precious sanctuary when I finally stood outside our house, and I breathed a sigh of relief. Danger over.

I opened the back door slowly, closed it and moved quietly across the kitchen. Then I just about jumped out of my skin.

"And where do you think you've been?" Mam was standing in the passage beside the coalhouse, still with her pinny on, arms folded. Folded arms were an ominous sign. "Err mm, I've been playing with Titch Irving and some other lads," I said, nervously, trying with all my might to avoid looking directly at mam. I couldn't tell her the truth about the dead dog and the escape.

Mam didn't seem impressed.

"And how did your shoes get in that state? They're your school shoes...look at them! Do you think I'm made of money?"

I looked down. I hadn't realised what a mess my feet were in. My shoes and socks were covered in a greenish yellow gunge with black bits of coal dust and there were dirty footmarks from the back door to where I stood. I looked up, mam's hand came up, and hovered. I shrank back. She was furious with me...but the hand fell back to her side. She had never hit us...well at least never very hard, but I realised I had been on the verge of a good whacking.

"Get those off now." she pointed to my shoes, "and your socks and pants, and get upstairs into the bath".

"It's not Sunday mam...it's not bath night."

She was breathing heavily.

"Just do as you're told. I've had the fire on, there's some hot water. Run a few inches and stand in the bath and get those feet and legs washed."

I pulled off the socks and shoes, left them on the kitchen floor and retreated quickly upstairs. "And make sure you're properly clean before you use the towel; I don't want any dirty marks on it," she shouted up the stairs...mam was not at all happy.

Twenty minutes later, feet now completely clean and clad in football socks I came downstairs as quietly as I could. Some of the stairs were squeaky but I knew which ones to avoid, and when to hang on to the banister. I made it down without a noise, not wanting to attract attention to myself.

I could hear mam and my sister Linda in the living room. They were watching telly; Come Dancing was on. Mam had saved money from her cleaning jobs, and she'd rented our first television. One of our neighbours who worked at the shipyard had to sign the agreement for the telly, and mam had to pay him the money every week. Only men, with regular jobs were allowed to sign agreements.

I loved the telly. I used to rush home after school to watch anything that was on at teatime: Popeye was a favourite, and Wacky Jacky but if it was one of the cowboys I was in heaven. The Range Rider, Lone Ranger, Wagon Train, The Cisco Kid...Oh those were the fellas, gunslingers all.

Linda was almost as tall as me, although three years younger, and was very close to mam. My older brother Kenny was six years older, and he had joined the army. He was terribly unhappy when we came to Blyth; he didn't fit in, he spoke with a broad Fife accent, and wouldn't change. He ended up fighting, on an almost daily basis. So, he'd pestered mam for weeks, to let him join the forces, pleading with her. Finally, her resistance crumbled, and she signed the forms to say he could take the Queen's shilling and join the Junior Leaders boy's army. That's where he was now, and he was living on his army base in Surrey...somewhere way down south. Mind you, he did write home a few times a month to let mam know how he was doing. He never took the time to write to me though.

Mam and Linda were oohing and aahing at the dancing on the telly as the ladies in their puffed-up dresses twirled around the floor, their smiling male partners with Brylcreemed hair, black suits and bow ties, looking for all the world like penguins.

I slithered into the living room, trying to be invisible. I noticed that mam had a length of old sheet in front of her on the carpet and she was cleaning the shoes I'd made such a mess of.

I quietly sat down on the armchair, beside the coffee table, still unnoticed. I leafed through the local newspaper, the Blyth News, feigning interest in the various articles. No acknowledgement from mam, my invisibility ruse was working. I kept turning the pages and eventually found something worthwhile on the sports pages and began reading about the Spartans pre-season friendly football match last Saturday against Darlington reserves.

Mam turned from the couch, duster, and polish tin in hand. She'd calmed down and didn't look at all angry now.

"There's half a crown on the kitchen bench for you Sid."

That was a surprise! What had I done to deserve that? Mam didn't have any money to be chucking about.

"Half a crown, for me...what for Mam? I told you I don't need any pocket money, you can't afford it, and anyway I'll have some odd jobs soon so I can help out."

"You're a good lad, Sid." Mam smiled. I liked it when she smiled because she was still nice looking, unlike some of the other kids' mothers. One of the lads up the other end of the street had a mother who looked like Old Mother Riley, and she shouted at you for nothing, screamed at you, when you passed her house. She was a bit nutty...and very, very scary.

"The money isn't from me," said mam, "somebody came while you were out. I'd told him about you wanting some odd jobs. He said if you're looking to make some pocket money he can help. There's some garden work for you, and some other things that he needs doing. He left half a crown...and said you'd get the other half when you've finished the jobs."

Wow....five bob, I'd only begun asking around a few days ago.

"Who is it mam? Is it Mr Harrison or Mr Winters? It must be someone around here... one of the neighbours?" I was beginning to feel rather proud of myself.

"No Sid, it's nobody from Hallside. It's one of the houses where I do some cleaning. The address is beside the money; they're nice people so be on your best behaviour, okay." Mam had a lot of little cleaning jobs and knew a lot of people.

"Ok mam, where do I have to go?"

"Devonworth, you know, over behind the Store, the big circle street. The number is on the paper."

My heart sank, Devonworth was where...where Titch said the dog murderer lived, surely it couldn't be one of the houses near to him, could it? What if he recognised me, walking past his house? What should I do?

"Devonworth, mam I've got loads of stuff to do tomorrow, I'll go next week."

Mam stopped dead in her tracks and turned to face me, suspicious. "What loads of stuff?" she looked at me quizzically. "That's news to me," she brought her right hand up to her face with her index finger over her lips, I knew from experience that gesture meant she didn't believe me.

The following silence was unnerving, then she ended it.

"You'll go tomorrow Sid." Mam wasn't asking, she was telling. "You can't ask people for jobs and then refuse them. You'll end up with a reputation for letting people down. Folk will start to think you're not reliable. It's not like you Sid. What on earth is the matter with you?"

"Nowt mam, nowt." I had to think quickly, my brain was working overtime and I was about to tell mam a lie again.

"It's just that I said I'd play for Titch's team over on the Cowpen fields tomorrow. Some lads are coming from Lindsay Avenue for a footy game - it's Titch's team against Ken Robinson's team and I'm in goal."

Mam's finger left her lips, and her arm dropped to her side. She believed me.

"Well, I suppose you are on your summer holidays...I'm cleaning at his house tomorrow; I'll tell Charlie you'll be there on Saturday without fail...okay?"

"Okay mam, thanks." The name Charlie was the clincher. Now I was terrified. I was hoping that there were some clean shorts in my drawer.

I tossed and turned all that night, all manner of horrible scenarios playing out in my mind. Then the following day, having laid down the lie, it had to be followed through. I needed to hide myself away for the whole afternoon so that mam would think I'd been playing football. The very idea of having to go anywhere near Charlie Chuck's house terrified me. What if he saw me...and started chasing me with a pencil?

I headed for Blyth, knowing mam wouldn't be working there today, and wandered aimlessly around the Crofton area, the old pit and around Park Road. Then, a wander down to Ridley Park, killing time, watching some lads playing on the putting green, Arnold Palmers in the making. There's only so long you can feign interest in someone knocking a ball into a hole with a stick, before your head clags up, and mine clagged up pretty quickly. So, I decided to have a mosey around the import dock Security was non-existent, no-one questioned my presence. The import dock was where some of the older lads used to go cigarette scrounging and buy papieros from the predominantly Polish sailors. The sailors wanted foreign currency and sold their cigarettes ridiculously cheaply. Blyth was awash at that time with Carmen, Spike, and Pall Mall cigarettes from the foreign sailors.

Cigarettes didn't interest me, which made the import dock boring, so I headed aimlessly for the other side of town, just killing time, and walked as far as the chain ferry.

I spent best part of an hour watching it clank back and forward across the river to Cambois, then back again, the occasional passenger disembarking. Most were walking, but some, pushing bicycles, and one really old bloke with a motorbike, a great big, old black and green thing with 'Matchless' picked out in paint on the fuel tank. I watched him for a few minutes, after he'd left the ferry. He was jumping up and down on a foot-pedal, waggling his hand on the grip at the same time and attempting to get the thing started. Then...'Yahoo'...he managed it, the motor, coughing and spluttering into life. Then, with a look of triumph, he donned a leather helmet that made him look like a fighter pilot and zipped happily away down Hodgson's Road.

Immediately after that, a moment of excitement - a fight outside the Golden Fleece pub. Two big blokes, shouting and cursing and punching lumps out of each other. It was all over in a matter of minutes, and then the protagonists headed back into the pub together, arms around each other's shoulders, as if nothing had happened.

After a while, deciding I'd wasted enough time, and scuffing my shoes, so it looked like I'd been playing football, I headed for home.

Tomorrow I was going to the house of the dog murderer... the man who had killed hundreds of people in the war... and someone who might remember a young lad from Red Rocks.

That Friday night, for the first time ever outside of a church or school...I said a little prayer: "Please God, don't let Charlie Chuck kill me, 'cos me mam can't afford a funeral."

CHAPTER 2

Charlie Chuck

———————————◆———————————

Sometimes Friday nights can really drag when you're looking forward to Saturday's adventures, a mosey down to Blyth beach for a game of pirates on the big concrete ship, then a "who can go highest on the swings" game or showing off on the monkey bars. But if the weather wasn't great.... a day out around Blyth market and, funds permitting, a bottle of pop at Seghini's cafe. That Friday night was different; it whizzed by, and no sooner had my head hit the pillow than my eyes fluttered open to the tapping on my bedroom door. Mam, informing me that breakfast was ready, and I needed to hurry up. Sunshine flooded through the thin curtains at my bedroom window, but I didn't feel sunny, I was feeling decidedly overcast. Dressing as quickly as I could, I headed downstairs, with a burgeoning feeling of dread.

Mam was at the sink washing the saucepan. Saturday breakfast was invariably porridge. I wasn't best pleased with porridge, because it stopped me achieving top marks in a spelling competition at my last school. I'd spelt it porage. Why, you might ask? Because that is precisely how it is spelt on Scott's Porage Oats boxes. I was annoyed with Scott's for not being able to spell correctly, and annoyed with my teacher, Mr Harrison, who wouldn't accept my spelling as correct. I missed out on a prize. It was probably just as well that I was starting afresh at my new school next term and not returning to Forster.

"Come on Sid, hurry up, you're being really slow. Charlie's expecting you at nine-thirty. Please don't be late."

"Okay mam," I was shovelling hot, claggy porridge into my mouth as fast as was possible for a ten-year old. Mam must have run out of milk. Saturday's porridge was usually milky white and nicely warm, not thick, grey, and hot like today's offering.

"Charlie says you can have some sandwiches at his house at dinnertime. I'll make your tea for five o'clock... we're having sausage and chips, all right?"

"Okay mam," I didn't like to tell her that it would probably be wasted, as I'd most likely be dead by then, and buried beside a dog. I didn't even ask her not to buy the cheap Co-op sausages, because they were full of water, and used to spit and hiss in the frying pan and tasted like squelchy cardboard. I couldn't be bothered, I had more serious things on my mind.

"I'm off now Sid. I've got the pub and the council offices to clean today. Linda is at Mrs Winter's house until I get back. Don't forget to lock the door on your way out."

"Righto mam." ...the door clicked shut, she was gone, and I was on my own.

Do I go...or do I stay...? I was in a Catch 22 situation, I was frightened to go, and frightened no to. The conflicting thoughts were battling each other inside my head. If I go, I'll end up dead, if I don't go mam will kill me anyway. Stay or go, - go or stay...what to do?

Mam had a favourite saying, "There's no point worrying, what's going to happen will happen whether you worry about it or not...so why worry".

With this thought in mind, I drew a deep breath, put on my jacket, and decided that I would face my last day on earth with as much bravery as I could muster. I'd left a note on my bed for mam to find which said, "It was Charlie Chuck that did it". No histrionics, just straight to the point.

I checked my door key on the string around my neck, put the latch on the front door, left by the back door, locking it as I left. Then with a purpose I set off for Devonworth Place and the home of Charlie Chuck. I had the half-crown in my pocket, and I fully intended to give my mam two bob of it, but I was in real need of a bar of chocolate as my final treat, or maybe a bag of midget gems, or even a few bars of cinder toffee. When you have money in your pocket the permutation of choices is endless. Decisions, decisions.

I had about five minutes to spare when I reached the Co-op on Brierley Road.

No-one except myself called it the Co-op, it was known to everyone as the Store.

The Store had its own Store Milkmen, Store Butchers, Store Bakers, all in their little vans, and local life revolved around these indispensable folk. One of mam's treasured treats when money wasn't too tight, was a vanilla slice from Billy the baker's van when he pulled up on our street.

The Store was an important part of all our lives, and everything seemed to revolve around it. My mam had a number which she had to say every time she bought anything at the store, and they gave you a little ticket. Every so often the tickets were counted up and mam would get a cash dividend, depending on how much money she had spent.

I nipped into the store and spent eightpence on my sweets. I had to wait in line behind a few early shoppers to pay my money over. The man in front of me had a whole pile of groceries to be totted up. I wondered why he was doing the shopping when that should have been his wife's job, then thought, maybe he lives on his own. Sometimes I just overthought things; mam would tell me repeatedly to stop overthinking and start overdoing instead, but I couldn't help it. Of course, it could be that his wife goes to work, and he's on the dole, or on night shift; maybe she's just bigger than him and he's frightened of her. Sometimes I needed to switch my brain off.

Finally, it was the man's turn and he paid, packed his purchases into two shopping bags, and made his way out. I handed over my half crown and gratefully accepted the sweets and the change, making sure to say thank you. Mam's rules: please and thank you cost nothing, make sure you distribute them freely. There was something reassuring about the chinking sound a pocket full of silver and copper makes, and you could count your money just by feeling the shape of the coins. Happier now, I shoved my sweets into my jacket pocket and headed for my date with destiny in Devonworth.

It had taken longer than expected at the store, so I started to jog, passing the man who had been in front of me at the till.

"Hey, young fella," I heard the voice boom behind me and knew instinctively it was intended for me. I stopped and turned to face the voice.

"You have drop this." He was holding up something in a white wrapper.

I patted my jacket pocket - sure enough, my cinder toffee was missing. 'How clumsy was that' I thought to myself.

"Thanks mister,", I said, gratefully accepting the returned bar from the outstretched hand.

"Why you in so much rush?" asked the man in a very strange accent. I immediately noticed he had missed his articles. Mam had been teaching me about articles and something called determiners...she was clever at English, and I hadn't understood it all, but it did make me notice that this man had dropped some of his.

"I have to get to someone's house to do some jobs. It's someone me mam knows so I can't be late." I turned to jog away.

"What number is house you go for jobs?"

I didn't know whether to tell him or not. Maybe I shouldn't even be doing jobs, and perhaps he would tell someone. Maybe he would get my mam into trouble with the government or the family allowance.

I turned to face him and gestured vaguely over to Devonworth. "Just over there."

"What is number of house you go?" He seemed very insistent.

Against my better judgement I told him.

He seemed pleased and he chuckled, "Aah, that's okay then, you are Marjorie's son; it is my house you are headed for. I am a little late myself. We will walk together."

It was the weirdest thing, now suddenly his English was perfect, and he wasn't dropping articles anymore, and he knew my mam's name was Marjorie.

Then the penny dropped. I was walking along with Charlie Chuck. Multiple murderer and dog destroyer. He wasn't wearing the combat jacket anymore; that's why I hadn't recognised him. We walked in silence for a short while.

"You're very quiet Sid." He knew my name!

"Your mother says you are always talking and asking questions."

I don't know why the words suddenly came out of my mouth, it was totally involuntary; perhaps I was annoyed that mam had been talking about me to strangers, and that spurred me into throwing caution to the wind. Maybe it was sheer fear, or I had a death wish and just wanted some truth. I can't honestly remember.

"Are you Charlie Chuck that killed lots of people in the war?"

We carried on walking. He didn't answer the question. He thought awhile then asked one of his own.

"Are you one of the boys who ran away when you saw me burying my dog?"

He had recognised me from the other evening. Now I was in for it, but strangely enough I was feeling courageous.

"Yes."

"Why did you run away?" There was no hint of a threat in his voice.

"Well...because you were burying a dog. Why would you do that?" I wasn't frightened now; in fact, I was having an outbreak of bravery, bordering on heroism. "Only a very bad person would kill a dog?"

The man stopped for a moment deep in thought, scratching at the stubble on his chin, I felt for a few moments that he was scanning my face with his piercing blue eyes, then, mind made up...he began...

"I'll tell you a little story," then he hesitated again, framing his words. "It was my precious dog, Bruno, you saw me burying...no, no that's not right...not just my dog, but also my best friend. He was with me from 1946, a puppy I rescued from being drowned...not wanted by anyone. I saved his life, and he lived with me all these years until he died?"

"You didn't kill him?" I looked at the man as I asked the question. He had tears in his eyes. He took a hanky out of his pocket and wiped at his nose.

"No, I didn't;" it may be difficult for you to believe, but Bruno knew that I had saved him. I don't know why I know that, or how I know that, but I do. Bruno would gladly have returned the compliment and would have given up his life to save me if the situation had ever arisen." He paused again, much longer this time, gathering his thoughts before he spoke again.

"I would give anything.... anything at all, any money I have, every piece of furniture in my house, just to spend one more hour with Bruno, just to hear one more bark, just one more long walk. He was more loyal than any human I have ever known. I will still talk to him every day, because wherever he is, he will hear my words; I will miss him for as long as I live, and I look forward, to that one special day in the future, when we will be reunited."

Wow, I didn't know what to say. I had listened to the cracking of his voice as he talked about his best friend. I felt guilty at having asked such blunt and insensitive questions. We had reached his house; he opened the front gate and beckoned me inside.

We stood together for a few seconds.

Charlie continued.

"Bruno had a stroke. There was no warning. He just collapsed, at my feet...his eyes, they told me, he knew.... we both knew. I called the vet, and he came to my house and gave Bruno an injection to put him to sleep....to take away his pain and his misery. He knew his life was at its end, and he trusted me to ease the ending. He had been struggling for many months, with getting old, with losing his eyesight, with losing his hearing, and at the end, he had a brain tumour. I held him in my arms while he went to sleep, he was fifteen and at the end of his time here on earth." Charlie's voice was raw and pained, tears streaking his cheeks.

I stood back and waited as Charlie struggled to compose himself. It took a long minute. I didn't know what to say other than "Sorry".

He patted me on the head, maybe thinking of his dead friend.

There was something, though, that I couldn't let go, something that just didn't seem right. I had to ask.

"Why didn't you keep him here?"

It was something that really bothered me, surely if you had something so precious you would keep it close to you. I was finding it difficult to understand why he had buried his dog miles away.

He took a moment, gathering his thoughts again, looking directly into my eyes, before replying, a half-smile, half-grimace creasing his face.

"If I made his grave here Sid, in the back garden, yes, he would be close...but think about it - this is not my house, it belongs to the council. When I move on somewhere else, when I die, or when someone else lives in this house... what then? What would happen to my best friend?" He took another moment before answering his own question.

"Maybe a gardener comes to live in this house. Maybe he digs up the garden and finds some old bones...maybe he thinks nothing of it and throws them in the dustbin. I couldn't bear the thought of that happening. Bruno is free of pain now...and he is in the countryside, where all animals should be, and he can wake up every night and chase rabbits and sniff out trails."

Charlie was smiling now, a hopeful smile. "When he goes to sleep every night, he has his favourite blanket to keep him warm, and a tennis ball, and his best toy, and he'll wait until it is time for me to join him, however long that may be. Then we'll be together again, I'm sure of it."

That was quite a speech from Charlie and his mood had lightened now. Those tumbling words had served to convince him that he had done the right thing. It had convinced me too. I felt sorry for this big man.

He put his hand on my shoulder, and we walked together up the front path to the house.

It was five o'clock on the dot when I returned home and opened the back door. I could hear the frying pan spitting and squeaking...Co-op sausages, I should have asked her earlier to go to Maddison's, or Shy's butchers - I usually did, it had become something of a ritual.

"Oh, you're back, are you?" said Mam, stating the obvious. "Did everything go alright?"

"Yeh, it was good," I replied.

"Did you get the jobs finished?"

"Yeh, but it was heavy. I had to carry about thirty buckets of coal from somebody's house along the street who works at Bates's pit. He sold half his load of coal to Charlie. Then I had to hoy them into the coalhouse. It took me ages. That wasn't all though. I had to help with cutting some timber 'cos Charlie's making a cold frame in the back garden. He let me do some sawing...until I got too tired. My right arm's sore and aching now."

"Oh, stop moaning," mam chided as she heaped sausages on to a plate, "You've been paid for it haven't you?"

I put two half crowns on the kitchen table and sat down in my usual place. "There you go mam." Charlie had given me five bob, on top of the half-crown advance.

Mam ruffled my hair. 'Thank you, Sid,'...then she paused. "We won't always be scratting for money you know; things will change soon." She didn't sound convincing, she sounded tired, worn down with working so many different jobs just to keep our heads above water.

A plate of sausage, chips and beans appeared miraculously in front of me. "Get your chops around that," mam chuckled. "You must be starving."

I tucked in, without mentioning the Co-op sausages, it would have spoiled the mood.

Mouth half-full of squelch I spluttered excitedly, "I'm going back to Charlie's tomorrow mam; he's got some more jobs for me to do".

Mam paused what she was doing but didn't reply.

I slept like a log that night, even after discovering that my note with the Charlie Chuck comment was nowhere to be found. Regardless, I was back at Charlie's door bright and early on Sunday morning...full of bacon and eggs, fried bread, and a few mushrooms. Sunday, as always, was breakfast treat day. I couldn't eat black pudding anymore though; cos mam told me it was made with pigs' blood. So, mam had all the black pudding to herself.

Charlie beamed broadly when he opened the door, glancing at his watch. The watch wasn't on his wrist, it was on a chain attached to his waistcoat and he produced it from his waistcoat pocket. In that moment I felt closer to Charlie, the waistcoat watch reminded me of my grandad. A grandad I hadn't seen for ages.

"Somebody's keen, fifteen minutes early. Come on in."

I was early for a reason. I had rehearsed a little speech. It wasn't in any way impressive or majestic, but it was heartfelt, and not bad for a ten-year-old.

We sat down together in the living room. I could hear a bumping and moaning from a bedroom upstairs.

Charlie noticed.

"It's the nurse, seeing to Martha," said Charlie simply.

Martha was Charlie's wife and she had cancer. He'd told me about it the previous day, without any prompting after I'd asked why he was doing the shopping. He didn't elaborate.

He just seemed resigned to expecting another loss in his life. I'd heard about cancer and knew it wasn't something nice.

I cleared my throat, "Erm mm, I want to say thank you for getting me some jobs to do and to say sorry for being rude yesterday...about your dog, I mean about your best friend, and sorry for asking too many questions".

Charlie laughed, and it was a genuine laugh. "Quite a speech from someone so young...your apology is kindly accepted, but don't stop asking questions. Questions are your only path to knowledge. They're how you find out about life, about right and wrong. Don't ever stop questioning."

I thought about this for a little while. "So, can I ask you any questions I like?"

Charlie laughed again, "Yes, of course, you may ask anything you like, but always remember there will be some questions I don't have the answer to, because I just don't know. Then, there will be some, of course, that I don't want to answer, for a variety of reasons." He paused momentarily. "I will tell you though, Sid, hand on heart, that I will always answer your questions as truthfully as I am able...unless of course it would hurt someone."

I processed this information carefully because grown-ups weren't usually this forthcoming with kids.

"Charlie, what do you mean about hurt someone?"

Charlie thought for a long while. He seemed to be wrestling with inner doubt, perhaps about myself, and while he thought he rolled a cigarette from the baccy tin in front of him. I was fascinated because he was rolling it with just one hand. It was just like watching a cowboy movie. Hopalong

Cassidy, right here in Cowpen Estate. Cigarette constructed, he put it to his mouth and lit it with a battered petrol lighter.

"Think about it like this," said Charlie reflectively, coughing, and puffing out a cloud of grey smoke. "What if your mam had been into Newcastle and came back with a new dress?..."

I interrupted, "Me mam hasn't got any money for a new dress".

"Sid, Sid, Sid," Charlie made a pressing gesture with his hands, a calming down gesture, "It's a what if...it's an example. I know your mam hasn't any spare money; just hold your horses for a minute."

Suitably chastised I fell silent.

He waited a moment or two to make sure I'd understood the message.

"So, Sid, your mam comes home from the 'Toon' with the first new dress she's had for a long time, and not a lot to spend on it. She goes upstairs, puts it on and then comes down and says to you...'well Sid, what do you think? Don't you think your mam looks like a star?' Then she twirls, waiting for you to answer. But you...you're not impressed - you cringe, you absolutely hate it, it looks awful, but your mam is standing in front of you with a hopeful smile on her face. She needs some back-up, she needs some positive noises, from her son. This is her first new dress for ages. What do you say?"

Now I saw what he was getting at.

Charlie didn't wait, he answered for me.

"Being a nice lad, a sensitive lad, you would say, 'Mam, wow, you look fantastic, you look really young. That dress is brilliant; it must have cost an absolute fortune, where did you get all the money from?"

He paused.

"If, however, you decided that the truth must always be told you would say, 'Mam you look awful, like mutton dressed as lamb. That dress must have been in the sale because no-one else wanted it. It looks like it's made from old curtains'."

I wasn't so thick that I didn't understand. The message was obvious.

"That's the difference between always being truthful and sometimes just being kind. Do you understand?"

I did. "So, it's okay sometimes to tell lies?"

Charlie shook his head. No, it's never right to tell a lie, but sometimes it's the kindest thing to do. You'll make up your own mind as you go through life."

We spent the rest of the day finishing the cold frame. Charlie had purloined some window frames with the glass still intact and they were to be the top opening section of the frame. He showed me how to attach hinges and fit them to the frame so that the top opened, and how to make a trough around the outside of the frame for drainage. How to make the back of the frame taller than the front, so any rainwater would run away and not lie on top, and so that you could use a stick to prop the bottom end of the frame open when it was a hot day, when the plants needed some air. I'd never even thought before about plants needing water, air, and sunshine. I'd always just thought that, well, they're only plants, aren't they? Charlie's teaching gave me a lifelong interest in gardening. He talked to me all day long and answered every question I asked, not just about growing vegetables and flowers but about anything I had on my mind...and I had lots and lots.

It was quite a pivotal moment in my life to find someone, an actual adult someone, who knew so many things and had lived so many experiences and was prepared to pass on some of this information to a little lad like me. The big question of the day however was...

"Charlie, who was Colonel Packin that's in the Lonnie Donegan song?"

Charlie gave a throaty laugh and didn't even pause to think, he was in his element and gave me an impromptu history lesson.

After mapping out a brief background to the conflict, he told me that Colonel Packin's real name was Colonel Pakenham, leader of the British army in America. Even though a peace treaty had been signed in Europe to halt the fighting, news of it hadn't reached the British and American soldiers who were battling each other in the southern states of America. Over Christmas 1814 and into January 1815, the British forces were soundly defeated around New Orleans and lost more than a thousand soldiers. The American forces lost only a fraction of that number and they were under the command of a man called Andrew Jackson, who would go on to become the American President.

I was totally surprised and spellbound at this man's breadth of knowledge; he was a gold mine just waiting to be excavated. Now I had something to tell Titch, but I was a little compromised. Should I tell Titch the source of this history information? Tell him that the bad man, Charlie Chuck, was actually a good man...and ruin Titch's reputation for knowing everything. Or should I just tell a little white lie and say I'd been to the library?

As it turned out I did neither. Colonel Packin was never mentioned again, and I decided to keep my newfound knowledge and my newfound mentor to myself.

CHAPTER 3

Plenty More Fish

———————————————■———————————————

Over the next few days, I had more in-depth conversations with mam than I had ever managed before. Mam had begun to treat me almost as a grown-up in the family, now that my brother was away, and I was managing to find a few odd jobs.

As well as my jobs at Charlie's I had been to the retirement bungalows in Redesdale and cleaned the windows of three of the old folks. I'd earned three bob and a bar of toffee. I gave mam the three bob and Linda and I shared the toffee. One of the old folks asked me inside for a cup of tea and a bun, and she was nice to me. I liked old people. They were always pleased to talk. The lady asked me to come back in two weeks and do her windows again. I could only do bungalows because all I had was a little set of ladders that had been for the bunk beds Kenny and I used to share. Mam had given me some old cloths to use, a bucket and a shammy leather. Window cleaning was turning into a little business.

I also ran messages for some of the neighbours in our street and received the odd threepence or a tanner. One of our pitman neighbours would sometimes ask me to run over to Carlo's shop on Briardale Road for five Woodbines. I was too young to buy cigarettes from the Co-op, but it didn't matter how old, or young, you were, you could always buy cigarettes - or tabs as Geordies call them, at Carlo's.

I had no jobs pending for the next few days and was looking forward to a game of football tomorrow over at Cowpen fields with Titch, John Norris and a few other lads from the estate.

It was Wednesday evening, and Linda was in bed. I was allowed to stay up until half past nine during the holidays but little by little this had extended to ten o'clock when mam always turned in for the night. The telly was on the blink, the screen kept going into lots of little lines and making a weird noise, and mam had someone coming the next day from Rediffusion to fix it. She was reading a book but put it down when I came in from the kitchen. I had just made myself a sugar sandwich as we had run out of jam.

I noticed the title of mam's book; it was Peyton Place. I didn't say anything because Titch told me it was one of the world's rudest books and the police could put you in jail just for reading it.

Mam seemed to be in a serious mood.

"Come and sit beside me Sid," she patted the couch and slid the book under a cushion.

"You'll be back at school a week on Monday...are you looking forward to it?"

That was a strange question to be asking.

"Ermmm, I think so."

"Only think so; is something the matter?"

"No mam, not really, nothing really, it's just...well...you know...Morpeth Road is miles away; why couldn't I just go to Bebside School?"

She took a few seconds to respond. "Your friend, Alan Irving, is going to Morpeth Road, and that other lad you know, George Wilkinson, is going there, too, and the Balmer twins, and they're all nice lads, so what's the matter."

"Nothing really mam; it's just that I was in school in Kirkcaldy, then we came here, and I had to start again at Forster School. Then eight months later I have to go to another school. When is it all going to settle down? I'm fed up with having to keep changing schools and changing friends."

Mam squeezed my arm. "I know Sid. I know it's been hard for you. It's been hard for us all...me, you, Linda, and then Kenny leaving for the army. Sometimes I could just have a good cry and give up, but I can't because I have two brilliant children at home who depend on me being strong." Then she paused.

"You weren't supposed to go to Morpeth Road School, you were supposed to go to Bebside with everyone else around us, but Morpeth Road is the best school in Blyth for helping people to grammar school...so somebody told me how to get you in."

"Told you...who?"

"It doesn't matter who, just a friend...an acquaintance, and somehow, I managed it." She paused for a second, gripping my arm even tighter. "Please try your best Sid, I'm hoping this will give you an opportunity to have yourself a better life than I've ever managed. Don't waste your life on...'

She checked herself, but I had a good idea of what would have come next.

"I promise mam." She was serious, and I knew that she had done whatever she had for my benefit. "Honest, I'll do my very best."

"Good, then that's all I can ask. Be the best that you can be every single day...and if you can't be your best...then be your second best."

She kissed me on the brow. I immediately thought she must have been reading too much Peyton Place. Brow kissing had no place in our family. It couldn't be the drink because mam never drank alcohol...and couldn't afford it anyway.

"Go on, off to bed, you're playing football tomorrow." She gave me a big smile.

I turned to go upstairs but then turned back. There was one question I'd been meaning to ask but hadn't the nerve to put it to Charlie or mam.

"Mam, why did Charlie talk with a foreign accent before he knew who I was, like he was French or something, then started speaking proper English?"

Mam seemed taken aback with the question, her mouth opened but nothing came out. It took a good few seconds before she replied.

"Have you asked Charlie?"

"No, I didn't like to because he's been good to me. I don't want to ask him one of those questions that he doesn't want to answer?"

Mam patted the seat beside her again. I walked over and sat down beside her.

"Sometimes you know...people have things happen in their life that they don't want anyone to know about. I wouldn't want to be telling anybody about that bad time with me and your dad. Sometimes you just need to accept that there are some things that are none of our business. If someone is good to us, treats us right, never does any harm, then we should speak as we find, and not listen to stupid rumours put about by nasty people."

"So, have you heard all the things that people say about Charlie?"

"Some."

"So, are they not true?"

"You'll have to ask him, Sid."

"But do you know what the truth is?" I wasn't about to let this go.

"Yes, I do."

"So, Charlie must have told you?"

Mam thought for a moment then gripped my wrist.

"Martha told me. She is very ill...no, that's not the truth, she may be dying, she doesn't think she has long left, and she wants to know that Charlie will be alright when she is gone. She put me straight on all the rumours and all the speculation. She's a good lady and he's a good man."

"So, what's the truth then, mam?"

She gripped my wrist even tighter. "If Charlie ever wants you to know he will tell you himself. I can't break Martha's confidence; it wouldn't be right. Just know that most of what you hear as rumours are just that...rumours, usually made up by sad little people with nothing better to do...so they create fantasies...lies, stories that they think can put a little excitement into their drab lives. Don't ever be like them Sid." She dropped my wrist.

"Go on; have you seen the time. Off to bed with you."

I did as I was bid and left mam sitting on the couch alone. Football tomorrow.

Tomorrow came soon enough.

I was up and about, bright and early. I even had time to take mam some tea and toast while she was still in bed and made my sister a soft-boiled egg with soldiers, not that she thanked me. Why should she? I was her brother. Mam still wasn't out of bed when I left.

I wanted to call in at Charlie's place on my way to the field and try to ask him some questions, but I could see from a distance that he was deep in conversation with a tall man, wearing a black coat, and there was a big fancy car parked on the road outside of the house. I gave them a body swerve, and I headed for the cut that ran through to Dunston Place and then over to the football fields. I was much too early and there weren't any of the lads about. I didn't want to knock on any doors as they were probably all having breakfast, so I moseyed down to the big green hut that stood halfway down the field to the side of the pitches. It was where the men's teams changed into their football kit before matches.

For some strange reason I immediately sensed danger as I approached the wooden building. I could hear voices, and smell cigarette smoke. I had a quick glance around the corner of the hut, then shrank swiftly back. Luckily for myself the four lads standing there had their backs turned. I knew two of them immediately: one was Bill Taggart, he lived at the bottom of Hallside on the corner with Axwell Drive, and one of the others, a blonde lad, was his pal. The other two were much bigger and must have been maybe fifteen or even older. They were all smoking and laughing. I held my breath and tried to make no noise whatsoever.

"Ha, ha, ha, so it was big Tommo that got that lass," chortled the biggest lad.

"Aye, she ditched that idiot she was with and gave Tommo a wank behind the chippy on Swaledale."

"Ha, ha, ha, that must have cost the ugly bugger a few bob."

It was the two older lads doing the talking.

I was terrified that they would turn around and find me, and of course that would mean a bit of a bashing for me, or at the very least a pushing around and a huge helping of ridicule. Fortunately, after another minute or so of holding my breath the biggest of the lads said, "Howay, it's borin' here man, there's naebody else comin' now, Fanta must have slept in, or gone straight there. Let's away doon Blyth and see if there's owt gannin on".

My luck was in, and without further ado they left without looking behind, and I breathed a huge sigh of relief.

I thanked my lucky stars, and as the morning had turned hot and sunny, I sat myself down and just waited in the shade of the huts. Half an hour later, Titch and John Norris appeared at the top of the field beside the rugby posts, and by the time I'd reached them another four or five lads had started kicking about.

I jogged up to join them.

"Where've you been?" asked Titch, noticing the direction I came from.

"Just talkin' wi' some lads," I answered. Titch looked unimpressed.

I beckoned him over, separating him from the group of lads who had begun passing a ball around with John Norris.

Titch looked interested now, football nestled under his arm. "So... what's the crack...what's up wi' you?"

I hoped I wasn't about to make a fool of myself. "I've just been listening to some of the big lads down at the shed, you know, Bill Taggart and some of the tough lads, and one of them said his friend had got a wank off a lass at the chip shop, but it must have cost him a few bob."

Titch just stared at me... "And?"

"And...so, do you know what a wank is?"

Titch looked taken aback for a second or two, staring blankly, right out of his comfort zone. Taking time to think, half turning away, then in a seeming lightbulb moment turned back towards me and snorted.

"Ya kiddin'...right, you don't even know what a wank is?"

I shook my head. "Never heard of it. Is it a Geordie word?"

"Nah man, well, kind of...sort of, it's just another fish, something like a cod or haddock but they look like a little shark, and they cost a bit more. When my dad gets overtime and has plenty of money, he sometimes has a wank. My mam doesn't...she likes fish cakes."

How did he know all this stuff? He just knew all these facts that no-one else did, or maybe it was just me who didn't know anything. "Don't say anything, Titch, to the other lads...about me not knowing."

"Are you playin' or what?" Titch smiled, winked, then bounced a football off my chest and ran off.

Problem solved; question answered.

Football that day wasn't so great. Everyone was thinking that the holidays were almost over, and we were going back to school soon. We just kicked about for a bit and did some shooting in, but somehow it felt different. After about an hour the lads started drifting away one by one, John Norris and a lad called Batesy were the last to go and I decided to turn it in, too. There were no big goodbyes.

I decided to go back home via Devonworth and see if I could spot Charlie. Nothing doing. There was still a big car outside of his house, but he wasn't out and about. It took me an absolute age to saunter home. I had no reason to rush; there was nothing pressing to be done, so I dawdled.

Something seemed strange as I approached home. Nothing tangible, just a feeling that something different was happening. I opened the back door quietly and I could hear voices in the living room - mam's, and a bloke's voice. It suddenly hit me that the car outside of Charlie's could mean that his wife was ill...or worse, had died. That must be it. Charlie must have come here to ask my mam to help.

Taking my shoes off at the kitchen door, I bundled into the living room and got the shock of my life. Sitting in the armchair was my brother Kenny. My mouth dropped open. It didn't even look like the brother who had left such a short while ago; he looked so different in his army uniform, and his hair cut so short, a crew cut.

With a huge grin creasing his face he said, "Hi young'un...I was wondering when you would turn up. Pleased to see me or what?"

I couldn't speak, his shoes were so shiny, his uniform with knife edge creases, and a collar and tie...for heaven's sake.

"Say something then," said mam from the couch.

"Hi Kenny," I squawked weakly, "you look different, how long are you home for?"

"Ha-ha, ha, thought you might say that. That's what everybody asks...how long before we can get rid of you again."

"No man, that's not what I meant. Just, I didn't know you were coming. It's a surprise, I didn't expect to see you sitting here."

"I've only got tonight and have to go back tomorrow; I got a 72-hour pass, but it takes a whole day on the train to get here, and a whole day back."

Kenny was bouncing Linda on his knee, and she was loving every minute of it. Kenny had always looked out for her. I know he had serious confrontations with dad in the few months leading up to the family leaving Scotland.

After my initial silence...the dam burst and questions came out in a torrent: what was the Ordnance Corps like? What were the other Junior Leaders like? What was the food like? Did the officers treat him OK? When was he going to get his first stripe? Had he been in any battles? Did he get to shoot real guns and throw proper grenades? Once I'd started, I couldn't stop. We talked for ages, barely noticing that mam and Linda had slipped out of the room.

Kenny told me about thunderflashes and sub machine guns, light machine guns and Carl Gustav rocket launchers. He told me about his pals at Blackdown, and how they had been out twice for a pint of beer at a place called Frimley

Green, even though they were all just sixteen. He told me how his uniform attracted lasses...and he had a girlfriend in one of the local villages...but that bit put me off, - who would want to attract lasses? Kenny laughed and told me I'd want to attract lasses myself when I was a few years older. I wasn't so sure about that.

We talked and talked and talked. I'd never had long conversations in the past with Kenny; he was always something of a loner and usually quiet, but he told me how much he enjoyed army life and how he was thinking of signing on for life because you were paid more money if you did. At present he was only signed up for six years, and six in the reserves, whatever that meant.

He asked me about mam and how she was coping, about how I was doing at school, what my pals were like. He made me promise that I would stick in at school so that I could get a good job when I turned 16 and not have to go into the army like him.

I told him about Titch, and how he was set on joining the army, too, even though he was only ten years old, but Kenny said, "There's better things out there for you and your pal than the army. You've always been the clever one, Sid; make it count and one day you can be in a job with loads of money and not have to make do with second best...mam needs someone in the family to be proud of."

I told him that mam already had that; she was extremely proud of him and that seemed to make him swell up. Then I made all the solemn promises about doing my best, hand on heart. Then we fell silent.

I did have one pressing question though.

"Kenny, do you know how the Germans lost the war?'"
I was showing off now, about to dazzle my brother with some
facts that he probably had no idea about...on second thoughts
maybe he did know, because he was in the army now and the
British army probably had loads of testicles, that's how we'd
won the war. Maybe Kenny even knew how to drive one.

Kenny thought for a minute. "Lots of reasons, I suppose,
mainly because the Americans came into the war to help us,
and Hitler made a mistake by attacking Russia and fighting
on two fronts...well, three fronts actually 'cos he was in
North Africa as well."

"Oh, I thought it was something different." I wasn't
expecting him to come out with that.

"Why...has your teacher told you something different?...
My sergeant told me all that stuff because he was in the war
and got wounded in Italy. Why do you think we beat the
Germans?"

"Because Hitler didn't have enough testicles," I blurted
out.

Kenny was still laughing minutes later when Mam and
Linda came in through the front door. He'd put me straight
in no uncertain terms...and even gave me a brief biology
lesson, explaining what testicles were, and on the changes
that would happen to me in a few years' time. I felt like a
right banana. Titch had really stitched me up with that one.

"What are you two laughing at," asked Mam as she
bundled through the front door with a stack of newspaper
parcels in her arms.

I looked anxiously at Kenny, but he was absolutely mint.
"Just telling Sid about one of the lads on our camp who goes

sleepwalking, and they found him one night on the athletics track, with no clothes on, starkers, jumping in and out of the sand in the long jump pit."

"Don't want to hear, don't want to hear," chirped Mam, "and not in front of your sister."

Linda just grinned and stuck out her tongue before skipping off and following mam through to the kitchen.

Vinegar has its own unique aroma when sprinkled on fish and chips and we could smell it from the living room. Mam came through to fetch us. "Come on then you two, it's out on the kitchen table for you. Get it while it's still hot."

We jumped up as one, my brother and I, and headed for the kitchen. To be fair, the fish and chips looked excellent, and mam had even bought mushy peas. Three big mugs of tea, with a glass of pop for Linda standing to the right of the plates. There was a ton and a half of chips on the plates and the fish were huge. Mam had cut hers in two to share with Linda. Even so, Linda's plate was still almost full, and mam's plate contained twice the amount of food she would normally eat. There was a plate piled high with half slices of bread and butter, cut diagonally like posh folk do, and there was even a fruit cake, cut into little wedges, on mam's willow pattern special occasion plate. She was really pushing the boat out for Kenny.

"Stick in until you stick out," said Mam, laughing at her own stock saying.

Kenny was like a hoover, attacking the food like a starving man. Mam was in a great mood. "Kenny, you should have tied racing colours to your knife and fork." We all laughed;

it was a time for laughter, we were all around the table and Kenny was home on leave.

"Come on Sid, you too. You're not usually this slow. Fill your bags."

I smiled at her weakly, toying with the chips.

"Don't tell me you can't eat it all...you're the family gannet."

"It's not that mam."

"Not what?" she looked puzzled now. "What on earth's up with you?"

"Nothin'...really nothin', it's not important. It's just... I wish you'd said you were going to the chippy?"

"Whatever for? You two were having a good time. I didn't want to ask one of you to go, it would have spoiled your conversation. Me and Linda were quite capable of walking to the chip shop for cod and chips; it's not dark or anything." Mam was still smiling and chuckling.

Then slowly her smile faded. "Unless of course it's Charlie...and his situation you're bothered about. Is that it?"

"No mam...well it is, sort of, a little bit, but it's not mostly about that mam."

"Then what is it Sid? You're being really daft."

"It's just that...you know, the cod's nice an' that...but I really fancied a wank."

Uproar, uproar, uproar, pandemonium!...I swear to God...tea shot out of both Kenny's nostrils all over the stack of bread and butter. My mam screeched, honestly screeched, it sounded like an owl, or a cat that had been kicked...Linda was laughing, giggling...at what, I had no clue. Mam started to choke, gasping, and banging the flat of her hand on the table. Kenny jumped up and began slapping her on the back. She gave a strangled cough and a squashed chip shot out of her mouth, landing on the fruit cake slices. Kenny gestured with his head for me to make myself scarce; he was snorting like a horse, with tears of laughter streaming down his cheeks. I slipped out of my seat, grabbed my jacket, and quickly exited via the front door, the sound of mam in the kitchen still screeching, "Oh my God, oh my God, what's happened to him?" following me as the door clunked shut behind me. My one and only thought was to make it to Charlie's...I hadn't a clue why I'd caused such a commotion.

CHAPTER 4

Calm After the Storm

———————————■———————————

The following weeks were, and to this day, remain ill remembered, vague and ephemeral. Distorted in my memory so that I can't swear with any degree of certainty that these remembering's are real or perhaps an illusion, conjured up to camouflage my humiliation.

Charlie swiftly sorted out the immediate 'fishy' problem that very first evening. I arrived at his house in a messed-up state, confused and tearful. He listened, and within half an hour he had made me a fried egg sandwich to make up for the meal I'd abandoned. Then he took himself off to explain to mam about the cod and chips gaffe, how it had originated from some older lads, and had been compounded by Titch's misinterpretation, and my own immature naivety. To say I was grateful is an understatement, however, for a little while afterwards I found it difficult to look mam in the eye. Whenever we spoke, the subject was studiously avoided, and my verbal faux pas became the veritable elephant in the room.

My brother returned to the army, without saying cheerio. My sister seemed to have a perpetual smirk on her lips whenever she saw me. I worried that maybe other people, the neighbours perhaps, had heard about my blunder...I couldn't be sure, and I had no desire to be the local figure of fun, fingers pointing, sniggers muffled. Because of these events I spent as much time as possible away from home and around at Charlie's house. He was the one person throughout that difficult period who saw me as an individual of value and not just as a child. The one adult at that grotty time who set about cultivating a set of values I could adhere to, and who gave me the encouragement to grow and flourish, who gave freely the gift of his experience.

During this phase I also began my education at my new school, Morpeth Road, and that too became a daily escape from home life. I looked forward eagerly to the daily routine and the making of new friends. I devoured every lesson, every session, an insatiable child hungry for knowledge. The big library in the town centre became like a second home for an hour each day, after the school bell liberated us, and in the reference section, foraging through those musty, and often shabby books, I soaked up all manner of scholarly delicacies. If truth be told, I discovered a reading banquet, and I relished every morsel.

It was at Charlie's however, that a template emerged, a framework for the living of life, which, when planted in my subconscious, lay dormant for a while, then set seed and quickly mushroomed.

During the following weeks Charlie explained to me how life really was, and how difficult it could be. How growing up could be torment. He gave me the truth unvarnished... warts and all. He assigned himself the male role-model post and set about steering me in a direction that he said he hoped would give my life some structure, some purpose, empathy, and compassion. Even so I didn't immediately discover the direction I would follow for the rest of my days. There was no St. Paul on the road to Damascus moment. I did however come to realise that life offers up an endless variety of paths, and the greatest difficulty one faces is in the choosing.

Charlie told me, "When you choose your route, follow it with your best endeavour, give it your best shot. Try to make each day better than the one before." Notwithstanding this advice, he also said, "if, after a while, you realise your choice hasn't worked out as you'd hoped, don't be afraid to admit your mistake; have the courage to begin again and find an alternative path."

It was at that moment he let slip a snippet of his past.

"I changed paths, Sid. I was set on teaching the sciences - you know, physics, chemistry, biology - but I changed, and I ended up as a professor of European history and modern languages. It's okay to do this. It doesn't mean you have failed; it means you are thinking deeply about your life."

I understood, like a child, for child I was. Some of the nuances escaped me, some of the language confusing. I didn't, for instance, know the meanings of the words, empathy, and compassion, and I hadn't a clue what physics were, but eager to learn I listened and remembered.

The Charlie conversations began in earnest several days after my calamitous fish and chip episode. My first day back at school proved happy and productive. I'd made friends with several of the new faces, as well as renewing acquaintance with many of the old ones. All in all, I'd experienced an excellent first day, and I'd promised to let Charlie know how it had gone.

The first lesson I recall being given, the one that sticks prominently in my memory, was succinct...short and sweet. Charlie was tidying the front garden when I arrived at his house. He smiled and gave me a salute as I opened the gate and closed it behind me. He must have noticed my enthusiasm and continued pottering about as he waited for me to speak. Without preamble, I unloaded. I spoke about my school day, full of good things and a feeling of exhilaration. New friends made, old pals reunited, a nice teacher, a friendly dinner lady, Mona. I talked about playing football and British bulldog, gaining top marks in a long division test. On and on I went. I must have talked non-stop for a whole five minutes before flagging, winding down, until finally, my brain seemed to dry up, and my mouth ran out of words.

Silence prevailed for a second or two.

"I'm happy too," smiled Charlie, filling the void."

"Cos I've had a good day at school?" I asked happily.

He paused in his reply. "Yes…of course, I'm pleased it's gone well for you Sid, extremely pleased, but also because the outlook for my Martha is much improved. There's some hope, and the doctor says he believes things are more promising, so I'm pleased too."

"Sorry, Charlie, I wasn't being rude…wi' talkin' so much. I'm really pleased that Mrs…Martha is getting better."

"Thanks very much young fellow. I'll let her know that you're pleased when I see her tonight at the hospital."

"Hospital?"

"Aye, lad, she's going to have an operation."

"To make her well?"

He paused again, choosing his next words carefully. "No Sid...there isn't any cure - not as such. At least not in the sense of Martha being completely healthy again. She will feel much improved for a while, hopefully a long while... and it means she will enjoy quite a chunk more of my company...if that's any consolation." He forced a laugh. "It will enable us to enjoy time together that we didn't think we would have. An opportunity to make peace with our lives...and say all the words we need to say, the ones we've somehow neglected."

Charlie was gazing into the distance as he finished speaking, inhabiting a private world. I remained quiet. He stroked at the stubble on his chin as he surveyed the looming clouds which were hampering the sun. He gave up a deep sigh. Then he jerked back into life, smiling, rubbing his big hands together. "Enough of me and my promising news. What else has been happening with you. Have you seen Titch today?"

"No...he wasn't at school. He's off with mumps."

"So have you been to his house?" Charlie asked.

I wasn't expecting that question, it flummoxed me for a moment; after all that had happened. I was a mite confused. "Why...why would I?"

Charlie shrugged, "To see how he is. He's poorly and he's your pal."

I snorted a response... "He's not me pal anymore. I've got to get him back for telling lies and for making me look stupid."

This seemed to displease Charlie, and he frowned, taking a moment out, choosing his next words carefully.

"Revenge...honestly, Sid, is that really what you want?"

"Aye, of course. I've got to get him back, but even worse than he got me, ten times worse, a hundred times worse, when I can think of something."

Charlie didn't comment immediately, but turned away, as if to go inside and leave me standing there, before pausing for a few seconds. Then, mind seemingly made up, he turned back, concern etching his face.

"Remember this Sid and remember it well. Revenge is a vicious circle, and it can be never ending. Take advice from one who knows this well, from one who has seen both sides of pointless spite, the futility of it." He paused to let his words sink in. "Your friend made a silly mistake, that's all, showing off, a childish blunder. But you.... you've turned his mistake into your grudge, and the grudge is rapidly growing into resentment. And next, the resentment will become hostility which will gnaw away at you. Then it will escalate, until it becomes hate and rage. Mark my words, Sid, no good ever comes from rage, from revenge." He stopped and thought for a moment.

"And what do you think will happen then Sid, after your revenge has been served up?...Do you honestly think you'll feel good about it, ehhh, take pleasure from it, or gain any happiness?"

He waited, but I didn't reply. He'd used a lot of long words, some of which puzzled me, and he wasn't being a friendly Charlie today.

Pause over, expecting no response, and receiving none, he answered for me.

"Sid, all you will feel is empty...and disappointed at the emptiness. You will exact your revenge, mete out his punishment, having put all your energy into it, and then, when it is done...nothing...a vacuum...and standing in front of you will be a hurt person who was once a friend." He paused again. "Then what happens?.... Your once friend becomes your enemy, and he seeks his revenge for the revenge you have inflicted upon him....and his revenge once accomplished must be answered, and so it continues, the circle is complete, and circles have no end."

He stared into my eyes, intently, then...it seemed he suddenly realised he was being intimidating, reprimanding a child, and his mood visibly lightened. He gave me a playful tap on the shoulder, as if to signify the lecture was over.

"Next time you're at the library Sid, see if you can find a copy of William Shakespeare's Hamlet. See what you make of it. I know you are young, and I know that life can sometimes feel overwhelming, but you are intelligent, and if you can discover why I've directed you to that play in particular... come and see me again, young Laertes, at my house here - Elsinore."

With that he walked into the house and shut the door firmly behind him. He left me standing outside, like one of those garden gnomes you often see, with a silly hat and fixed smile. I was missing the hat. Out of the corner of my eye I saw the living room curtains move but pretended not to notice. I turned and headed for home, a tad upset at his unexpected response, and the fact that he hadn't more time for me. I decided however that tomorrow after school I would track down the Hamlet book and endeavour to find out why he had called me young Lergi…and find out who the mysterious Elsie and Nora were?

Two days later I was back in his garden. I'd used the time productively; in a manner I hoped would please Charlie. It was a balmy late afternoon with a delicate, meandering breeze, picking its way gently here and there, and a curious quiet around the entire circle of Devonworth Place, with its scruffy central wasteland, ugly and unkempt, dog muck and discarded cigarette packets, strewn indiscriminately among the tussocks of grass eking out an existence. No buzz of traffic, or children shouting, no barking dogs or screeching women. The whole neighbourhood seemed to have collectively decided upon an early evening siesta.

When I came through his front gate and entered the garden, Charlie was sitting on a long wooden bench, beneath the front window. He was smoking. Sitting beside him on the bench was a woman of enormous proportions. I had to look twice because I couldn't believe my eyes the first time. She was huge. Not tall, just wide.

"Afternoon Sid," Charlie gave a wave.

"Hi Charlie," I waved back, but my eyes were fixed on the big woman.

"Hello Sid," the lump said, with a big smile. "My name is Helena, Martha's sister. I've heard many good things about you from Charlie."

I opened my mouth to reply, but no sound came out. I realised I was being rude, just staring, but my brain wasn't functioning normally. Helena couldn't help but notice, and she laughed, a high, giggly laugh, which sounded totally alien, coming from such a large woman, a chortling bouncy castle.

Charlie had a half smile on his lips. He could feel my awkwardness.

It was Helena who spoke next.

"You're wondering why I'm so big, aren't you Sid?" … she attempted a smile, a forced affair, which quickly faded; then, in an instant, she regained her jollity.

"You think I might have swallowed Billy Bunter." At this, both Charlie and Helena began chuckling, nudging each other with elbows. I was just completely embarrassed, unable to respond, feeling very much like a child in the company of adults sharing secret adult stuff. They both saw my uneasiness and the laughter subsided.

"Helena has diabetes, type one," said Charlie, offering up an explanation.

I was none the wiser.

"What's that?" was all I could muster, as I made my way over to the bench, to sit down and join them.

"It's a disease," explained Charlie, "a nasty disease, which can be helped with a drug - something called insulin. Insulin can help to control diabetes, but it also makes you eat, not because you want to, or when you want to, but because you must, to maintain a blood sugar level, to stay alive, and in staying alive you pile on weight. It's not a nice disease to have…but at least it's not a death sentence nowadays."

Helena chipped in. "There's something inside our bodies…inside my body, an organ, called a pancreas. Mine has stopped working and needs help." She held her arms up. "Which is why I am like I am."

"Sorry for being rude…and staring," I offered.

"There's no need to be sorry, Sid. It's a natural reaction. I get it all the time, believe me, I've become used to it."

I thought about this, "But it's not nice, for people to stare, if it's not your fault."

She raised her eyebrows. "Well, actually Sid, it wouldn't be nice, or polite, even if it were my fault."

That response made me think. Another lesson learned. It made me think about the little fat lad at my new school who we'd all nicknamed Porky Pig. On reflection, I wasn't impressed with myself. I felt a little ashamed. Maybe he had a disease, too.

"Anyway Sid, just realise that we need to hear a person's story, about their life and the obstacles they face before we become judgemental."

I knew what she meant immediately. My mam had talked about these things, and she'd given me one of her stock sayings.

"You mean, don't judge a book by its cover…. don't you?

Helena seemed impressed. "Yes Sid, that's it precisely. We must use our ears, to really understand a person, and not to accept as truth what our eyes tell us. Light travels faster than sound, but bad words can travel many miles before good words are out of bed."

"Ok, I understand." I replied because I had understood. It made sense, and she was using a metaphor…and mam had explained about metaphors.

"Also, you need to know," Helena continued, "inside this body you see before you, there's a thin woman, and she's screaming out...desperate to escape".

I didn't reply, no response was expected. I just nodded.

"But I can usually shut her up with half a dozen pasties."

Charlie and Helena began laughing loudly, doing the elbow nudging thing again. It made me laugh too, although I kept my elbows to myself.

Helena was very nice, I decided. She was genuinely friendly, listened intently when spoken to, was humorous in a self-deprecating sort of way, and extremely intelligent. When she said something, you listened, because it was invariably important, or funny, or a bit of both.

Ten minutes after the half dozen pasties moment we were sitting in Charlie's living room, chatting away. I'd been asking questions non-stop. Charlie and I sat together on the couch, with Helena perched in the big old armchair, which was stuffed with horsehair. I'd sat on it once before, with my short trousers on and it scratched the back of my legs like crazy.

"So, what's been going on with you, little fella?" Charlie asked, at the same time as Helena pointed to her watch and got up from the chair.

"I need to go and get ready Charlie," she said, and looked at me apologetically.

"Sorry Sid, I've really enjoyed your company, but I have a taxi coming soon, to take me to the hospital to see my sister."

"I've liked your company as well," I answered shyly, not making eye contact.

"Well, thank you for that, and make sure you listen to Carol. He knows what he's talking about. He'll never give you bad advice," she said as she left the room. "See you soon, Sid." Then she was gone, with the sounds of her laboured progress following her up the stairs.

Carol? What did she mean by calling Charlie a girl's name? I filed the question away, to be revisited at a later date.

"So, to repeat, what have you been up to, Sid?" Charlie asked again.

It was the moment I'd been waiting for. I cleared my throat. He was about to be incredibly impressed.

"To be, or not to be, that is the question:
Whether 'tis nobler in the mind to suffer
The slings and arrows of outrageous fortune,
Or to take arms against a sea of troubles."

I finished, waiting for his response, the first four lines were all I'd learned.

"That's it..."

A nod of approval from Charlie;. I'd been expecting enthusiasm.

"Very good Sid, excellent in fact, and I really do mean excellent. You don't usually encounter Shakespeare until you're much older. Remember the speech well and learn the remainder. Some words will make little sense, because it's written in old English, and many of them sound confusing. However, if you make it to university, and I'm sure you have all the qualities to do so, you will encounter Shakespeare regularly, and if you can quote that speech, at the right time, in the right circumstance, it will impress people, believe me."

He waited until his words had sunk in.

"Apart from that, I was really hoping that you might discover a lesson in Hamlet, rather than learn some lines of Hamlet's soliloquy. You know, about the things we were discussing when you were last here?"

I wasn't sure why he'd called Hamlet's speech a solwolliky but the beam on my face must have been so obvious. I had prepared myself for this very moment. Mam had talked me through the meaning of Hamlet.

"Shakespeare's message is that revenge is really stupid, and it messes your life up. There were three men in Hamlet, all wanting revenge for different reasons; they were all trying to kill each other, and it ate them up, made them all loopy, especially Hamlet. So, the play is mostly about that, me mam says, but not just about that. That's what you meant, isn't it?"

"Yes…but have you done anything else, about what we discussed?"

I nodded, "I know who Laertes is, and Fortinbras, and I know about Elsinore, too - it was Hamlet's castle in Denmark."

"I was hoping…" Charlie began, but I didn't let him finish.

"Ohh, aye, and I've been to Titch's house as well. I never said anything about…you know, the bad stuff? I took him a packet of Spangles, out of me own money, but I had to give them to his mam cos she wouldn't let me in just in case I got the mumps. Then she even told me off for calling him Titch. Anyway, I've stopped thinking about gettin' him back, 'cos it was some of my fault an' all for believin' him.

Charlie's smile was huge. He pulled a shilling out of his pocket. 'You did a good thing, Sid…Here, take this, to pay for the Spangles."

I shook my head. "No thanks Charlie, I didn't do it for money. Titch is my pal. I don't want you paying for stuff that I should have done without being told."

Charlie put his big hand on my shoulder and gave me a friendly shake. "I'm proud of you, Sid. You're growing up, and you're growing up right."

At that moment, Helena's head appeared around the door.

"No sign of the taxi?" she asked.

"It'll be a few minutes yet," replied Charlie. "Have you got your coat on....got Martha's grapes...enough money for the taxi?"

"Carol, for the love of God, stop fussing...I'm a big girl now." She turned to look at me. 'Isn't that right Sid?" We all laughed at the same time.

"Do you want dropping off at home, Sid?" she asked.

"You mean, in the taxi?"

"Aye, but you don't have to."

"Aye," I replied. "I've never been in a taxi before. Is that okay Charlie?"

"Certainly, and if truth be told, I'll be glad to have a bit of peace and quiet when you two have gone." He gave me a nudge, to indicate he didn't mean it.

Helena took my jacket down from one of the hooks in the front passage and handed it to me.

"That's a nice jacket Sid. Very fashionable." She gave a friendly smile.

"No, it's not," I snapped back, rudely, immediately regretting it. Helena didn't deserve rudeness from a stroppy kid, but I had a monkey on my back, years of being galled with my lot in life.

"It's not even mine... like most of my clothes, they're second hand. They used to be my brother's clothes. It's not fair - my sister doesn't have to wear old clothes. Linda's clothes are always new. She always smells of polo mints or pear drops; me though, I smell of Kenny and mothballs, and walk around in pants that don't fit properly, and have to wear shirts with collars a size too big that make me look like 'Plug' out of the Bash St Kids."

I was on the verge of tears and felt Helena's big meaty arm around my shoulder. Then she hunkered down in front of me as best she could. She looked me in the eye.

"Me too, Sid. My father died when I was very young. My mother had three daughters and I was the youngest. I wore hand-me-downs all my life, my sisters' clothes, some of them Martha's. I didn't complain because I knew mother was struggling. I knew money was tight and she was doing her best. Then, as time went by, I outgrew my sisters and couldn't wear their clothes anymore."

My own travails were diminishing now that Helena was in full flow. Her story made mine fade in comparison.

"What did you do then, when you were too big for your sisters' clothes?"

She gave me a big smile," Funny you should ask...at fourteen years of age I'd shot up so quickly...I was almost on an eye level with my mother, and I had to start wearing her old clothes and that was even worse."

"Why...were they tatty and stuff?"

She laughed, "No Sid, certainly not, but it was terribly embarrassing having to walk to school, wearing a wedding dress".

Then the three of us laughed and laughed, the image in my head of a young lassie in school wearing a wedding dress, even though I knew it was a joke, gave me pause for thought, and my own problem faded into insignificance.

Then I had a thought. "There's a poor lass at my school, she gets free school meals, and she comes to school in sandshoes without socks, and her clothes are always tatty, and even if it's cold she doesn't have a coat or a jumper, and everybody calls her bad names and make fun of her."

Charlie and Helena were both staring at me, concerned.

I was in the spotlight. Two adults were waiting for me to continue. I was struggling. "Just saying...about that lass, that's all."

"Have you thought about doing something about it then?" queried Helena.

I shrugged. "I don't call her names or anything...not me. But what can I do? I'm only a kid. It's up to her mam and dad to do things, isn't it? I can't think of anything that I can do, so it's probably best to do nothing."

"Well, that's one way of looking at it," Charlie offered. "Or, you could have a good think about different ways of helping."

Then Helena chipped in. "You know Sid... there are many ways of doing something, but there's only one way of doing nothing." She paused, letting her words sink in. "D'you understand?"

I didn't have time to reply. A car horn was sounding, outside. The Silver Streak taxi had arrived. We had to rush. Charlie ruffled my hair as I brushed past him in my eagerness for a new adventure. My first time in a taxi.

It would be some time before I saw either of them again.

CHAPTER 5

The Bella Gang

———————————◆———————————

The longest break in my relationship with Charlie, up to that point, wasn't due to any kind of fallout. The following week was just chocker-block with lots of exciting things to do, adventures to be adventured, plans to make, experiences to be experienced, kids' stuff. Every day there seemed to be something different happening.

First, we had to start collecting wood for bonfire night, although the big day was almost two months away. Wood collected in the meantime had to be stored in back gardens, so that it wouldn't be nicked by the Devonworth mob. I had two broken wood pallets in our garden, and mam wasn't pleased, she said we looked like a rubbish tip...and we did.

It had been decided that our bonfire would be on waste ground at the bottom of Axwell Drive, opposite the Tilmouth house, and we'd need the older lads to stand guard, those that could stay out late, once we'd started building it...'cos we knew the Devonworth crew would try to sabotage it. Additional odd jobs had also to be found, so that I could generate enough money for a box of Standard bangers. I was much too old for sparklers now, and if enough money could be earned, I might be able to buy a jumping jack, maybe even a rocket.

Also, we had to plan a battle, all of us Cowpen lads, because a fight had been arranged for the following weekend. The Cowpen Gang against the Bella Gang. I don't know who did the arranging, and I didn't really care. It was a badge of honour to be called to the front line to fight those heathens, and my invitation to be part of the gang was yet another milestone in my quest for acceptance as just an ordinary Blyth lad.

Rumour had it that the Bella Gang were a bunch of Neanderthals. Low browed and communicating with grunts, and nicknamed the great unwashed. They lived over in bandit country, in houses without inside toilets. Known to us as the Isabella Colliery rows, their toilets were situated away from the houses, across a back lane, and one Bella lad, it was said, had been knocked down by a car, in his frantic rush to have a poo.

Bella kids, allegedly, lived on raw potatoes and bashed old people with sticks, and it was common knowledge that dogs and cats kept well away from the Bella 'cos they knew they would be eaten.

Therefore, it was up to us, the decent kids of Cowpen, with proper toilets, to sort these Neanderthals out. We were full of bravado and boast, we were going to wipe the floor with that bunch of donkeys. Unfortunately, that wasn't how it turned out.

On the Saturday evening in question, the weather wasn't the best, and, honestly, neither was the fight with the Bella gang. Frustratingly, it turned out to be something of a fiasco.

We congregated at seven o'clock. Twenty or so lads turned up for the fight, Taggart, Fowlers, Trude, Bates, Armstrong, Ash, Connor, and a plethora of faces and names I didn't recognise. I was a little dubious too, as to our readiness for a gang fight, when a lad called Roly turned up with a bow and arrow; last year's Christmas present no doubt, although, to be fair, he had removed the rubber sucker from the business end of the arrow and sharpened it. In a side pocket...his backup, a pea-shooter, and around his head a Sitting Bull Indian headdress with half a dozen feathers.

The fight was to take place on a grassy mound which stood to one side of the track, or cut, that led from Hallside, down to the Bella heap. The mound was roughly halfway between Cowpen and the Isabella houses. Most of us warriors had loaded our pockets with stones, and some were carrying various lengths of wood to use as clubs or swords.

The Bella lads were already in possession of the grassy mound when we first spied them and made our advance. They didn't look formidable, so this was going to be easy. Actually, they didn't look much different to us, and that surprised me. Weren't they supposed to be half-wits?

Someone in our midst shouted 'Cheeaarrgge'. In truth, it might have been myself; I was on a high. The battle began, when, as a group, we ran forward about twenty paces, no-one wanting to be in front. Roly fired his arrow and hit one of our own lads in the back of the head. A few stones were thrown in the general direction of the opposition, then....'whoosh'...a volley of projectiles scattered us. The Bella lads were much better prepared than us and had catapults...not the plastic ones...but big metal ones and they were firing not only stones, but ball bearings. Batesy was hit in the leg and gave a huge howl, Stan Fowler shouted 'retreat' as a ball bearing smashed into the fence beside his head. Another lad was hit in the chest, and we all turned and ran like a herd of wildebeests being chased by lions.

There's not much more to say about this infamous battle. It was over almost before it had started. We all ran back into Hallside and scattered. I took the opportunity to peel off from the crowd and head for home without waiting for the inevitable outcome. The battle petered out, seemingly with a few more stones and marbles fired. Our leader had a fight with their leader in someone's garden, and afterwards everyone split up and went home for supper. Tales of heroism and valiant deeds were dreamt up, fabricated, and eventually presented as fact. I heard many tales of derring-do over the next few days.

The truth is, we lost, the Bella lads won, and they, as victors, sauntered off home, to feast on cats and bash their grannies.

The day before the Bella debacle, it had been mam's banana day. A ritual which played itself out once a month, over an entire weekend, when mam received maintenance money in the post from dad.

Mam would have a smile so wide when she bought bananas. We had to treat this delicacy, she instructed us, with respect, indeed with a kind of reverence. Many was the time, she told us, how fervently she had longed for the tasting of a banana during the war years and for several years afterwards. Until, at long last, as the 1950s dawned, bananas returned to the grocers' shops. They ceased being rationed and were scarce no more. In mam's mind's eye however, they would always be scarce, something to be treasured.

Mam would give the fruit pride of place in a fancy smoked-glass bowl she called Lalique, and on which she'd squandered a whole shilling at a Salvation Army jumble sale. The bananas were always left alone over the weekend, a hand of fat yellow fingers, not to be touched, but admired. On Saturday and Sunday, they were only for show, our status symbol, just in case we had visitors. They stood, proudly, on a tall, slim unit at the living room window. Mam's net curtains were jardiniere style with a central bow which allowed passing folk to glance into the house, and what they would spot once a month would be mam's bowl of bananas. This was important, because, in truth, as newcomers, we rarely had visitors, unexpected or otherwise, and the fruit needed seeing.

Poor people...mam reasoned, would never leave bananas lying around in bowls - they would scoff them off as quickly as possible - and so, these exotic yellow fellows were our proclamation to the world, or at least anyone who cared to notice, that we were significant, not poor, and not unimportant. That we, the Brown family were worthwhile. Visitors or not, with the weekend over, on banana Mondays, we came straight home from school. We could have a whole banana each for tea, but it had to be accompanied by two slices of buttered bread, to fill us up, and only after we had finished our plateful of chips.

The day preceding banana day, however, Titch returned to school, now fully recovered from the mumps. He was as bright as a button, and completely unaware of my embarrassing episode. I didn't enlighten him.

It was noticeable to all of us that Titch had lost a little bit of weight. What he hadn't lost, however, was his ability to spin a yarn. It was morning playtime on his first day back, and he was holding court. There were five of us gathered around Titch, taking cover from a rain squall, in the big shed opposite the classrooms. We were hanging on his every word.

A lad, nicknamed Willick asked the first question, "What happens then Titch, when you get the mumps, what's it like?"

Titch surveyed his gathered audience like a modern-day rock-star. He waited before answering, knowing how to wring the maximum effect from an elongated pause. He scrunched up his face and rolled his eyes.

"Honestly, nee kiddin', it's even worse than having a broken leg or a heart attack. 'Cos sometimes, if you've been lucky, or if you're not really very ill, you only get one little mump, two at the most. Me though...I had loads...more than twenty, all inside my throat and my head. My neck swelled right up, and my head got massive, so that I looked like a turnip."

Then a long pause, "Oh, aye, and I had the hottest fever ever recorded in Blyth. There's only ever been one hotter, and that was somewhere in Africa. Doctor Campbell told my mam that if he'd come to the house half an hour later, I would've been rushed to hospital in an emergency ambulance. Not the Blyth hospital mind you, but the General in Newcastle, and they would've put me in an iron lung."

"Phwwaarrr, Titch, you must have been really scared," one of the Balmer twins chipped in. "How did they get you better?"

"Well...the doctor told my mam to give me lots of Lucozade, the big bottles not the little 'uns, and plenty of soup, and half an aspirin. I had to have some warm towels wrapped around my neck and had to sleep a lot."

"That doesn't sound very serious," said Derek Raisbeck. "I have Lucozade sometimes, and soup, so that's not medicine."

Titch was having none of it. "See, that's all you know... and you're wrong. Lucozade has a special thing in it that kills mumps. That's why it tastes fizzy. It makes your mumps burst...but it only happens while you're asleep, so you don't notice, and they don't go off with a bang."

We were all enthralled. We hadn't known any of that. "Is that why you're so skinny now?" I queried.

Titch shook his head, "Nah, it's just 'cos of the soup. That's all I was allowed for nearly a week. Chicken soup and tomato soup, and I hate tomato soup, but my mam said I had to have it, for vitamins. So, I used to pretend to eat it, and then when she went downstairs, I used to sneak along the landing, and flush it down the toilet."

We all laughed. That's just the kind of thing we expected from Titch. He was pleased with the laughter...playing to the gallery.

"Then, when I was getting better, mam brought me fried egg, sausages and beans, but my throat was still sore, and I could only eat the egg and beans. So, I tiptoed to the toilet and tried to flush the sausages away, but they just kept coming back up, like two massive poos."

We were all giggling away now. Titch in his element, the centre of attention.

"What happened then?" Willick was wide eyed and believing it all.

Titch had a huge grin on his face. "I had to stick my hand down the netty and fish them out afore mam came back."

Now we were in stitches. I'd heard his stories before, but I wasn't sure if this was the truth or another one of his tall tales. "So did your mam catch you, flushing the sausages."

"Nah, I got back into bed, in the nick of time. I put the bangers back on the plate before she came to take it away, and I told her I still had a sore throat and couldn't swallow them."

"Was your mam annoyed with you?" I asked.

Titch kept his face poker straight when he answered. "Nah... she just said not to worry, she'd give them to me dad for his tea."

He had all five of us in hysterics now, and he was loving it.

"The thing is...my dad really liked them. He wanted to know where my mam had bought those tasty sausages from."

Ding-ding-ding, the bell went. Playtime over, we all laughed our way back to the classroom.

There was also a slight altercation with Mr Hunter, our teacher, during that week. I hadn't intended to be a clever clogs, but that was the way it turned out.

I really liked Mr Hunter and he was always very fair with all his pupils. He didn't do favourites and if we worked hard, listened, and learned, he was invariably pleased.

Titch was now back in class, and we sat in rows, in alphabetical order. As my surname began with a 'B' I was in the first row, four seats from the front, behind the Balmer twins and Batesy. Titch was in the second row, an 'I', and he sat to my left-hand side, immediately opposite, across the aisle, just before Lamb, and Lawton. It meant we could have a good whisper, occasionally.

It was during a lesson break that I decided to tell Titch about Charlie Chuck.

I'd given it a great deal of thought and decided that it was wrong to keep secrets from my pal. So I told him, just little bits at first, tentatively, and rather nervously, expecting disdain, but he didn't seem surprised. In truth, he surprised me, informing me that while he had been absent with mumps, he'd told his dad about the dog burying episode, and in return his dad had been telling him all he knew about Charlie.

He knew for instance that Charlie wasn't his actual name, although he didn't know what his real name was. I did though...but I didn't let on that I knew. He said that Charlie was originally from Poland and had killed loads of Germans when they invaded his country. Then, he managed to escape, because the Nazis were searching for him, and he managed to make it to England and joined our army. "So," said Titch, "Charlie Chuck is alright". His dad however, had still warned him to keep away.

Wow, I was amazed. Titch hadn't only been palming his dad off with lavvy flavour sausages during his enforced absence. He'd also been doing some research on my new-found mentor.

I happened to be telling him all about my Hamlet episode with Charlie when Mr Hunter returned to the classroom. I was showing off to Titch with my 'to be, or not to be' soliloquy. I'd learned another few lines in the meantime.

Mr Hunter overheard and wandered up the aisle.

"That's very impressive Sid."

"Thank you, sir...it's from Hamlet. It's something that a man called William Shakespeare wrote about revenge and stuff."

Mr Hunter smiled, "Yes Sid, I do know Hamlet," then he paused. "Alas poor Yorick, I knew him well," followed by a superior smile. "It's not something you need to know for the time being though."

I was a little surprised at such a deflating comment from a teacher. Why wouldn't I want to know things about Shakespeare if I could?

I almost stopped the next words from escaping but couldn't quite manage it, and other people in the class were listening now.

"Shakespeare didn't write it like that sir. 'Alas poor Yorick, I knew him well...that's what everybody thinks it is. But it isn't. He wrote it different...'alas poor Yorick! I knew him, Horatio; a fellow of infinite jest.'"

Mr Hunter glared at me, obviously annoyed. The classroom was so quiet, you could have heard a pin drop. "Very good, Sid, you're right of course." He was not a happy teacher, being corrected by a kid. "But like I said, you don't need to know that for now." Titch was glaring at me, making his eyes bigger, telling me to shut up. I did.

Mr Hunter threw me a look which I took to mean, 'clever little git, now you're in the bad books'. Then he turned away and walked to his desk at the front of the classroom. Conversation ended.

"Alright everybody, pencils, and paper out. I want you to spell all the months of the year, in their correct order." He glared at me once again, "That includes of course, Mr clever-clogs Shakespeare".

Gales of laughter - it seemed the entire class was laughing at me. Inside I was really hurting, embarrassed at being ridiculed. I didn't understand.

Clever clogs became my nickname for weeks after, until, like all things, the moment passed, and life returned to normality.

That day was not one of my best. I needed to talk to Charlie, for advice. I would do that on Monday evening, after banana tea-time.

Before that, however, on the Saturday night, we received a surprise from Mam. She'd arranged a railway trip to Newbiggin for us the very next day, and an early start was required. Mam had received extra money in the post from dad and she'd decided we deserved a family treat.

Dawn had barely time to peek over the horizon when we were woken for breakfast, both Linda and I bleary-eyed, and having to be almost force-fed with eggy bread and mugs of tea before departure. I'd never been to Newbiggin, and wasn't sure where it was, but I'd heard some of the other lads talking about the Ashington – Newbiggin train. Mam said it was further north than Blyth, at the seaside, so the day promised some excitement and sandy sandwiches.

We were to leave from Newsham, so we set off early, and followed the track, through the fields from Cowpen, passing very close to the spot where Charlie had buried Bruno. Then, past Buglass' farm and the row of retired miners' cottages, on down Phoenix Street and then to Newsham station. Why we ended up at little Newsham station when

Blyth had a much bigger one, I couldn't say. Maybe the fare was cheaper from there.

The train ride was exciting, my first experience of rail travel. Tickets to buy, tickets to be checked and clipped, doors slamming, and men in uniforms, seemingly very important, blowing whistles, waving arms to the train driver, and shouts of "all aboard".

Arriving on the platform just in time, we boarded our designated carriage, and after finding seats, the train pulled away, tentatively at first, the carriages giving a little jolt, before we began slowly, picking up speed.

It wasn't the Flying Scotsman, and we didn't break any records, but soon, the rhythm of the wheels on tracks became soothingly hypnotic, diddle-de-dum, diddle-de-dum, diddle-de-dum, while through the windows, scrawny trees, and banks of pit waste meandered past. It was by no means the Orient Express, but I thought it was brilliant. Paris, Munich, Vienna, and Budapest it wasn't. Instead, we had our own exotic and intriguing stations - Newsham, Bebside, Bedlington and Ashington before our arrival in Newbiggin, our local version of Istanbul. To a rail travel novice of 10 years, it was a little slice of heaven.

The journey was over way too soon, I wished it could have been longer, but on arrival, we alighted from the train, exited the little station, and immediately made a beeline for the beach. Mam had been carrying the blanket, to put down on the sand, while I was stuck with the towel and the heavy bag of sandwiches and pop. Linda as per usual carried nothing but a grin, and just skipped along, without a care in the world.

I'd really love to say that it was a fantastic day, but it wasn't. Newbiggin was incredibly boring, and a huge disappointment. We would have had much more fun at Blyth beach. Mam of course pretended it was brilliant. She felt obliged to, after spending what little money she had on the day trip. The sand, however, on what masqueraded as a beach, wasn't sandy at all, wasn't inviting by any means, it was a depressing grey colour with flecks of black, tiny little bits of coal and coal dust, having accumulated for years from the surrounding mines. It was sparse too, unlike Blyth, where the golden sand was sometimes so high that it muscled its way up, onto the promenade.

Here, however, down at the water's edge, there was also a faint black line, identifying how far the tide had come in. A pathfinder for the mining waste, dug up and dumped at sea, and which was now finding its way back to land.

If you peered into the little rock pools which had formed, tiny jags of jet black seemed to sparkle like diamonds when the sun caught them at just the right angle. I don't know if anything was living in those rock pools...other than maybe, tiny crabs, and winkles with emphysema.

There was, at least, an ice-cream van, hot-dog van and a café, and a mysterious wooden booth, but that was about your lot. Even the shuggy boats were out of order for some reason. Mam tried to make the most of a poor situation and made a big thing of digging holes in the sand and then burying her feet.... yippee. I feigned enthusiasm, just so mam wouldn't be disappointed. It was difficult though, to ignore how dirty her feet had become from the mucky beach. Also, she was desperate for us to watch the Punch and Judy show. A throwback to her childhood and nicer times, a reminder of her days of innocence and happiness. Those were her Kinghorn beach memories, of which she had spoken so fondly in her rare moments of Fife reminiscence.

The mysterious wooden booth suddenly lost its mystery. It was the setting for Punch and Judy. Why they called Punch and Judy a show, I'll never know. We sat in front of that little booth amongst the gathered crowd, while some bloke, hiding inside the wooden box, stuck his hand up a puppet, held it above his head, and moved it around a little puppet stage whilst talking in a squeaky voice. We were, in effect, watching a caricature of domestic violence, as the main character 'Punch', bashed his wife over the head with a little baseball bat and chucked a baby onto the floor. A policeman puppet popped up, told him off, and then chased him off stage. 'That's the way to do it'...indeed.

Enthralling it wasn't. Mam laughed at it, I didn't know why, because it wasn't funny in the slightest, and it made me wonder how she could be amused at something like that, after all the rubbish experiences she had with dad. It made me feel a little sad, and a little annoyed. All the other kids who were watching the show laughed, too. Perhaps I was missing something, and maybe I was overthinking again.

After that torment, it was time to eat. The sandwiches, as expected, ended up sandy. We had egg and tomato, or seaside sandwiches, as mam called them, with a pile of banana sandwiches, too. Mam was really pushing the boat out, sacrificing bananas before Monday. Dandelion and burdock, our choice of pop, was alright, and drinkable, but we'd have preferred American cream soda. Not that it would have tasted any better, but if it said American on the label, it must be excellent...right?

Linda palled up with another girl for a while and spent some time paddling in the sea and then joining in a bat and ball game with the girl's family. They spent a while exploring those little rock pools and fishing out tiny crabs, so at least she found some enjoyment.

But for me, the whole day dragged. It wasn't enjoyed, it was endured. I endured with a fixed smile so as not to spoil it. I told mam it had been a brilliant day, but maybe next time we should make do with Blyth beach and save the train fare. That seemed to please her.

Boring day or not, by going home time the sea air had hit the three of us hard. We were totally shattered. Small mercies, at least I didn't have the pop and sandwiches to carry home, but I carried the blanket for mam.

I could quite easily have fallen asleep on the return journey, the rhythmic sound of train wheels on tracks now doubly hypnotic, but I was determined to extract every minute of pleasure from that surprise outing. Destination reached, the return walk from Newsham to Cowpen saw all three of us dragging our feet. It was by now quite dark, and conversation was at a premium, all three of us being too tired to chatter. We returned by way of Winship Street, turning right, past the little school then on down a little track that ran parallel to the pit railway line. Until finally, we made our way through the Isabella Colliery rows.

This change of route kept me on my guard. I was nervous as we walked down the back lane of the row of houses standing closest to Cowpen, houses to the right, toilets to the left, and hoping no-one would recognise one of the Cowpen gang heroes. Luckily, there wasn't a soul about, except a little black dog, which seemed very nervous as it ran past us. I subconsciously urged it to keep running before it became a Bella banquet. Apart from that, nothing, and we escaped enemy territory without a hint of confrontation.

By the time we reached our house we were completely drained of energy. My sis and I trudged upstairs to get washed, then into our pyjamas, whilst Mam managed to rustle up some supper for us, wearily it must be said, but nevertheless, it was welcomed. Then, a kiss for Linda, and a punch on the arm for me, before packing us both off to bed.

During the night I got out of bed to use the toilet. I heard the crackle of the television and mam's snores from downstairs. She'd fallen asleep on the couch. I took a blanket downstairs, switched off the telly and covered mam up.

Tomorrow was Monday, she would have cleaning jobs to go to, and I was going to see Charlie after banana tea-time.

CHAPTER 6

Life Lessons.

———————————————■———————————————

As it happened, there was no banana treat that Monday after school. Mam had used all the bananas for our sandwiches on the Newbiggin trip, so teatime turned out to be a routine affair. Well, virtually routine, apart from mam's pointed question at the tea table.

"Sid, what on earth has happened to your eye? You've been fighting at school, haven't you? What have I told you about fighting?"

My left eye was noticeably bruised and sore, the pupil beginning to turn yellow, and my eyelid half closed. I'd been wondering when the inevitable grilling would begin, but there was no way I could tell mam the truth, I couldn't tell anyone what had really happened. It was too painful and embarrassing, another of my misjudgements.

"Fighting is stupid Sid, it's pointless. You sort your differences out by talking, not by bashing each other. How many times have I said?...I mean, for heaven's sake, please not again, I've had this with Kenny...I'm sick of it." She was ranting...not making sense...really annoyed.

"I want you to tell me the honest truth. Who were you fighting with.? I don't want anyone's mother turning up at my door and causing a scene because you've bashed her lad, so come on, out with it. What's your story?" Mam was going ballistic.

I wasn't a fighter; I wasn't frightened of a fight, but I wasn't any good at it, unlike some of the other lads at my school. I was a talker, a thinker, and now I needed to talk and think my way out of this situation. Mam didn't deserve a lie, and lying is never good, as Charlie had told me, but sometimes it's acceptable, if the truth is going to hurt someone. This was one of those occasions. Telling the truth would absolutely hurt someone - the someone being me.

"Me... fighting mam? You must be joking. Why do you think I'm such a good runner? The only thing I've had a fight with is a cricket ball. We were playing cricket at school cos Fred Douglas brought a bat and a corker, and I was standing too close when he whacked the ball and it hit me in the face. It knocked me over, and everybody thought I'd been knocked out. Mona, the dinner lady, came and helped me up, and took me inside, into the porch, and she washed my face and put some smelly antiseptic cream on." I began to walk around the table, "Here, mam, have a sniff, you can still smell it, I think".

Mam put her hand in the air to stop my progress. My acting had been exquisite. She believed me.

"That was a silly thing to do, Sid. Your eye is all bloodshot. I'll see if I can find an eyepatch in the medicine tin." She was simmering gently now, having cooled down from boiling.

"Mam, mam, I was just standin' in the wrong place - it's nobody's fault."

She was rummaging through an old Crawford's shortbread tin, in the bottom kitchen drawer, mam's medical war chest. Her hand shot up, holding a white eyepatch. A big smile of victory creased her face.

"Here, put this on. It'll keep any dirt out and stop the light from hurting."

She moved behind my chair and put the patch in place, over my eye, the elastic tight around my head.

"There, that'll keep you right," she chuckled. "Don't get into any more arguments with cricket balls."

Linda had been watching the entire episode from the other side of the table. She wasn't a chatterbox, and rarely spoke, other than to mam, but she made an exception on this occasion. Staring quizzically at my eyepatch.

"Do you want me to go up to Mrs Thompson's house mam?"

Mam frowned. "Mrs Thompson's,? No, why would I?"

Linda began giggling, "To ask if we can borrow her parrot to put on Sid's shoulder."

Mam laughed, Linda continued giggling, and even I managed to crack a smile, more in relief at being believed. It was funny though.

I went around to Charlie's, immediately after teatime. It had been a week since my last visit, and I was having withdrawal symptoms.

I was pleased to see that Helena was still at Charlie's when he opened the front door and ushered me in. She gave a huge grin when I walked into the sitting room.

"Sid, where have you been? We've missed you. Our lives have been empty without you."

I knew it was rubbish, but I was pleased. At least it was nice rubbish.

"Hi Helena, my life has been empty, too," I fired back, "I don't know how I've managed to survive".

She gave me a thumbs up, and a welcoming smile.

I responded to her initial question. "I've been busy at school and doing other stuff. Helping me mam".

"Good for you, Sid. How did you get your black eye?"

The question was direct, not unexpected, but I'd hoped the black eye would be ignored, put away as just the general hurly burly of kids' lives. But she was concerned.

"Got smacked!" I replied.

"Did you smack him back?" she asked, a question I hoped I wouldn't have to answer. I didn't want to lie.

"No."

"Why?"

I was now in a quandary, tell a lie to preserve my status, or tell the truth and look like a real Jessie.

The truth prevailed. "It wasn't a lad."

Helena looked concerned. She said no more, but waited, for what seemed an interminably long time, until I continued.

"It was a lass punched me in the face. That lass I was tellin' you about, who hasn't got any decent clothes."

The pause in conversation seemed endless. No-one spoke, no-one offered a comment. I felt obliged to carry on.

"She punched me in the face 'cos I gave her one of my brother's old jumpers that's too small for me now."

Still no response.

"I was being kind...she hasn't got anything, no good clothes or anything, but she told me I was a snob who thinks I'm better than her. But that's not right; I was just wanting to give her my brother's jumper, so she could be warm. I wasn't trying to be better than her."

Helena and Charlie were exchanging meaningful glances. They were concerned. I felt I wasn't explaining very well.

"See, I told you. I shouldn't have done anything at all. I've tried to do something nice, but all I've got is a punch in the face."

Helena smiled. "A punch in the face, but for all the right reasons. You attempted to do something nice, Sid, but you did it in the wrong way."

"What d'ye mean, wrong way? I was being nice."

"She didn't see it like that Sid...did she? She thought you were being superior, better than her."

"I wasn't. I was trying to be kind."

Charlie piped up, "There are many ways of being kind, Sid. What's the girl's name?"

"Errr, I don't know." I shrugged; I'd never even asked her. "It could be Lilian...maybe, or Gillian, something like that."

"So", said Helena, "if someone who didn't know your name, walked up to you and gave you an old pair of pants, without any explanation, would you be happy, or would you perhaps think about punching them in the face, for treating you like a poor person, like rubbish?"

"Aahh did give an explanation, Aahh told her I'd brought a jumper cos aahh knew she didn't have any decent clothes."

"Oh Sid, Oh Sid, how simple it must be to be ten years old again." Helena broke in, a forlorn look written large across her face.

"She may be poor, but she doesn't want to be told that she is...she doesn't need a handout, she needs a hand up. She doesn't need charity, she needs friends. She probably wants someone to ask her name, and to talk to her, ask her how she's feeling, how best to help, how is she coping?"

Charlie chipped in again.

"That person could be you."

Then he seemed to realise that enough was enough.

"That's it for today; enough advice for now, give your head a chance to process it; to think things through. I'm sure you'll figure things out all by yourself, without Helena and me". We can't keep heaping pressure on you. Life is life, and what you make of it is up to you."

Charlie winked, "Anyway, Helena is going to London tomorrow evening".

"What for?" I asked, happy that the conversation was taking a different tack. "Is she going on the train?"

"Aye, she is," Charlie confirmed, and smiled at Helena.

"She's going to enjoy an opera...aren't you?"

Helena grinned, "You don't even like opera, Carol. You're a Philistine."

I was not part of the conversation. An outsider, looking in.

"What's opera?" I ventured.

Helena responded immediately. "It's life, beautiful life, but lived on a higher plane, it's sublime, it elevates the soul and makes life bearable, wonderful..." Her voice tailed away.

Charlie chipped in, "Take no notice, she talks rubbish and she's biased. Opera is unreal. It's just like a play, with music and squeaky voices. It's where the leading character gets stabbed in the back, and instead of dying, or at least shouting 'ouch', he starts to sing... I mean...seriously? and always in Italian. It's pure fantasy and absolute rubbish."

Helena laughed, "And it isn't all over until the fat lady sings."

"Then don't and it will go on for ever."

Charlie and Helena laughed together, lifelong pals. They possessed a magnetism that is difficult to explain

There's a certain beauty in friendships, a bond, which is sometimes more than friendship, and which transcends the norms of human existence. Those two had that bond, and I hoped I would experience that sort of connection, with someone, someday.

"Is London really big?" I asked, excitedly. I'd heard tales about London from a lass at school who had relatives there, and she said it was huge, much bigger than Newcastle.

"Yes," was the brief reply from Helena.

"So, how come you're going there, to the opera. Have you got some friends in London?"

"Yes," another brief reply. Not unfriendly, just brief.

Charlie chipped in, "Helena has an important friend in London, a politician, a Liberal politician, Lubbock".

I was out of my depth but enjoying the experience. "What's a Lubbock, and what's a Liberal?"

Charlie laughed. "Maybe you're just a little young for these conversations. A liberal is just a member of a political party, like the Labour party, or the Conservatives."

"Are they any good, the Liberals, you know, like the Labour party, or are they nasty, like the Conservatives?"

Charlie and Helena were making eye contact, deciding perhaps if I was too young. Helena shrugged her shoulders, giving Charlie the green light.

"Sid, I will tell you what I think, but this is only my opinion. Remember, opinions are like snowflakes, each one is different. You'll have your own snowflake when you have more experience of life."

I was instantly confused. Snowflakes....ehhh, what was that all about?"

"Lubbock is a person, Eric Lubbock, a Liberal candidate for a little bit of London called Orpington. And yes, he's a good bloke."

Got it, Lubbock was a who, not a what.

"Liberals are generally good people, with good intentions, but perhaps not...very...errrmm, capable, no-no-no, perhaps efficient is the word I'm looking for." Charlie paused, deep in thought, then continued. "Best to explain what I think with an example." He cleared his throat.

"Imagine, Sid, you're out on a bike ride, and fickle fate takes a hand."

I immediately piped up.

"Charlie...I haven't got a bike. Mam says she'll try and get me one if I pass the eleven plus."

"There you go again Sid, interrupting. Remember, we've been here once before, it's an example, a what if, an illustration of a point I'm trying to make. Now can you please use those extremely large ears of yours instead of opening that monstrously large mouth."

That put me back in my box. I gave a little grin and shut up. I was too used to Charlie by now to take offence.

He smiled at me and continued.

"So, you're out on your bike ride, and fickle fate takes a hand. You have a flat tyre and you're stuck. Then a Liberal sees you at the roadside and stops to give you a hand, sees the problem and tries to fix things. But being a bit of a bungler, although well-intentioned he only succeeds in damaging some of your spokes and setting your bike on fire."

A little snort from Helena. A brief laugh from me.

"Then someone from the Labour party pulls up. He knows how to fix your tyre, but he needs to call five of his friends. One to deal with the rubber, one to handle the metal bits, one for the glue and two to supervise. Then, a dispute, because the rubber person thinks that the metal person had touched his rubber bits. They end up arguing with each other and nothing gets done.

"Finally, a Conservative pulls up in his car. Sees that you have a problem, winds down his window, shouts 'ha-ha, that'll teach you, peasant,' and drives away to boast to his friends at how he'd laughed at a poor person."

I was only ten, but I understood more than they thought I did. Mam had told me what she thought about politics, about politicians, about Tories - she called them. Labour believed in people, she said. Tories only believe in money and themselves, and I believed mam.

"So, what are your saying Charlie? My mam says that the Conservatives are selfish. She says they're not nice."

"Aye, not nice, your mam's right. Not the ordinary people, who vote Tory; they're just ordinary folk who've fallen for a big lie. Unfortunately, the Tories, the big important ones, they control the banks, the press, the newspapers. One day they will destroy this country, so that a few thousand rich people can live in extravagance, while the rest of the population struggle." He paused. "And one day, when scientists discover the centre of the universe, most Tories will be surprised to find they're not it."

"Enough, enough," cried Helena. "Sid's far too young to be listening to the rantings of old people." She gave my arm a squeeze, before continuing, "Age lends you a certain perspective on life, Sid. When you've lived some more of it yourself, you'll understand".

I thought about this for a moment, "So, what's it like, being old...getting older?" I hesitated, "Sorry for being rude, it's just...well, I can't think what it must be like to be old. Do you still have things that you want to do...you know, like places to see, and stuff you want to accomplish?"

She thought for a moment. "The old horse in the stable still yearns to run," she replied," but perhaps not in the Grand National." It sort of made sense, so I filed that reply away, to dissect later.

"So, can you remember what it's like, being young...like me?"

A big smile from Helena. "Yes, of course...in my head, I'm still young. It's the one place where you never age. So, the great thing about being old is that you don't lose all the other ages you've been."

That made perfect sense. Mam had said something similar.

"And you're looking forward to all the ages that you're going to be," I volunteered.

They both looked at me with something approaching astonishment.

My involvement with adult conversation was over for the day. It was Charlie's turn to visit Martha in hospital. Another taxi ride home. Silver Streak would be getting fed up with me.

CHAPTER 7

October Song

———————————————■———————————————

September was over and October was racing on at a frenetic pace. Visits to Charlie were sparse. Martha was home now, after her operation, but required lots of rest as part of her recuperation. Charlie was her full-time carer and had minimal spare time. Helena stayed to help for a while, but she also had a life of her own, and soon returned to her work in London. She'd been intentionally vague when I asked what she did in London; unforthcoming, so I assumed it must be important, or private, but didn't press it.

What I did discover over the next few months, was that my life had subtly changed. Lessons learned from those frequent Charlie and Helena visits altered my thinking, made me question things I'd taken for granted, helped me look at the world and the people around me with fresh eyes. I was still a ten-year-old, but my head was awash with adult opinion. A precarious position indeed, which would require careful management.

Mam and I were back to normal now, and when we talked it was as if nothing out of the normal had happened. She made no further reference to my silly indiscretion, and it made possible my escape from self-imposed purgatory. The elephant disappeared from the room.

Then an unexpected development, which caught me completely off guard. Mam paid a surprise visit to Morpeth Road one morning. I was shocked to see her coming in through the school gate, and then heading purposefully for the headmaster's office. It was playtime and I was in the school field, a cavalry trooper, fighting pesky redskins, and she didn't see me. I was puzzled and also nervous as to the reason for her visit. For several hours afterwards I was fully expecting a summons to the headmaster's office, for a telling-off maybe, or to be told some bad news. But the anticipated call never came, and it baffled me for the remainder of the day.

I questioned her about it at tea-time.

"What were you doing at my school today, mam?"

She looked surprised. "Oh, you saw me then. I had a look around for you."

There was a long pause, and she turned back to the saucepan on the cooker, fishing eggs out with a tablespoon, their statutory three and a half minutes of boiling now over.

"Just a progress report Sid, you know. I wanted to find out how you were doing at school." She didn't face me, she kept her back turned. I knew she wasn't being entirely honest.

"And what did Tweddle say?" I left the Mr out purposely. If she picked me up on it, that was normal. If she didn't, she was hiding something.

She didn't. "He said everything is satisfactory, you're doing great. In the top set. I'm very pleased, obviously."

I was feeling uncomfortable. I didn't like mam being cagey, and when she turned from the stove she avoided eye-contact.

"Will you see to these Sid?" she pushed the eggcups towards me. "I have to pop out for ten minutes. Pick up some cleaning money." She was avoiding any further questions.

"Ok mam."

She brushed past to reach her cardigan in the passage. "Remember...'

"Yeh, yeh, yeh," I interrupted, "little end down, big end up. Gulliver's Travels".

"Thanks Sid, back soon." Then she was gone.

Now I was more mystified than ever. What on earth had she really been doing at my school. The problem is, when you're fed a half-truth you begin to fill in the other half with speculation, with imaginings, and you conjure up all manner of fanciful outcomes to the problems you've created. Maybe I'd be moving school again. Or going back to Kirkcaldy. Perhaps mam couldn't afford to pay for school dinners, and I'd be on the free-meal register. Maybe, mam didn't know Mr Hunter was married, and she fancied him. Worse still, maybe she fancied Mr Tweddle, who must have been over a hundred years old! How daft had my thinking become? But by the same token, it could be true that she'd been at my school for a progress report, like she'd said...but if so, why be so evasive?

When she returned, I avoided questioning her. Being unable to give a straight answer was so unlike mam. Our following chat was stilted and awkward. My elephant had departed, but mam had created a new one. God only knew which corner of the room it would be sitting in. It would be several days before the subject was broached again.

The answer to mam's school visit came in two parts, both surprising, and each one leaving me a little sheepish for having doubted her. It was the last Friday before October half term, known in Blyth as 'blackberry week' or 'tatie picking week'. The final school bell had rung, and there was a buzz of excitement. This was our last week off school before the hugest of the huge holidays, Christmas. After this short break was over, we would all begin ticking off the weeks, and then the days, as the big celebration drew ever closer.

I was in as much of a hurry as anyone to remove myself from school premises, much as I enjoyed the learning. Yesterday we'd all been laughing and singing our hearts out in the big shed, "One more day of school, one more day of sorrow, one more day in this old dump, and we'll be free tomorrow." Mr Hunter, who really was a good stick, as far as teachers go, popped his head around the corner of the shed, and instead of telling us off, he joined in with the singing. We were so surprised. That one moment entrenched him as the favourite teacher of all the fourth year, not just his own class.

As the bell went, there was a mad scramble for the classroom door.

Mr Hunter caught my eye, "Sid, can you wait behind for a minute?"

"Yes sir." I didn't know what I'd done. I was pretty sure that it couldn't be anything serious.

He waited until everyone else had exited.

Titch was looking in from the hall and Mr Hunter saw his face at the window. He made a shooing gesture and Titch turned and trotted away down the corridor.

Turning back to me, he said. "Now then Sidney, you're probably aware that your mother was here recently."

I kept quiet, not sure how to respond.

"Among other things, she asked me why I'd told you not to read Shakespeare."

Suddenly, everything was making sense. Mam must have been here to tell Mr Hunter off. I'd told her what he'd said to me, about not needing to know anything about Shakespeare.

"So, I'll tell you exactly what I told her." He cleared his throat.

"I said that I didn't tell you not to read or appreciate Shakespeare. What I meant to say, and perhaps I should have made it much clearer, is that you need to focus on basic maths and English, sums and spelling, problems, and punctuation.

"What is needed for now Sidney, is your concentration on schoolwork so that you pass the eleven plus exam. If you can do that then it is out of my hands. You'll go to grammar school and then you can broaden your horizons, broaden your knowledge, expand your appreciation of literature.

If you do go to grammar school, as I myself did, then you will be encouraged to read Shakespeare, and Dickens, and Wordsworth and the Brontës", but Sidney, you must pass the exam first. Please, please, please, just concentrate on your schoolwork. It gives me great satisfaction to see the boys and girls that I teach, attain their full potential. I've told your mother as much. I guarantee there will be no Shakespeare questions in the eleven plus, and not a single reference to Hamlet."

I just stood there quietly, mouth open.

He smiled at me, stroked his moustache, then made a thumb gesture towards the door. "Right Sid, all done, tell your mam I've spoken to you. Now bugger off and enjoy your holidays."

I did as I was told. It was the first time I'd heard a teacher say bugger. It wouldn't be the last.

What Mr Hunter said to me that day was also a life lesson. Charlie, and to a certain extent, Helena, had proffered so many pearls of wisdom. Grown-up lessons to mull over and absorb, and for that I was thankful. This one from my teacher however, struck an immediate chord. Concentrate on the things I could control, those that I needed as a kid, to further my ambition. Don't forget about all the other stuff, the clever stuff, but put it on the back burner until the exam is over, and hopefully passed.

Thank you, Mr Hunter, your words were direct, but they were good words. Other than your reference to the Brontës of course. That puzzled me. Brontës were what cowboys rode, surely? And they were usually bucking, weren't they? I'd have to ask Charlie.

I was feeling quite breezy as I walked down the corridor. One mystery cleared up; mam's visit explained.

Titch was waiting for me in the porch. We'd arranged to walk home together with George Wilkinson. Titch was looking interested, Willick was holding my coat.

"So, what did Hunter want you for?" Titch asked.

"Nowt much, just stuff," I replied, nonchalantly, as I took my coat from Willick.

"Howay man, Sid, it must have been summat." Titch was a little edgy. There was something going on, and he wasn't in the loop.

"Honest man, Titch, it wasn't owt special. Just stuff to do wi' me mam, and grammar school...nowt important."

"What about grammar school; what did he say?" he was becoming more agitated by the second.

"Can't tell you Titch, I'm sworn to secrecy."

"Don't be daft Sid; howay man, what's it all about?"

Willick chipped in, "Aye, what did he say. Is it anything about the eleven plus? Something about the questions?"

Even today, looking back, it's still a mystery how I managed to tell such a huge lie with a straight face. I'll never know, but I did, and I remember the words sounded weird coming out of my mouth.

"Hunter says that because I know so much Shakespeare, one of the teachers at grammar school told him that I'm guaranteed a place and I don't need to take the eleven plus. I won't be coming back here. After blackberry week I'm supposed to go straight to grammar school."

Silence, from both of them. We walked on for a little while, not talking. I had the weirdest feeling of power. I felt jealousy emanating from the pair. I knew it was a lie, they didn't.

We must have walked half a mile, heading towards the allotments, past the boulders, which was what we called the area where the council stored their main concrete drains for the new housing estates. We spotted Ken Robinson and Andy Reid hiding inside one of the big drains, puffing away on a sly cigarette. We ignored them and walked on.

Then Willick spoke. "What's the name of the teacher?"

"Ehhh?" I wasn't expecting that.

"The teacher that says you can go to grammar."

"Ohhh, him." I was thinking on the fly. "Mr Winkle...he teaches frimology".

I don't know where this stuff was coming from. My mouth had taken over and left my brain way behind.

"Ehhh?" said Titch. "What's that.... frill.... flimbo?"

"Frimology," I corrected him.

"So, what is it?"

"Errrmm, it's like science...but about insects and ants and worms," I explained, grasping at straws.

"That's biology," Willick interrupted. He was one of the class smarties.

"Zactly," I declared. "See Titch, Willick is really clever. He knows that Frimology is part of biology."

Titch was silent, Willick puffed up with the compliment.

Titch piped up again. "Anyway...I don't believe it, 'cos there's no such name as Mr Winkle....it's just made up."

"There are people called Winkle," said Willick, jumping in. That's where my name comes from...Wilkinson...and Wilkin and Wilkes - it comes from a name in Austria and Germany... and it's where we get the name for periwinkles...'cos I've got that in my 'Knowledge' magazine...so it is right about that."

I'd thought my lie was going to be jumped on, until Willick pulled it out of the fire, and inadvertently saved the day.

"See, Titch, you don't know everything," I said rather harshly, then tempered it with, "you do know most things, but it's right, there is a teacher called Mr Winkle."...I'd decided to go with the flow.

Then I calmed things down. I was looking for a way out of my own lie, "Anyway, I'll have to see what mam says, 'cos I don't think she can afford my uniform just yet."

I quickly changed the subject. "I know a brilliant place for blackberries if you want to come with me tomorrow. I saw it from the train last week and I bet there'll be bucketloads."

Grammar school was forgotten for the present, although Titch still seemed a little miffed; and we were soon engrossed in planning our foray into bramble country. How many bags would we need, maybe jars, a big stick to move the prickly brambles, and a pail maybe? Titch took leave of us at the top of Brierley Road, a quick wave and then he was trotting away down Dene View. Willick and I walked on to his house.

"Is that right, about you goin' to grammar," Willick asked, obviously still doubtful. He wasn't daft.

"Nah, I was just winding Titch up. Like he does with us. Hunter just told me to concentrate on sums and spellin' instead of learning Shakespeare."

Willick grinned. "Titch believes you though, doesn't he?"

"Aye so don't say nowt, okay. It's our secret."

Another grin from Willick. He liked being part of a secret.

I left him at his house and headed across the wasteland opposite the Co-op for home. We'd all arranged to meet up the next morning for our first blackberry safari.

Four of us met up, very early on that Saturday, outside of my house. I could see that mam was pleased that I had a few friends. She'd gone through absolute torture with Kenny when we'd first moved to Blyth, with his inability to fit in and make pals.

Titch, Willick and I were joined by Batesy from Axwell Drive, a lad from our school who I'd only met up with a few times. I knew him of course, because we were in the same class, and we'd endured the Bella gang debacle together, but usually we moved in different circles, and although we were on nodding terms we'd never been pals.

I'd sort of hoped to take the lead on this outing, having boasted about knowing a good spot for blackies, but Titch insisted that Batesy take the lead because his dad was reputedly the best blackie finder in Cowpen, and his mam would be making the blackberry and apple pies when we returned. Not only that, the pies would also be the best we'd ever tasted. I was a little dubious about that pronouncement, because of Titch's dismal recent record, but I gave in gracefully.

As it turned out he was spot on with everything he'd said.

That Saturday morning, armed with bowls, bags and sticks, we four blackieteers set off in search of our prey. There was a chill in the air and the sun shone shyly, hinting perhaps at warmth to come, as we trudged through the fields between Cowpen and Newsham.

I couldn't understand why Batesy was leading us past hedgerows with a profusion of bramble bushes and not giving them a glance. I stopped to search one of the bushes.

"Nah Hawky," Batesy said, "picked clean man. Yer might find the odd blackie, but these are the easy bushes. Everybody's had a go at these ones. They never look any further than the brambles at the side of the path. Trust me, I'll show you where me and my dad go; we'll get loads."

He did, and we did.

We didn't head towards Newsham, but the opposite direction towards Bebside. About a quarter of a mile further on, along the dirt track, following Batesy's directions, we clambered over a broken fence, then up over the railway line, down the other side, over another rickety fence, and finally, into a narrow belt of land between the railway line and the banks of colliery waste. We alighted there, facing a long, unbroken profusion of bramble bushes.

Batesy grinned, triumphant, arm outstretched. "Get pickin' lads."

To say we discovered a bountiful harvest would be a gross understatement. Those hedgerows were bursting with the biggest, the best, and most juicy blackberries that the world had ever beheld...at least that's how we all remembered it. Batesy showed me how to pick the blackies carefully between thumb and forefinger, so as not to squash the plump, ripe fruit, and to look under the bushes, parting the grass to ferret out the rogue stems which held the fattest berries, and which had evaded the birds.

But even if you're armed with a stout stick you still end up scratched. Little bloody cuts and painful scrapes, tiny thorns embedded in your skin, and all made worse because we were all members of the short trouser brigade. Nobody wore long trousers until senior school, and that made those jaggy bushes complete purgatory. Woollen jumpers clicked and pulled, t-shirts, trousers and bare skin stained here and there in deep red. Absolute heaven.

In less than two hours our bags and bowls were full to capacity, and there was a feeling of exhilaration at a job well done, a hard-won victory. It was pointless picking any more fruit. We had no room for more.

"Leave some for the birds," said Batesy, "they need to eat as well, and maybe we can come back again later in the week. Anybody want a sandwich and a slowsh of pop?"

He'd been the only one of us who had come prepared. He'd brought a haversack with him, containing some sandwiches and a bottle of pop. I was impressed that he was sharing, he didn't need to. We were all thirsty and grateful for a mouthful of lemonade, and then hungrily devouring the little packet of sandwiches. There were four of us and only four sandwiches, and they were only jam, but they went down like caviar. Then Titch generously produced a packet of Murray Mints, the too good to hurry mints, and he shared these out amongst our little gang.

Sitting on a little patch of grass, and all four of us now fed and watered, mouths sucking on Murray Mints, we felt like a complete unit. We rested there for a while, tired and happy, before wearily packing up and heading for Batesy's house to display our bounty.

On the way home we passed two groups of blackie hunters, foraging away in the very bushes that we'd ignored. As we approached the first group, Batesy whispered, "Don't say anything about our secret place, it's only for our gang, not for anyone else".

I was pleased as punch. I now belonged to a secret gang. As we passed the foragers, we could feel the envious glances as they viewed our abundance of fruit.

"Hey lad," a voice, presumably the dad of the group, asked, "where did yer get all them blackies?"

We stayed silent and let Batesy do the talking. "From here, where you're lookin' now; we came really early and picked them clean."

"Knew it," said the dad figure, "thought somebody had beaten us to it. Do you know any other places?"

"Golf course is supposed to be good," Batesy replied, "it's a bit of a way though, but it could be good".

"Thanks lad," the dad figure replied. "Wish we'd started out as early as you lot. Bet your mams will be pleased."

We carried on, and I asked, "Is it really good at the golf course for blackies, or were you just kidding?"

"Aye, it's not bad," Batesy replied, "but that place will have been picked ower an' all. Yer have to find the hidden places to get the best blackies. There's been folk out pickin' for a few weeks now. So, mind that you keep our place to yourself, or everybody will be ower there before you can say Jack Robinson. It's just for us lot." He was telling, not asking. I didn't know who Jack Robinson was, but I didn't care. I was now officially part of a gang.

We dropped off all the blackies at Batesy's house on Axwell. Titch had pulled me to one side and in a very serious tone, told me to stop calling him Batesy. "You only use last names when you're mad at someone, like... 'here Irving ye little pig' for example. You have to use nicknames or first names, else people think you're bein' cheeky and you get into bother."

"Rubbish," said Batesy who had overheard. "Call me what you like Hawky. Jim or Batesy is fine; I don't mind as long as it gets my attention. I call you Sid or sometimes Hawky. Titch is Titch or sometimes Alan, Willick is Willick or sometimes George. Tek nae notice, please yourself."

Conversation finished. Titch hushed, problem over.

Batesy's mam couldn't believe her eyes when she saw the huge piles of blackies we presented. She was a little woman with white hair, slim and smart and wearing glasses.

"Heavens above, you lads, I'll have to make more pastry, lots more, and I'll need a lot more apples. Jim, get me purse. Can you run down to the store and buy some for me?"

We were standing in their kitchen. The big kitchen table was covered in flour and there were tin plates and dishes greased in preparation.

"Want ter come with us, Sid?" Batesy asked.

"I'll come," said Titch.

"Oh no, you don't Alan Irving. You're going to help me wash these blackberries in salt water to get rid of the green stalks and the little worms," Mrs Bates insisted. "I need someone who's a good worker."

Titch grinned; he loved being important.

"I've got to go home Mrs Bates. My mam's needing a hand with the shopping," said Willick, making his excuses, probably realising for the first time that some of the blackies had fruit worms in them, and he'd already popped more than a few in his mouth.

"Okay son. Nice to see you. Don't forget to come back for your pie if your mam wants one of course."

"What time, Mrs Bates...when will they be ready."

"I'll tell you what, George, I'll send one of the lads around to your house when they're ready and still warm, okay. Tell your mam to get a pan of Bird's custard on. It won't be until much later, probably after teatime, early evening."

Willick made his escape...it may have been true about his mam's shopping, but I doubted it.

Batesy and I set off for the store, and when we returned with the apples Titch was still hard at it, fishing saltwater-soaked berries out of the sink, filling up the colanders standing on the bench, and then rinsing them under the cold-water tap. He seemed happy enough. Truth is we'd been very lucky to get to the store when we did. With it being a Saturday, the apples we managed to buy were the very last available.

Another pair of hands had joined the effort when we returned.

"Hi Mrs Connor."

"Hi Jim, I've been press-ganged by your mam" she chuckled. "you know, with your Ann not being.... errrmm... available," she said, diplomatically.

Mrs Bates had been joined by another lady called Sylvia, one of the neighbours, and she immediately set to work on the apples, peeling, coring and slicing, before half-cooking. With the number of pies to be made, Sylvia's oven had been roped in as a reserve, and there was much to-ing and fro-ing between the two ovens, four houses apart.

I was fascinated as I stood to one side in the Bates kitchen, keeping well out of the way. I watched closely as the skilled hands of Batesy's mam and Mrs Connor rolled and fitted the pastry to the plates, loading in smooth half cooked apples while palming in the berries. They pastry topped the pie, making three little top cuts to let the pie breathe, then trimming and sealing the pastry edges and making a bonny pattern with a fork. After the egg wash, they sprinkled caster sugar over the uncooked pies before they went in the oven. It was a labour of love and the two women only stopped when the last pie was out, cooling on the table. Both looked as if they'd just finished a shift at the pit, completely tired out.

I'd been roped in for deliveries, with my mother's complete agreement, and it was our job - me, Titch and Batesy - to take the fruits of our labour to family and neighbours. It was quite ironic really. Titch had the furthest to go so he only had three pies to deliver, one for his own house, one for Willick's house, and one to be taken to Charlie Chuck's. I thought he'd be a bit put out, having to deliver to Charlie's, but to be fair, he didn't complain or refuse.

The easiest way for distribution, was to place the warm pie into a clean towel and knot the top to make a handle so that you could carry two at a time. I ferried out five pies, one to the Bowman house, one to Beresford, one to Winters and of course, my last delivery was to my own house, but for some reason we'd been allocated two pies. I assumed it must be because we were the blackie finders and deserved more, but I couldn't remember Titch and Willick getting two pies.

Batesy had more to do than me, but his deliveries were all short journeys to houses in Axwell. That pleased him, because it meant he had to deliver to the Thompson's house across the street, and he told me he really liked their daughter, Carol - she was a stunner, he'd said.

I'd never seen so many pies all together in one place in my short life, and to be honest, I've never seen that many since. I often wondered where all the dishes came from.

It was dark outside when I finally arrived home with my final pie delivery. Mam was waiting and I could smell the custard bubbling away as I came in through the back door. We feasted that night, the three of us. One pie only, with the reserve put away in the pantry, but it was ample, more than ample. I was fit to burst after my last mouthful, but it was exactly as Titch had told us. They were the best tasting pies of all time, it was like eating heaven, dripping in custard. Surprise upon surprise, who'd have thought a kid's adventurous day out could end up being so luscious. In my diary entry it said 'best blackies of all time, yum'.

Sunday was something of a surprise too. The second reason for mam's school visit was about to be revealed. I'd risen early and made mam a cup of tea and a slice of toast. Linda was still asleep, so I didn't bother her. I felt the need to visit Charlie's and bring him up to speed with all that had been happening. I set off after breakfast.

I spent a happy few hours that day chatting with Charlie and Martha. It was the first time I'd really spoken to her, now that she was home from hospital, and I discovered she was so much like her sister Helena, not in size, but in personality. Because, when she talked, you listened, you paid attention, owing to the fact her words were pointed, and meaningful, and she spiced them all with a wry sense of humour.

Charlie waxed lyrical about the blackie and apple pie and said that the cook deserved an award from the Queen. Martha, too, said she'd had a little try of the pie but Charlie had wolfed most of it. Cancer wasn't mentioned, but we skirted around the meaning of life. I just had no frame of reference for understanding, how anyone could face knowing that dying was on the horizon, and yet still be so stoic.

We talked about my own situation. My school, and my learning. I told Charlie about Mr Hunter and what he'd said about Shakespeare, thinking Charlie would be annoyed. Instead, he was supportive of Mr Hunter.

"Listen to him Sid; he's your teacher, and he knows how to give you all the tools you need for the exam…just listen, learn, and pass. It may be that I've been trying to teach you how to be an adult, before you've experienced being a child. Been forcing your growing, instead of letting it develop naturally." He gave me a big grin. "Enjoy these years… because when they're gone, they're gone, and honestly, they're the best ones of your life."

We went on and talked about mam, and how she was happier at present than she'd been for years, even though she was now on her own and dad was no longer in our lives.

It was Martha who remarked, after a studied pause, "You know Sid, you'll discover as life goes on, that some people are like clouds, when they're gone, the sun shines".

I had another pearl of wisdom to file away.

Martha though, was still very fatigued, and before long we had to conclude our little chat. She needed lots of bed rest and our conversation drew to a natural close. I was aware she was flagging, so I took the initiative.

"Sorry Martha, and Charlie. I have to go, stuff to do, kid's stuff. I can't spend all day chatting with grumpy old folk. I need to have a sensible conversation with young people."

They both laughed, and Charlie winked. He realised I was being very grown up and giving them some space.

I took my leave, said my goodbyes, and headed for home. I was about to walk into another huge surprise.

I took my time going home, there was nothing planned for the rest of the day, so I wandered past Titch's house, past Willick's, past Batesy's, maybe hoping for another trip out to the blackberry patch. There was no-one about until I bumped into Stan Fowler. We said our hi-yas' and we chewed the fat for a few minutes, going over our shared experiences of the Bella gang disaster. By the time we'd finished analysing the fight, you'd have thought that we'd actually won it, talking up our own miniscule contributions, and making heroes of the Cowpen lads.

We took leave of one another, and I meandered on home, taking the cut from Redesdale through to Rookery Close. As I came out of the cul-de-sac and onto Hallside, I ground to a stuttering halt. My head couldn't accept what I was seeing. I blinked and rubbed my eyes to make sure I wasn't imagining things.

There were two lasses, with a rope tied to the lamppost along from our house, and they were skipping. One was my sister, and she was doing the rope turning. The other lass, doing the skipping and singing at the top of her voice, 'Up the Mississippi, if you miss a beat you're out,' was the very lass from Morpeth Road school who'd smacked me in the eye.

I must have stood there for a full minute, just staring, and trying to make sense of it. What on earth was she doing at my house? How on earth did she even know where we lived? Why do lasses even like skipping? I was still doing my statue impression, when a beat must have been missed up the Mississippi, and the skipping lass was out.

Linda and the lass both turned and noticed me at the same time.

"Hi Sid," "Hi Sid," two greetings, as if everything was all tickety-boo and nothing out of the ordinary was happening. I lumbered forward but couldn't reply. My mouth dropped open. I was trying to make some sense of the situation. Two smiling faces came closer, little by little, and unless I was mistaken, the lass was wearing one of my sister's dresses. Then, they were directly in front of me. Both within touching distance, both still smiling. My mouth was fixed, still stuck on open. I must have looked like a post-box. Knowing what the lass was capable of, I was half-prepared to duck, if I needed to.

The lass smiled. A huge smile, and for the first time I realized how nice looking she was. My mouth finally moved, and I managed a weak smile in return.

"Sorry," the lass said.

"Ehhh...what?" my brain was sloshing with treacle.

"Sorry...ye know, for smackin' ye in the face like. It was wrong." The apology was heartfelt and genuine.

"Ahh thought you were tryin' to show us up, like some of the other'uns at school, but Linda told me you were just tryin to be kind. She says that you're really kind, but sometimes a bit stupid."

I couldn't help but smile at that. I was chuffed that Linda had called me really kind, and I couldn't argue with the sometimes-stupid remark after my recent escapades. We all laughed together, genuine, hearty laughs, and Linda came and took my hand as we walked to the house. But then, I had the weirdest, warm feeling when the lass took my other hand and gave it a squeeze. I'd never held a girl's hand before, other than Linda's, and after a second or two, I squeezed back.

The girl's name was Mildred. I'd never heard that name before and didn't know such a name existed until then. Her mam was inside, talking to my mam when we came into the sitting room.

She, too, was attractive, but tired looking also. I could have sworn that the dress and cardigan she was wearing belonged to mam, but maybe they were just common clothes.

She smiled as I came through. "Hello. You must be Sidney, who tried to be kind to my lassie?"

I didn't know how to respond. Being kind usually ended up with me covered in bruises, but I couldn't pretend to be someone else.

"I errr, errrmm, just didn't do it very well. I wasn't bein' rude or owt, I thought I might be helping."

"Thank you, Sidney, your kindness is most appreciated, by me at least. I promise not to punch you."

We all had a chuckle at that, even mam, and she made no mention of my having lied about my black eye.

The second blackie and apple pie had been commandeered for this very occasion and it wasn't long before we were all sitting at the kitchen table, tucking into pie and custard.

To cut a long story short, mam made a new friend. Charlie had told her what I'd been up to, with the jumper, and how I deserved better than the reception I'd received. Mam, it seems, had been proud of my attempt to show some kindness and made it her secret business to track down the girl and her mother to see if there was anything we could all do, to chip in and help.

That Sunday was the day that Mrs McClair, her daughter Mildred, and West Highland terrier Wilf, became our new extended family. Mildred, who was very petite, and slightly smaller than Linda, although almost three years older, found herself in possession of a pile of new clothes, or at least, new to her. She didn't take offence at being given the clothing, she was grateful, and she also realised that the people doing the giving, were decent folk.

I didn't delve too deeply into why they found themselves in such a fix. I remembered what mam had said, about things being none of our business sometimes. I left those kind of questions for a later date when I could probably get some answers from mam. I wasn't going to ask Mildred, but I decided there and then, I would listen if she ever needed to talk. I was secretly pleased that I'd be seeing more of this new lass. I really liked her smile.

They stayed with us until early evening and then mam, Linda and myself walked them home. Of course, I ended up carrying the bags with the clothes in. It wasn't too far to their house in Malvin's Close, in the street nearest to Cowpen, and before we left them at their front door, I arranged to walk to school with Mildred the next day.

I was around at Mildred's, pot-hot, the following morning. I had been looking forward to seeing her again, and being enthusiastic, I turned up early, but she was waiting for me.

"Hi Mrs McClair," I gave a little salute as her mam opened the door.

"Woof, woof," was the greeting from the little westie at her feet. I wasn't great with dogs because we'd never had one, but Mildred had told me that Wilf was really friendly. I hunkered down on my knees as instructed, and let the little fella sniff me. He seemed eminently satisfied and let me give his head a scratch before shooting past me into the front garden for a wee.

Mildred came out of the house, fastening the coat she'd acquired from my sister. She looked like a different person today. She was actually in the year below me at school, even though there was only three months between our birthdays. I really liked her, who would have thought? Her clothes were nice and clean, her shoes shiny, her hair tied back and glinting. Much as her attire was impressive, the nicest thing she had was her smile. It wasn't so much a smile as a twinkle. It gave me a warm feeling when the smile was directed at me.

We set off for school, but hadn't walked more than a hundred paces when she asked,

"Will you call me Milly please, Sid?"

"Aye, whatever you want. Why?"

"'Cos Mildred's an old-fashioned name. It's what me gran was called. I don't like me name very much."

"Aye, okay."

"And can you leave me before we get to the school gates."

"Ehhh, what's that all about?" it suddenly crossed my mind that she didn't want to be seen with me. It made me feel empty.

"Are you ashamed of me or summat?"

"No Sid, not that, but your friends might laugh at you for walkin' to school with Raggedy Annie - that's what they call me."

In that moment I felt so sorry for her, so bad about all the times I'd just ignored the jibes when I'd heard them. How low she must have felt.

"Any friend who laughs at me, or you, won't be a friend again. Me mam says you and your mam are part of the family now."

"Sid...you don't have to do this. Honest, I'm used to being laughed at, but you might end up with no friends."

I thought about that for a moment.

"Milly...I'll tell you one of the things a very wise person called Charlie, once said to me when I had very few friends. He said, "It's better to be by yourself than poorly accompanied"."

"Ehhh?" She'd missed the meaning.

"Milly, it just means that being in company with the wrong people is worse than being alone."

She smiled an acknowledgement.

"Here, anyway, take these." I handed her a large packet of fruit gums.

"A present, Sid, for me?"

"Nah, from me mam. She says kids are fickle. Once you hand out a few sweets and let them know that all your clothes have arrived from your old home, you'll have more friends than you can shake a stick at."

She gave a little laugh and took my hand. I didn't refuse.

As it happened, we bumped into Ken Robinson and Derek Raisbeck, also on their way to school. They saw us, waved, and crossed the road onto our side. We dropped hands.

"Don't forget the sweets," I whispered.

"Hi Hawky," shouted Raisbeck.'

"Hi Decka. Hi Ken. D'yer want a bullet. Milly's got some fruit gums."

"Aye," enthusiastically, from both of them. They were there like greyhounds released from traps, hands out.

"This is Milly; she's in 3A; she's one of my relatives."

"Hi Milly," they both acknowledged her. I was sure that they hadn't recognised her as the girl from school who had been the butt of so many jibes. "Got any more bullets?"

She grinned. "Aye, okay, just one more each. The rest are to share with the lasses at school."

She gave them another and as soon as they had them in their paws, they were off to catch up with another two lads in front.

Ten seconds later the other two lads, Ray Lindores and Mickey Linney, were stood in front of her with hands out. "Hi Molly, Decka says you've got some bullets; can we have one?"

"It's Milly."...She laughed and gave them one each.

"Belter...thanks Molly." Then they were away, to catch up with the others. No comments, no bad words, no confrontations.

"Thanks Sid," was all she said as she nudged me, the words heartfelt, and her whole demeanour changed in those few minutes.

I wasn't aware at the time just how big a part we would both play in each other's lives.

For the time being I just needed to carry on being a kid.

CHAPTER 8

Dark and Light

———————————◼———————————

October fizzled out and November made its entrance. Halloween was a damp squib as far as I was concerned. I don't know why I'd never taken to it and disliked it so much.

I couldn't understand why kids, much like myself, would stick their heads into a bowl of water to pick up an apple with their teeth, when the sensible thing to do would be to just reach in with their hands to save themselves a soaking. Why on earth was that supposed to be fun?...I found it to be so mind-numbing, so tedious. Even at ten years of age I found the whole concept of All Hallows Eve pointless. Maybe I was missing something. Perhaps I was growing up too quickly. Probably I was just boring.

Linda and Milly had fun though, walking around with a candle inside a hollowed-out swede, and fair enough, mam and Olive tried their best to make it interesting, but honestly, I began to realise that there must be something seriously wrong with me, because the girls enjoyed the evening - the same one that I found exceedingly irritating. Milly even took the opportunity to tell me off. She said I needed to have some fun and stop being so serious. "Things don't always have to make sense Sidney, not when you're a kid...you're allowed to have silly fun."

Halloween was on a Tuesday. The following Sunday was bonfire night, and I would love to say it was brilliant, honestly, I would; an awesome evening with crowds of children, 'oohing' and 'aahing' as Standard fireworks zipped forth and lit up the sky. Catherine wheels, whizzing and spinning away spectacularly on fence posts, Roman candles dazzling and burning incandescent, and jumping jacks hopping their erratic path around the central bonfire...itself a massive, blazing wooden stack, stunningly magnificent...and forcing the gathered crowd to retreat to a healthy distance because of the great heat it was throwing out, and spectacularly topped by the most realistic Guy Fawkes ever.

That's what I would love to say, but I can't. It rained... not the heavy, torrential rain with streams gurgling down kerbsides, and drains struggling to cope. It was the drizzly, depressing stuff that clung to your clothes before soaking through, wetting you by degrees. Not heavy enough to keep folk indoors, but claggy, and disheartening enough to turn what should have been an upbeat and cheerful evening into something drab and dismal.

We congregated opposite the Tilmouth house as the bonfire was lit and we were all initially enthusiastic. It glowed brightly for a while, as some old rolls and sheets of linoleum in the central core of the bonfire blazed intensely for a few minutes as the tar took hold, before waning and spluttering out gradually. Then the remainder of the bonfire fizzled and popped its way into obscurity, smoking heavily as the fine drizzle turned all the combustibles soggy.

The sad guy, or Mr Fawkes, sitting atop of the pile, lost his head almost immediately. It plummeted into the smouldering linoleum. Not a head to be proud of, it has to be said, but an old, pink bulbous vase with painted eyes and lips, a battered hat the crowning glory, surely the product of an enthusiastic amateur. Then, almost immediately after that, Guy Fawkes tatty old cardigan burst open as the lumpen body, legs and all, tumbled into the waning fire, the straw and rolled up newspaper stuffed inside it, burning black...and reluctantly.

One of the dads tried to encourage the fire and get it blazing again by chucking some petrol on, and initially it made a whoosh, singeing his hair and making him stagger backwards, then within seconds, it died away once more.

Ours wasn't the only bonfire to be struggling. Looking from the top of Axwell bank we could see the Devonworth bonfire in the near distance, and that too was a paltry affair, glowing bright initially and then dwindling into insignificance.

Our bangers wouldn't bang, they only popped, jumpy jacks limped, and Catherine wheels wouldn't spin. One Fowler rocket left its milk bottle launch pad and made it into the night sky, up to about lamp post height, then must have thought better of it, and fell back to earth, hitting that same unlucky bloke with the singed hair on the shoulder before tumbling to ground. I bet he wished he'd stayed indoors. And irony upon ironies, the only things to sparkle that night were the sparklers, the only folk to find any enjoyment that bonfire night, were the tiny folk, the under sevens.

It was a dreary, disheartening evening and I walked back down Axwell with Batesy and one of the Connor lads when everyone began drifting away. It was a pointless exercise, standing in the drizzle, shivering, and pretending to be having a fantastic time.

"That's an hour of my life that I'll never get back," said Batesy. "Wasn't worth comin' out for."

I agreed, wholeheartedly, and I agreed in my best Blyth speak which, whilst still not perfect, had been coming on in leaps and bounds.

"Aahh know. Aah've bought a box of twelve bangers and aah've only got seven left. Four of them never even worked. I couldn't get them to light properly; me box of matches were damp. And the other banger that I managed to light when they weren't damp, didn't bang, it just farted, and me jumpy jack didn't even jump, it didn't even hop; it just fell to bits."

At that moment, I was so annoyed at having saved up for weeks and then having wasted the money on a non-event.

I didn't have the same resources as Batesy, who'd been pushing Roly Forman around in a wheelbarrow, dressed up as a guy, and making loads of money 'penny for the guying' outside of the local pubs and clubs for the past week. One drunk had even given them a ten-bob note. And Batesy hadn't even bought a single firework. He'd kept the money for his Christmas fund and told me, "Nae point spendin' dosh on fireworks when aah' can watch everybody else's for nowt."

But he gave me some advice. "Don't worry about the bangers; keep them as dry as you can in the box, somewhere warm, and we'll go and do some of the drainpipes over at the Bella next week. Get our own back on the Bella gang. Frighten the life out of them."

"Drainpipes, what's that about?" I was a little lost.

Batesy looked at me quizzically, struggling to understand why I'd not heard of the drainpipe wheeze. So he shrugged and raised his eyebrows.

"Don't know what you did up in Jockland for fun, but it can't have been up to much if you never did drainpipes." The Connor lad laughed, and Batesy threw me a grin before explaining.

"Well, what you do is, you sneak up to a hoose and you light the banger, stick it up the bottom of a drainpipe and block the end off, wi' a clod of grass or somethin', do it quick and mek sure it's in tight. Then run like buggery, 'cos when it bangs, it bangs and rattles through all the other pipes, aall roond the hoose. Meks the people inside cack tha'sels." He was chuckling gleefully.

"Honest, is it that bad?" I thought he must be exaggerating.

"Yeh, it's super canny, makes a belter of a noise. Me and Roly did one of the new un's last year up at Leeches. The folk had just moved in, and when the explosion went off you should have heard the wifey screamin'...she must have thought the hoose was collapsin'. Got a right good chasin' off the gadgey. Nearly got caught an' all; he was really fast for an owld bloke, must've been nearly forty or somethin'. We had to leg it quick, ower some fences and back gardens. Got lucky though 'cos the bloke tripped ower a brick or summat and went splat." He smiled at the memory.

"Don't worry about it though, 'cos we could do some car exhausts instead, if the bangers don't dry out very good. Mind, we'll need some taties to jam up the tail pipes."

With that we'd come to the parting of the ways, needing to go in different directions. Batesy gave a pretend salute.

"Like aah said before, keep your bangers warm and dry, Sid. They might still be alright if the gunpowder dries out. Hey, but mek sure they don't go off in yer hoose. We'll do a plan at school, next week."

He gave a big grin. "Got to go." With that, he signified the conversation was over, and without further ado he jogged away with the Connor lad, down Axwell. I broke into a trot, too, and made my way past the old folks' houses in Redesdale and on through the cut to Hallside. It had been a thoroughly miserable Guy Fawkes night and I was happy to be going home.

Next day, I calculated it was exactly seven weeks until Christmas. We never did get to stick bangers up drainpipes, or taties up car exhausts. Batesy and Willick came down with mumps or measles, or something equally nasty, both at the same time, and although Willick was back at school after little more than a week, Batesy was absent for a lot longer. I wasn't worried about catching measles - apparently, I'd already had them, when we lived in Kirkcaldy, or so mam said. Not that I remembered.

My bangers were a write off anyway. I dried them out, but they went all wrinkly, and the powder just turned to clag, so they were eventually binned, and as the weeks rolled by and life moved on, I forgot about the wasted money, and happily I found myself spending much more time with Milly, and our newfound friends.

Mam, being mam, had helped Mrs McClair to find some work. On Blyth market days she'd found her a job on a fruit and vegetable stall that stood with its back to the Central cinema. On other days she worked with mam when they cleaned together at the library, and some of the offices and shops in town. She also worked two nights every weekend at the Red House pub, serving behind the bar, as well as a few afternoons at Cowpen Club and The Sidney.

Because of her mam's new work situation, Milly spent a lot of time at our house and sometimes slept over.

It was Friday and Saturday nights however, that became a fun time at our house. Milly's mam worked at the pub on those evenings, and she stayed with us, bunking in with mam in her three-quarter bed, so that she didn't have a long walk home in the dark.

Mam and Olive - Olive being Mrs McClair's first name - had become really close friends, and it was so nice to see the two of them interact, smiling, talking, laughing and planning together. They were both of a similar age, and mam seemed to take on a new lease of life.

On those weekend nights, we kids were allowed to stay up late; the girls staying in to guard the house, while mam and I would put Wilf's lead on, and the three of us would make the short journey, to meet Olive outside the Red House at the end of her shift. We would walk with her back to ours, making sure she was safe and not pestered by anyone worse the wear for drink. Olive always complained, saying there was no need to be putting ourselves out, but mam insisted. I was beginning to feel very grown up, escorting a lady home in the dark.

Olive would invariably bring back three packets of Tudor beefy crisps, and a dozen or so blackjacks for the kids, and a single bottle of Newcastle amber ale for the two adults to share. Who'd have thought it, mam drinking beer and having a good old laugh; it was really nice to hear, especially after the tough year she'd had.

Wilf wasn't forgotten either and there was always a piece of ham or beef for him wrapped up in a hanky, having been purloined from one of the staff sandwiches.

When bed-time beckoned Milly shared Linda's room, and they had formed a bond like sisters, whilst I, for my troubles, shared my bedroom with Wilf.

Wilf couldn't be left on his own overnight in his own house, because he would disturb the neighbours, and howl, with something that Olive called night separation complex; I thought it must just be an excuse, or he must be a real wimpy dog, but what did I know, and anyway, for some strange reason, Wilf had taken a liking to me. I'm convinced he thought I was some kind of exotic two-legged canine.

We'd made a little blanket pile for him next to my bed, and he was quite happy to snuggle down there at night... for a while...but as soon as I was in bed and the light was switched off, he'd wait a few minutes and then I'd hear him snuffling, and then scratching at my mattress, before giving a little whimper to make me feel guilty. Every night that he stayed at ours, without fail, he somehow wormed his way up onto the bed with me, and for a little dog he took up loads of space, I kid you not. I would end up on those nights clinging to the edge of my mattress whilst Wilf splayed out full stretch, usually on his back, legs akimbo, and snoring like a human.

It was a Saturday morning, early December, with Christmas creeping ever closer. That particular Saturday was about to change all our lives, although it wouldn't be immediately apparent.

Milly and Olive had spent Friday night at our house, and by the time we three kids and Wilf had roused ourselves and filtered downstairs, the grown-ups had departed for work.

As I was supposedly the most mature of the trio, I was supposed to be in charge when the adults were missing, but it was Milly and Linda who sorted the breakfast, and they worked together in tandem like regular sisters, as if they'd been doing it for years. Porridge for all four of us, because Wilf loved porridge too, without the salt or sugar of course, and he wolfed it down after it had cooled, then licked his bowl clean.

We were at a bit of a loose end, that morning. The girls wanted to have a trip down to Blyth market, and then have a mooch around the shops, to do some Christmas window shopping. I couldn't be bothered; it wasn't my cup of tea. As much as I enjoyed Milly's company, and my sister's company, too, nowadays, there was no way I could face an afternoon of trailing around, looking at things I didn't have the money to buy. I'd reluctantly accompanied them the previous week on their window-shop and the whole experience had me almost climbing walls. Their conversation was embarrassing.

"Linda, when I'm married I'm going to have a couch like that in my sitting room, oh, and with a black and white pouffe, like that one there, for my husband to put his feet on when he comes in from the pit, after I've made his tea, and he's had a wash...and stuff."

"I'm not getting married Milly, 'cos men are just bigheads, and they just drink lots of beer, and go to the toilet, and don't put the seat back down, so I'm having my own bungalow and it's going to have net curtains like those ones

127

there, something like me mam's but not so fancy, and big red velvet pull curtains that you can tie back with velvet ropes, so that they look like a stage...like what you see in a play."

"Well, I think that's daft, about men being bigheads, and it's best if they have the seat up anyway, 'cos sometimes they don't aim very good, and miss. So I definitely am getting married, 'cos my husband will just drink tea and pop, and you can be one of my bridesmaids, probably the chief one, and you'll have to wear a pink dress, and scatter some rose petals up the church aisle before they start playing 'Here Comes the Bride'...Oh look, have you seen that duffel coat? Look at the toggles, it's fantastic...I'll get my husband to buy me one just like it."

I promise you, I kept myself sane by constantly going over Hamlet's soliloquy in my head, attempting to be word perfect. I went over all my times tables, especially the nines, which I always struggled with, and all the while trying to ignore the crassness of the conversation that the two girls were having.

The only saving grace, was that I didn't bump into any of my friends. Wilf and I endured this for a full afternoon, and it wore the pair of us down, hours fruitlessly, and needlessly spent, and I swore never to tag along with them on a window-shop again.

Girls, at that time, were still an alien species to me; I didn't have a clue what made them tick. I found them extremely baffling, totally bewildering, positively perplexing, and there were probably a further ten adjectives which would be just as descriptive of my failure to understand the workings of their bizarre and cranky minds. Why would anyone go window shopping?...just looking at things, imagining what you would do with those things, or where you would put them, at some indeterminate point in the future, if you had enough money, and a house to put them in. Honestly...what was the point?

Skipping - that was another one. What was that all about? Lasses just jumped up and down but didn't go anywhere and found it necessary to chant daft tunes about knowin' boys that were double jointed and being disappointed when they kissed them, or somethin'...ehhh?

Then there was Hopscotch, another daft lasses' game, numbers one to ten chalked on paving stones, when they would chuck an empty polish tin onto a number and hop around on one leg, then two legs, missing the edges of the pavers, then picking the tin up, or something like that - I didn't know the rules, didn't want to know the rules - it was totally senseless, totally stupid, totally incomprehensible.

And the worst one of all...the farmer wants a wife, oh yeah'...why? Is the farmer daft or something? Has he had his marbles removed? Surely, investing in a working brain would be smarter. If he's listened to anyone with a smidgeon of sense, they'll have told him that when he gets married his wife will probably spend her days skipping or playing hopscotch...or heaven forbid, window shopping. Stay single, you silly old fool...stay sane.

Lasses were definitely an alien species.

They didn't have a clue about conkers, or muggies, or Japs and English or monty-cuddy. They didn't appreciate Davy Crockett; in fact, I can't remember ever seeing a lass with a Davy Crockett hat. They didn't like Roy Rogers or

Ivanhoe. They weren't interested in football or trainsets, Airfix models, or forts and soldiers.

I had a sister and a new friend who, even though I couldn't punch my way out of a wet paper bag, I would gladly have fought for, and defended with all my might. But even so, after weighing up all their pros and cons, I concluded that girls' heads didn't work properly.

So, that morning, we decided to part company. The girls would take their window-shopping trip, and I would have the pleasure of Wilf's company until teatime. The sky was dull and overcast when we left the house and went our separate ways. I walked as far as the bus-stop with the girls before we took our leave. I'd thought about taking Wilf for a walk through the fields, where I'd have an opportunity to let him off the lead, but it looked for all the world like rain was coming and coming soon. So, on a whim, I headed for Charlie's.

Little did I realise what the day had in store. It would turn out to be, paradoxically, one of my best ever days, and also one of my most disappointing.

CHAPTER 9

No News is Good News

———————————————————■———————————————————

When I arrived, there was a spanking new, silver Jaguar outside of Charlie's house. I was impressed - who wouldn't be? - and immediately thought it must be a doctor's car. Someone seeing to Martha perhaps. Doctors had loads of money, didn't they? There were a few of the local kids clustered around the motor, stroking it, fondling it, running their hands over it and marvelling at it. A Morris Minor it was not...this was the car of an important person, and it was parked outside of a council house on Cowpen Estate.

I ignored the kids, not my problem, nothing to do with me. I remember thinking though, that if I owned a car like that, I'd have been out like a shot, probably with two snarling Alsatians, and the ground around the car would be littered with half-eaten children.

I knocked on Charlie's door. I could hear sounds from inside, but no reply to my knocking. I rapped on the door again, louder this time. I waited, and waited, but once again no reply. There was music quietly playing in the house but for some reason, Charlie wasn't answering. I kept on knocking, and now I was feeling a wee bit embarrassed, somewhat conspicuous. Those kids were watching me as I knocked. I realised I was sticking out like a sore thumb; my presence at the door was drawing their attention and my being overlooked and ignored was busy playing out in public. I couldn't stand there for ever. I'd have no skin left on my knuckles if I continued. Time to beat a retreat.

I forced a half-smile as I walked away. "Mustn't be in," said for the benefit of the kids, as well as myself. I was positive someone was in that house. But why no answer? Wilf trotted alongside me as I made my escape from the house. I wasn't so much annoyed, more baffled than anything. Something wasn't right.

I'd only walked a short distance when I heard a shout from behind me.

"Hey...Hawky, hang on a mo' man."

I turned. It was Batesy, with Titch and the bow and arrow lad, Roly. Batesy was carrying a big carrier bag, Titch was carrying a pair of shiny shoes. Roly thankfully had ditched the feathered headdress, but for some reason was rolling an old, warped bicycle wheel around. What an odd trio they made.

"Where ye' been," I forced out, attempting some joviality, even though I didn't feel it. We walked as we talked.

"Just to Jimmy's, along the street. Jimmy Riddell...my dad's friend. He's been out on his boat and caught loads of fish, so he's payin' me mam back for the blackie and apple pie." Batesy held up the bulging bag, which absolutely stank of fish and the sea. "Been to Charlie's have yer?"

"Aye, how do you know Charlie?"

"My dad knows him. Helped Charlie get loads of topsoil from the allotments, for his garden, and I've brought a few bogie loads of coal around when Charlie's been a bit short."

"I thought everybody was frightened of Charlie...you know, and say bad things about him."

Titch, at that point, looked away...sheepish.

"Nah," said Batesy, "only the donkeys talk like that. Charlie's okay: people talk rubbish sometimes." I decided I definitely liked Batesy.

At this point, Roly had run out of patience with the wheel and he sent it careering down the road. It performed a huge arc and bumped over the kerb into the central wilderness, wobbling erratically, before coming to rest on a clump of grass.

"Whose dog is it?" Batesy asked, kneeling down, and giving Wilf a scratch under the chin.

Now there was a question and a half. It would have taken a while to work my way through that whole explanation.

"It's my cousin's dog...Millie...well, her mam's dog actually."

"Didn't know you had an auntie in Blyth," said Batesy, innocently, as Wilf pushed his chin forward for more scratching.

This was becoming tricky. I wasn't good at subterfuge, and I felt as if I was complicating matters unnecessarily.

"We just call her auntie...you know...like she's just me mam's best friend...'

I tailed off.

Batesy just shrugged. "Aye, I've got a few of them myself," and thought nothing more of it.

Titch chirped up at that very moment. "That teacher at the grammar, Mr Winker. I go to dancin' with his daughter."

I wasn't sure that he had the name right but couldn't remember. A figment of my imagination now had a daughter.

"Winker?" Asked Batesy, "really?"

"It's Winkle," I remembered, correcting him, even though I'd made it up and the man didn't exist.

Titch seemed oblivious anyway...in a world of his own.

"Teaches science, her dad. She's gonna be me girlfriend."

"In yer dreams," Batesy chuckled. "If it's that lass with the black hair I seen yer with, she's ower bonny for you."

"Bet yer a shillin'," Titch replied, a little narked at being disbelieved.

"Nah...but I'll bet you a selection box," Batesy responded. "Loser has to pay up on Boxin' Day."

"Right...yer on. Sid and Roly, you're witnesses." Titch sounded hugely confident.

"It'll cost yer a bounty," Roly chipped in.

"Done," Titch agreed, "Or a crunchie if there's no bounty."

I was listening to this with an air of incredulity. I wasn't sure what to say or do next. He couldn't in all honesty win the bet because the girl's father didn't exist, at least not the one that I'd conjured up.

"If she's not yer girlfriend before Christmas...you lose, right?"

"That's not gonna happen," Titch grinned cheekily. Then, as we reached the phone box on Brierley, he tucked the dancing shoes under his arm and gave a smart salute. "See yer at school," then turned on his heels and jogged away towards his house.

"D'yer think he'll win the bet?" I asked Batesy.

"Probably, knowin' Titch. Even if she won't be his girlfriend he'll offer to give her half a selection box if she'll say she is, just for one day...He's crafty like that."

I had to agree with that observation.

"I couldn't be bothered with it though," Batesy observed, "doin' all that dancin' stuff at the Roxy".

"Me neither," I agreed. Then we walked on in silence for a while before I chirped up, "Was your measles really bad? 'Cos you've been off school for ages."

Batesy looked bemused. "Measles? I haven't had measles...well, I have, but that was years ago. Anyway, I'll be back on Monday."

"So why have you been off school?"

"I got knocked out," Batesy lifted his fringe of hair out of the way. He had a fading scar, right across his forehead, along the hairline, and not yet completely healed. Then he held out his left hand and showed me another scar. "Six stitches in me head, three stitches in me hand, and I had a couple of cracked ribs an' all."

"So, how did yer get knocked out?" I was fascinated now because the scars looked really impressive.

"Don't know, can't remember."

"Ehhh, yer kiddin'. How can you not remember getting a scar like that."

"Look Hawky, I'm not kiddin', I just can't remember," he sounded annoyed, "Ahh just woke up in hospital."

"Hospital...does anybody else know what happened?"

He shrugged, "Seems like somebody told the police that I was with a bunch of lads, and we were goin' down the hairpin bend on a trolley, or a big bogie or summat. Must have fell off or crashed."

"Who were you with?"

"Don't know, I can't remember. There wasn't anyone else there when the ambulance men found me. One of the lads must have told somebody what happened, or phoned for an ambulance, then nicked off."

"D'yer think you might remember soon?"

"Look, Hawky...I don't know, right. I've even had the police askin' questions, 'cos they thought I'd been bashed up or somethin'. I don't know who I was with, or what happened. Me head's just a load of mush about that day...aahh really can't remember one thing about it, not a single one, an' you keep repeatin' questions won't make me memory come back...okay?'

Batesy was annoyed, so I shut up, but I had the distinct impression that he did know who he had been with that day, and it was nothing to do with a trolley crash...but for whatever reason he was keeping tight-lipped.

I changed the subject.

"Just been to Charlie's but no-one would answer the door. I hope Martha's all right."

He seemed relieved that the subject had changed, and he answered my query quickly. "She'll be down in London, with Charlie. Jimmy says that somebody's lookin' after the house while they're away. Somebody with a really posh car, obviously."

That was a worrying development, "Ehhh, London. Are they away to a hospital for Martha?' Then I had another thought. "Maybe they've gone to the opera with Helena or somethin?'"

Batesy looked at me with an expression of incredulity. "What are you on about Hawky? Opera...hospital? They've gone to London to pick up their cheque from Littlewoods... or Vernon's, can't remember which."

"Cheque for what...what's Littlewoods?"

Now Batesy was looking nonplussed. "The pools, the football pools, man, Charlie's won a load of money on the pools."

I didn't know what to say. If that was true, it was totally out of character for Charlie who was utterly anti-gambling.

Roly had left us by that point. No goodbyes, or salutes; we noticed that he'd just wandered away towards the Co-op, hands in pockets, without a by your leave...not a word. A strange lad indeed.

"I thought you'd have been the first to know about Charlie's win. He's pretty close to your family...isn't he?"

I was really perplexed. Astonished in fact. Charlie never did games of chance. I knew that for certain. He'd been so scathing in his remarks when I'd told him about dad and his gambling.

"Aye, me mam did a lot for them when Martha was really ill. Charlie appreciated that. He's been good to me mam... and me an' all of course. But I haven't been around at his much, not for a while."

"Well...no doubt you'll get all the news when they're back from London next week. You'll probably end up wi' a few quid an' all." By this time, we were at the top end of Hortondale.

"Got to go Hawky, me mam'll be waitin' for the fish; they'll need gutting, and they stink."

We split up then, with several cheerio's, Batesy heading down Axwell and me heading for home. My head was all over the place. How come Batesy knew about Charlie's win but I didn't?

Mam was in the house when Wilf and I returned. She'd only had one of the solicitor's offices to clean down Regent Street today, an hour's work. She was sitting on the couch, feet up, with a cup of tea when we bundled through into the living room.

"I didn't expect to see you Sid. I thought you were headed into Blyth with the girls."

I didn't reply to that. "Did you know that Charlie had won some money on the football pools mam?"

"Yes, he told me a few days ago. Last time I was around at his doing some housework."

"So why didn't you tell me mam?" I was still feeling a bit put out.

"Because Charlie wanted to tell you himself - his decision."

"But I haven't been round to Charlie's for a week, so how could he tell me?" I snapped, petulantly.

Mam snapped back, "Don't you dare take that tone with me young man. They wanted to tell you themselves. It's no-one's fault but your own if you've been too busy to visit Charlie's."

"Aye...but, well...you know. Batesy just told me. He knows and I didn't, an' that's not fair."

"Oh for heaven's sake, Sid. Stop being such a baby. What does it matter if Jim knew before you? You don't own Charlie...you know? He'll tell you all about it the next time he sees you, no doubt."

I had to make do with that. It was pointless to keep nipping away at something I couldn't change.

"Sorry mam," I said, contrition being my chosen path.

"Okay Sid, it's okay. It didn't cross my mind that you'd be upset. Well, to be honest, I didn't give it a second thought... you know, I've had lots of other things on my mind."

"Aye mam, I know...Are you stayin' in this afternoon?"

"Yes," mam chuckled, "I thought I'd have a lazy day. What do you want to know for?"

"Just...could you have a lazy day with Wilf...you know? So that I can go down Blyth? Wilf doesn't like being in Blyth with all the traffic and the crowds. He hated it last time we were there, and some kids were tryin' ter be funny, you know...barkin' at him, and chuckin' stuff."

"Wilf will be fine here; get yourself away Sid. Anyway, look, he's tired out, his little legs must be sore." Sure enough, Wilf was lying on his side beside the fireplace, eyes closed, squeaking softly and legs waggling as he meandered through a dream.

"Do you need some bus fare?"

"No mam, I've got nearly three bob in me tin. I'm just gonna have a look for some comics at that little shop opposite the shipyard, you know, beside the Traveller's."

"Okay Sid, enjoy yourself. If you see the lasses remind them that tea is at five thirty. It's just pie and peas, so nothing spoiling, and Olive doesn't start at the pub until seven. If you're back in time, though, you could nip up to Swaledale for a few bags of chips, it would save me peeling taties, and putting the chip pan on."

With that thought in mind I was off. Released from responsibility. When I emptied my tin, the expected three bob turned out to be almost four...riches indeed. It was really chilly outside so I decided to dig into my cash mountain and hop on the 49 bus from Brierley to Blyth.

Surprise upon surprise, Batesy was waiting at the bus stop when I arrived. I didn't see him at first, he was behind a big bloke who was puffing away on a pipe. I spotted the bus in the distance, turning in from Dene View Drive, and the bloke saw it too, stepping forward to knock the dottle out of his pipe on the lamppost.

"Hi Hawky, where yer off to?" I heard Batesy's voice and turned, as he came into view from behind the pipe man.

I was startled to see him. "Hi Batesy. I'm off to Blyth, just moochin' really. Maybe get some Justice League, or Flash at that shop beside the Traveller's."

"Aye, good stuff." He agreed, "I'm after some Biggles myself; well, saying that, I will be when I've got some proper dosh."

"Any ones in particular?"

"I've got five or six, but I'm tryin' to find some of the early ones, just for collectin' really...readin' as well, obviously, but I'd like to track down the first ones that Ginger is mentioned in. I've been lookin' around jumble sales and second-hand shops." Batesy was enthused, talking about Biggles, obviously a fan of W.E. Johns.

The bus pulled up, a double decker. We both headed upstairs and sat in the front seats. We had the top deck virtually to ourselves.

"What one's have you got...Biggles, like?" I was interested now because I had quite a collection myself.

"I've got Biggles of 266, Biggles in Australia, Pirate Treasure, Biggles in the Gobi, and Biggles Cuts it Fine. I've got Foreign Legionnaire as well but it's damaged - there's two pages missing - so it doesn't really count. I can't keep that in me collection."

"If you want to come to mine next week sometime, I'll show you my Biggles collection. I've got fifteen...mostly from my Grandad and some of them are in Modern Boy magazine. I've got the first book with Ginger in, the Black Peril."

Batesy looked amazed. "Honest?"

"Yeh, had them for a while. They're the original one's an' all, not the ones that they're printin' again. But I haven't been able to add to them really...you know, 'cos money's been scarce, but you're welcome to have a look, or to borrow some."

"Wow, cheers Hawky...I'll come sometime when your cousin and aunty aren't about. Don't like to intrude...it ain't polite." Batesy grinned. Polite and Batesy weren't words you'd normally expect to see together in a sentence. Which, as it turned out later, was to be to my advantage.

I got off the bus beside the Traveller's Rest. Batesy stayed on - he had some pies and sausage to get for his mam at Shy's and Maddison's - but he said he'd catch up with me as soon as he'd finished, and we were to meet in Seghini's cafe.

The little second-hand book shop close to the pub was run by two old women. Really nice they were, and somehow they always seemed to have a good stock of Marvel, DC, and other American comics. I loved the Justice League of America, and Flash and Aquaman, and whenever they had a different selection in I used to pore over them for ages before deciding which to buy. Today however was easy. There were only four and I bought them all, jumping up and down inside myself because one of them was a 'Legion of Superheroes'.

I was in comic heaven. My cash stash however, was now seriously depleted.

I bade the ladies goodbye, thanking them for the comics and set off to walk into the town centre.

Batesy was already inside Seghini's when I arrived. He was sitting at one of the furthest tables. I calculated that I had enough money for one pop and my bus fare home.

He gave a big grin when he saw me, and I sat myself down. "D'yer want a coke or a tea or an orange juice," he asked.

"Errrmm, I'll just get me own thanks, 'cos I can't buy you one back," I replied sheepishly.

"Don't be daft. I've got enough on me. You can return the favour sometime when I've got nowt...so, tea, juice or coke, what's it to be?" He stood up, not about to take no for an answer.

"Coke...thanks." That had been a decent gesture.

"Sidney Brown," a loud and unwelcome voice boomed out from an adjacent table, "not on the scrounge again are we?" Batesy heard it, too, as he walked off to order. He half-turned, with his back pressed up against the counter, and seemed to be weighing up the lad behind the voice.

I hadn't noticed him when I came in. The lad's name was Vincent, a posh moron, and an erstwhile bully. His dad was something important, some sort of head doctor, and they lived in one of the big houses beside Ridley Park. He was the most disliked person in our school, at least by the lads that I usually knocked about with. But he was supposed to be tough, so we generally tried to give him a wide berth. He was a conceited, self-opinionated kid, and one could only wonder what his parents must be like.

I didn't reply to his opening remark.

"Brought one of your bananas to eat?" he laughed, and even his laugh was an irritating cackle. Someone must have told him about our banana days.

"Or are they being saved for your teatime?" another snort.

Batesy returned with two cokes, put them down and noisily scraped a chair over to Vincent's table. He sat down to face him. I immediately sensed danger...a fight brewing.

"So, Vincent," Jim gave him a huge mock-friendly grin, "still trying to torment folk? We've done this before, haven't we? Do you remember the last time?" Then the grin disappeared to be replaced with an angry stare, "Whatever you're having for your tea...or dinner, I suppose that's what you call it in your house...well, you'll be needing some teeth to chew it with...and you're in danger of losing most of yours".

Vincent gave a snort, "Is that a threat, Bates? You caught me by surprise last time...and just so you know, my dad does lots of work with the police, so be warned. He's their top behavioural psychologist."

"No Vincent, not a threat, it's a promise. And just so you know, my dad's a top pitman, he works on the washer... washing lots of coal for the police." Batesy was being sarcastic.

"Take it as a friendly warning, unless of course you think you were just unlucky last time we had a ding-dong. Want to try again? Do you want to take this little chat outside?"

There was no response. A long suffocating pause.

Batesy grinned again, "Thought not...so it's probably best if you keep your gob to yourself...okay?"

No reply. Vincent wasn't so sure of himself now. You could see the doubt written across his face. Weighing up the odds no doubt. To back down or to money up. Confront or concede. He didn't move.

"By the way," asked Batesy in a contemptuous tone, "me and Sid aren't having bananas for tea, we're having pie and chips...yum, yum! What are you having for your dinner this evening...caviar no doubt?"

Vincent, although subdued, still had some cockiness left in him.

"Well, it will be decent food, but it won't be bananas or whatever else you people eat in council houses. And we won't be having caviar actually. Mum says we're having rump steak with all the trimmings," he replied haughtily, head back, and peering down his nose at both of us.

"Ha, ha-ha," Batesy's laughter was overdone, a forced response.

"You're kiddin' surely?" he snorted. "You're showing off because you're going to be sitting down to chew on a chunk of cow's bum?' Ha, ha-ha." He continued laughing, then stood up and pulled his seat back over to our table.

The aggravation in the air was palatable. Batesy was still expecting Vincent to fight, and his next comment was intended for me, but loud enough so that Vincent would overhear.

"Rump's the cheapest cut of meat you can get now... since that kid in Bedlington went and died with cackabetis."

The statement had the desired effect - he'd been overheard.

"Tosh, nonsense, what a load of rubbish; there's no such thing." Vincent was feeling some boldness returning.

Batesy turned to face him, and stared hard, and gave a little shake of his head, "I wasn't talking to you...was I? But for your information, mister know-all, read last Tuesday's

Chronicle; everybody knows about it. The lad's funeral was on Monday. There's photos of the church and everything, and the coffin an' all, and loads of people cryin' an' that. The kid was only twelve or somethin' and he died in Newcastle General, from that disease he got from rump steak. All because the butcher hadn't wiped the cow's arse properly."

I struggled to keep a straight face, but inside I was giggling uncontrollably. Strangely enough, I remember I was also feeling remorse for that poor fictitious lad.

I knew Batesy was battling to keep a lid on his anger as he stood up, walked across, and leaned over Vincent's table... their faces only inches apart, Vincent's wide eyes showing how nervous he was.

"Ask your dad if it's true or not, okay. If it turns out to be a lie get some of his police friends to come and arrest me." He reached over and took a piece of Vincent's cheek between thumb and forefinger and gave a squeeze.

"You enjoy your buttocks, Vince boy." He turned his back and returned to our table, waiting for the response.

There was none, no reaction to the thumb and forefinger squeeze, which should have been the starting gun for a battle. Vincent had capitulated, his head dropped. No fight expected. That's as much as I can honestly remember. Vincent, without looking in our direction, left almost immediately, his tail between his legs, and we left soon after, both of us ready for home. I never did say thank you to Batesy, but there again, I don't think he wanted me to. That one confrontation will always stick in my mind, for various reasons, and in all the years since, I've never once had a fancy for rump steak, even with a toilet roll handy.

My diary entry says, 'Batesy', 'Vince', cow's arse, funny, Jim coming next week for Biggles, Charlie back Tuesday.

I can't remember seeing Vincent again after that. Maybe I did, or maybe he just deliberately avoided us after that altercation. Maybe he had his rump steak and got a disease. I know that's a lousy thing to say. I do remember, however, that was the start of my friendship with Batesy and it would last for a few years at least.

CHAPTER 10

A Strange Turn of Events

Christmas came hurtling down the tracks, like an express train, and what a strange Christmas it would turn out to be.

Martha and Charlie must have won big...huge big, not little big, that much was obvious. Certainly, many thousands, but the exact amount, I still don't know to this day, mainly because I was too polite to ask. Peoples' financial affairs were private matters - mam had drummed that into me and asking about them was vulgar. I spent a few hours with the pair of them, early one evening, just after their return, and we chatted for ages, about everything and nothing. I remember how good it felt, to be back asking questions, trying out ideas, listening to grown up opinions and words of wisdom.

I was made aware, during that session, that the Brontës, who Mr Hunter had referred to during our Shakespeare chat, were a family of authors, and not cowboy's horses as I'd initially assumed. I knew that already of course, I'd looked it up in the library, and asked mam, too, but I was quite happy to sit back and let Martha think she was teaching me a new fact.

Martha also gave me a brief English lesson. Out of the blue, she asked if I'd been following the news to keep myself abreast of current affairs.

"Only the proper news, like on the telly, about the Russians buildin' a wall in Germany, and about how we've vaccinated them people from Tristan da Cunha," I replied.

"It's evacuated, Sid, not vaccinated." She was correcting me, and she was in teacher mode. "Evacuate means to move someone from a place of danger to a safer place. That's what we're doing with the people from Tristan da Cunha, because of the volcano erupting on their little island."

Hang on a minute, I thought to myself, vaccinated was the proper word, I'm sure I'd heard them say that on the telly. "Evacuated, Martha...not vaccinated, are you sure?"

"Yes Sid, I'm sure; vaccinated, is the past tense of vaccinate...which means to inoculate or treat someone with a vaccine, to produce immunity against a disease. And that is certainly not what the poor folk from that island think is happening."

No way was I going to contradict Martha - she was too clever, - "Okay Martha, I'll remember...evacuate." I was happy to be corrected, and happy to have them both back.

I wasn't peeved anymore. I'd got over it, especially when I learned that it was Martha who had entered the pools competition but had put Charlie's name on the coupon. That firmed up my belief in Charlie's strong principles. He was still anti-gambling, but he wasn't about to refuse the money.

My personal experience of gambling had up to that point been unproductive. Twenty-four whole pennies lost on a penny arcade game at Spanish City in Whitley Bay, and a whole bag of glassy marbles lost to a lad called Richie Cavner at Morpeth Road School. He was brilliant at marbles, unfortunately I wasn't, and I still haven't forgiven him to this day. But seriously, I knew from snippets I'd overheard from mam, about the big amounts of money my dad had lost by betting on dogs, horses and card games, but I'd never heard about anyone, certainly not anyone I knew, who'd won a lot of money on the football pools.

It was during that same evening, they informed me that mam, Olive, Milly, myself and Linda were all to benefit from Charlie's largesse, and that was brilliant news. No figures were mentioned, or expected, but Martha told me how brilliant my mam had been, and what a great comfort, to have her assistance when the cancer was at its most dreadful. Charlie agreed wholeheartedly and told me that he'd never be able to repay mam's kindness but with the pools win, he could at least make a start.

I hadn't known until then, how involved mam had been, but those words from Martha and Charlie filled me with pride.

After making all the bequests, I was told, they intended to purchase a house, but it wouldn't be in Blyth. And afterwards, Martha's intention was to use her half of the remaining money to make Helena's life much easier, and also to pay for a full-time carer, so that she could take some of the weight of responsibility from Charlie's shoulders. Charlie, in turn, joked that he was going to purchase a ready-made cold frame, so that no other kids ended up with sore arms.

The flip side of the coin however was not so palatable. Charlie and Martha, in the very near future would be moving down south, to Sussex, so that they could be closer to Helena, their only living relative. It appeared I was soon to be Charlie-less. That troubled me in a different way, too, because what would happen when Martha died, and it was an accepted fact that it would happen in the not-too-distant future. Charlie would be left on his own, without Martha, and miles away from us...it was a worry.

I was so disappointed, and why I felt like that is perhaps not too difficult to fathom. Charlie had been, for a number of months, a stabilising influence in my life. A male role-model, or a father figure in fact, even though he was older than my grandad. Taking a problem to Charlie was like cutting the problem in two, halving it. And once out in the open...the problem generally shrank, became manageable, and easier to tackle. "If you want to devour a big cake, cut it into pieces first," was Charlie's advice. Don't try to gobble it all at once, eat it one slice at a time, problem solved.

Another of his pearls – "If you find that the same old problem keeps cropping up, change the way you tackle it. Because, if you keep on doing what you've always done, you'll carry on getting the result you've always got."

And just that day, when I asked if the money would change him, Charlie said that winning a huge amount of money might change a person's life but it doesn't alter their personality. "If you're kind before you get it, you'll be kind afterwards, and if you're stupid before you get it, you're going to be stupid afterwards," he said.

So, I was sad, initially, until I took a step back and really thought about it. Then I changed my mind. Martha would be close to her sister and they'd have some important, quality time together. Charlie would have some help at hand if Martha became very ill...and I would have somewhere to visit at the other end of the country...probably in a posh house that they'd bought...and what a train ride that would be.

Thinking about it more deeply, I would also have two mature pen pals, and we could exchange letters, to let them know how I was doing at school, and to get advice when I needed it. We could maybe even do phone calls because Charlie would definitely be able to afford a phone now, and even if we didn't have a phone of our own I'd be able to use the one in the phone box on Brierley and get Charlie to ring me back. All sorted, no need for despondency.

Batesy didn't come around to look at my Biggles collection as promised. There was stuff going on at his house that he didn't want to talk about. His sister had just had a bairn and moved back home with baby and husband.

I'd been at the bus stop with mam a few days previously, when Mrs Bates came past, pushing a pram. Her first grandchild. She stopped to talk, and mam made a fuss of the baby, putting some silver under the pillow. "Ohhh, look Sid, isn't that a beautiful little boy?"

I don't know where she'd been looking, or maybe she needed a trip to the optician, but all I could see was a wrinkly monkey.

"Have they picked a name yet?" asked mam.

"Brian William," Mrs Bates replied, "but we have to call him Billy."

The name was the clincher for me, Billy...it wasn't a little wrinkly monkey it was a little wrinkly goat. I was chuckling inside, to myself.

"Aahh, that's nice," said mam, diplomatically. "Well must be off, good luck with the sleepless nights, Peg." We said our goodbyes and parted company.

"That must be a bit of a squeeze for them," mam commented when Mrs Bates was out of earshot. "That'll be seven of them in that house."

"And callin' the baby Billy Bates, that's a bit daft," I said.

"It's not Bates," mam corrected. "It's Long, that's the dad's name."

I was confused. "Batesy said they lived on the farm at Horton, and they've got a gold Labrador dog."

"Aye," replied mam, "don't know what happened with the dog, but the husband was finished at the farm and they had to move out. He drives a lorry for Wood's pop now."

"Aahh, right, but why did you call Mrs Bates, Peg?"

Mam laughed. "Why do your pals call you Hawky?"

"Cos that's me nickname...obviously." I replied.

"There's your answer then," mam gave me a nudge, and left it at that.

Mam confirmed what I already knew, when she told me one evening, on the run up to Christmas, that Charlie and Martha had gifted her a big chunk of money. Enough, she reckoned, to make us comfortable for a good while, maybe even enough to buy us a pair of flats down Disraeli Street, or one of the other streets beside my school. Mam also told me that they'd made sure that Olive and Millie would be okay, too. I'd already been told that, but it still pleased me no-end to have it confirmed. Mam said that, apart from Helena, we were the only folk that Charlie and Martha considered as family. Martha had already told me as much, and I knew in what high regard they held mam. However, it would be many years before I managed to discover what had happened to their real family.

The most brilliant news, from a kids' point of view, however, was the twenty pounds each, for myself, Millie, and Linda, to be spent on whatever we wanted for Christmas. A gift from Martha and Charlie. Martha wasn't anywhere near well enough to be going shopping, mam said, and Charlie, being a man, wouldn't have had a clue what to buy for three kids of our age, so they'd decided to give us money, to choose gifts for ourselves, and have a big splurge.

Twenty pounds was huge. That was a week's wage for a footballer, one of the top one's, mind you, not an ordinary one. And miners were only paid about fifteen or twenty pounds, and they had to pay some of it back to the government for tax or something. I'd heard mam talking with our next-door neighbour, and she'd been moaning about it.

In effect, we three kids were to be unleashed with a veritable fortune.

Well, actually only two of us kids, myself and Millie were to be let loose with the whole amount. Linda was to have a day in Newcastle with mam, for her spending spree, and she didn't complain. That was far too much cash for a seven-year-old lass to be carting around, mam said, and I think it quite unnerved her.

One evening, Mam and Olive sat down with Millie and I, to say that they trusted us, and the money from Charlie was ours to do with what we wanted. But they also asked us to stick together, if possible, when shopping. We were advised to leave most of the money in the house unless we were certain what we were going to buy. Otherwise, to use it for shopping in little chunks, and to take out only what we needed. Maybe do some window shopping first...I couldn't believe it - window shopping.

They were quite adamant however and stressed that it was a lot of money we had, and not everyone outside of our family circle was as honest as us, but that we would be okay, as long as we were sensible. We were given the whole parental guidance speech. We listened, like obedient children, which of course we were, and agreed to all the parameters.

Milly and I arranged to go shopping together in Blyth. I was so excited to know we were going to have money in our pockets, and to be honest, I didn't know where to start. Think!...Billy Bunter with the run of a tuck shop...and you'd have a good idea of my enthusiasm. 'Yaroo.....!'

The present from Charlie and Martha had arrived in a white envelope, with 'Happy Christmas Sidney' written on the front, with a little hand-drawn smiley face. Mam had handed it over with a huge, happy grin. She didn't say a word, she was just overjoyed. The change in mam was massive, like the contrast between a rainy day indoors and a sunny day at the beach.

I'd sat on my bed the previous evening, with the money spread out before me. Fifteen, one-pound notes and ten ten-shilling notes, plus of course the one and a tanner of my own. I counted it over and over, and one of the times I came up with twenty-one, so, I had to count it over, again and again, just to make sure, and yep, it was definitely twenty. I decided I must be the richest kid in Blyth at that very moment... probably even richer than Vincent.

Mam, Olive and Linda were off to Newcastle, which was unusual because the two adults would normally have been working. Wilf was enjoying full board at Charlie and Martha's house and had spent the previous day there, too. I think Charlie was enjoying having a dog around again, so much so that it was almost impossible to find him without a huge grin on his face.

Yesterday had been our final school day. Milly, not being the school outcast any longer, had been one of the stars of the nativity play, and her mam, in the audience, had almost laughed her head off when Milly came on the little stage dressed as a sheep. My mam wasn't there. I wasn't in the nativity play, and anyway, on the same day, Linda was appearing in her own nativity play at Bebside school, and of course mam couldn't miss that. I never did ask why Linda and I were sent to different schools. It was just what it was.

The last day of school before Christmas was always exciting. Carols being sung, and plays being enacted with parents watching, cards from your pals, delivered by one of the kids dressed up as Santa. Every single kid wanting the clock to go faster so we could escape and start the holiday properly. Cards for your teacher and little gifts. Kids boasting to each other about the presents they were expecting, and that brilliant feeling, the fluttering tummy, that every child should have with the big day just around the corner. There was a definite air of magic about those final few hours of school, a feeling of...something special approaching.

I enjoyed the day so much; a complete contrast to last Christmas, when I'd been the new kid, with no friends to speak of, and feeling like an alien, abandoned on a strange planet. Christmas then had been sparse. No cards from schoolfriends. A few gifts only from mam, a sock with an orange, apple and nuts...and a book. The same for my sister and brother...and I don't think mam had a single present to open.

Many of our removal boxes still hadn't been unpacked so we didn't even put up a tree, and I can still remember the gloominess of that Christmas day morning, all of us so uncertain about what the future held. Even the lady from next door arriving with three Cadbury selection stockings didn't lift the gloom. It made us feel like charity cases... something like, I imagine, how Milly must have felt with my old jumper fiasco.

So, Blyth it was to be for the two little rich kids. Olive had been to work at the pub the previous evening, which meant Milly and I left from my house. The two grown-ups and Linda had set off very early as they were expecting big crowds in Newcastle with Christmas only nine days away. Linda was looking forward to the trip, and excited about seeing Fenwick's Christmas window. Milly, however, was a little subdued. I didn't know why, because we were now flush with cash, but I reasoned that she'd let me know what the matter was in her own good time.

We took the bus, a single decker, but it was a very quiet journey. Milly seemed to be grappling with some inner turmoil. Being really close friends, we would normally have been chatting away about everything and nothing, sorting out all the world's problems with our childish solutions. I was becoming quite concerned at our lack of interaction because she seemed to be immersed in some problem that she didn't feel comfortable discussing.

"D'yer fancy goin' to Seghini's first, to mek a plan?" I put the question out there as the bus pulled into the bus station. She gave me a funny look, then dropped her gaze, as we made our way to the front of the bus and alighted. "Aye, okay Sid," was the limited response.

We both couldn't help but notice though, as we walked across the square, when Titch passed in front of us, with a big grin on his face as he sauntered along, with an attractive dark-haired lass, about six inches taller than him. He didn't say anything but winked at us and walked on. The lass seemed to give us a questioning stare...and Milly looked swiftly away.

We continued, and I made a mental note as we crossed over from the bus station to Hedley Young's and walked on to Seghini's.

The café was quite busy, a Saturday rush, and more older people than you would normally see, but we managed to find seats quite close to the door.

"What can I get you Milly?"

"Just a glass of pop please."

"D'yer not want an Eccles cake or somethin', or some chocolate?"

"No thank you Sid, just pop."

Now I was definitely concerned. Our chatter had been like two strangers, not our usual casual banter. We didn't usually do polite with each other. I was just going to have to tackle this head on and ask what was up.

I'd just sat down at the table with Milly's pop, and a tea and wagon wheel for myself, when, who should walk in but Batesy.

"Hi Sid, hi Milly," he sat down in the spare seat, looking around as he did so, "What are you up to?"

"Just doin' a bit of shoppin' for Christmas presents, like," I put my hand in my pocket. "D'yer want a coke or summat, it's my turn."

"Nah, I was just lookin' for Roly; we're supposed to be goin' to the match."

"What match? I didn't know the Spartans were at home."

"Sunderland man, they're playin' Walsall today, and we'll be late if he doesn't turn up soon."

"How ye gettin' there?"

"'Got me ticket for the match bus. Leaves from the bus station whenever Sunderland's at home."

"Has Roly got a ticket?"

Batesy grunted, "Says he has...but you know, Roly is Roly."

"Aye, I know what you mean, but I thought ye'd have been Newcastle, like," I commented. Most of the lads at school were Newcastle fans.

"Nah, bunch of stinkies. Got a draw at their place a few weeks ago. We'll stuff them at Roker."

"D'yer go to every home game, like?" I was just making conversation now, not being particularly interested in Newcastle or Sunderland. My brother and I used to follow Rangers, or Hearts, but without enthusiasm.

"This is just my second time this season. Too expensive, but Charlie sent five quid for me...just 'cos I helped him wi' the allotment soil and some coal. He's given me mam and dad some dosh an' all. That was good of him. So, I can go to the match and I'll still have a canny bit left for presents. You'll probably be gettin' a fiver soon an' all Sid." With that he stood up, took a last look around the café and started for the door. "Anyway, you two, nice to see you, but I got to go... or aall miss the bus...ta-raa." And with that, he was out of the door and off.

Milly and I looked at each other as the whirlwind departed. I raised my eyebrows, she raised hers, shrugged and gave me a big smile.

That was more like it. Now for the pressing question.

"So, Milly McClair...are you goin' ter tell me what's been the matter with you? 'Cos you haven't been the normal cheeky Milly," I finished off with a big grin and pulled a funny face.

She smiled. "If the wind changes you'll stay like that."

"Aye, well it'll probably be an improvement," I chuckled, "so what's the problem? 'Cos something's been botherin' yer." I was trying to be nonchalant, rocking on the back legs of the chair...like all good kids do.

She wasn't making eye contact but looking down at her pop when she answered. "There's two things actually, Sid."

"Aye, okay, so take them one at a time. You can tell me anythin' and if there's a problem, then we'll sort it out together. Problems don't seem so scary when you share them." Oh, deary me, I sounded just like Charlie.

Milly gave me one of her nicest smiles, her twinkly one. "The first thing, Sid, is that I don't want to spend any of the money on me. I want to spend it on mam, and your mam, Linda, Charlie, Martha...and you of course...I want

to spend it on the people who've changed my life around."
She had real tears in her eyes, and her nose had begun to
run. I didn't know how to deal with an emotional girl, and
of course I didn't have a hanky to hand.

I tried to ignore the tears, looking anywhere, other than
directly at Milly.

"Aye, me an' all. I've been thinkin' the same thing
meself. Your mam and my mam have a bit of money now,
so they'll be makin' sure that we have a good Christmas. So,
I think the same as you. I'd like to get somethin' really nice
for mam, and Olive, Linda, Charlie, Martha...and somethin'
for Batesy an' all, but I've already got an idea about that. Oh
aye, and a ball and some dog biscuits for Wilf." I paused,
and scratched my head, "I haven't left anyone out have I...?"

"Now you're teasin', Sid Brown," the tears were in retreat
and the smile was back. She did have a hanky, tucked up her
sleeve. She took it out and wiped her nose.

"I suppose I am, but I never bought anythin' for a lass
before, so I'm strugglin' a bit...any suggestions?"

She was feeling better now, the normal Milly was returning.

"I don't need anythin' Sid. "We've got a house to live in,
and I've got a nice family now...and I've got you."

I wasn't expecting that. Everybody wants something for
Christmas. Having a nice family...and me, was true, but she
couldn't wrap us up and stick us under the tree.

"That's daft like, it's Christmas and you have to have a
good present, not just a selection box or socks and stuff. It
has to be summat special. I was gonna have a look around
for a duffel coat for you today, while you're with me, so you

can try it on......cos I remember you said to Linda that you'd seen a nice one wi' brilliant toggles on."

Milly's eyes filled up again, and her nose...well it wasn't running, but it had begun a slow jog.

"Ohhh Sid, that's a lovely thing to do," she wiped her nose again, "but me mam's buyin' me a duffel coat. I saw her shoppin' list last night. I know I shouldn't have looked but I didn't want to buy any of the same things as her. She's got a big, long list of presents for me, and you and Linda...Ohhh aye, and she's buyin' somethin' for Kenny an' all."

Oh, my goodness, Kenny. I'd almost forgotten about my own brother, with no family for Christmas. I wrote myself a mental note to be revisited later. I'd need to be quick, too, because I'd need to send his present in a parcel, and Christmas was just over a week away. Maybe mam would let me put Kenny's present in her parcel so I could save the postage.

"Okay, no duffel coat, but I have to buy somethin' good, somethin' that you really want. I don't want to give you a rubbish present so that you have to pretend, and go 'ooohh that's lovely', when your face is saying 'yuk, that's a pile of cack'. 'Cos I'd be really embarrassed...and disappointed."

Milly smiled, a cautious smile, so unlike her normal grin. She was struggling with what was to come next. Then she spoke, timidly, her voice faltering.

"There's one thing...that I would really like."

"Name it and it's yours," said I, jauntily, "as long as it's not more than twenty quid."

"Shhh' man, Sid, be quiet, you're talkin' really loud."

I gave her a puzzled look.

"About the money an' that," she whispered. "Somebody might hear, somebody not nice, that wants to steal it."

"Okay," I whispered back, "now what is it that you'd really like?"

She didn't look at me as she began, speaking softly, "I heard some of the older lasses talkin' at school, ones out of your class."

I didn't respond, other than with a questioning frown.

"June Marshall and Linda Maddison. Ohhh, and Jennifer Minter and some other un's."

She paused, and I just shrugged. I was stumped, and Milly seemed to be struggling again. I waited for her to continue, leaning back in my chair, and sipping at my tea, which was now lukewarm.

When she started, it all came tumbling out, the drip-drip-drip suddenly became a torrent.

"One of them said that you were the nicest lad in the class and she's gonna ask you to be her boyfriend. But that's not right, and it's not fair, because I like you more than any of them, and I don't just want to be your new sister or just your friend, I want to be your girlfriend, because you're the nicest lad in the whole world...and I keep thinkin' about you all the time, even when I'm on me own at home...so there... that's it..." She began crying, properly this time.

Bang, clatter...crash... "ouch". I'd been rocking my chair on two legs, but now the chair had its four legs, but they were sticking in the air and I was flat on my back, giving my head a good bang in the process. The tea was now decorating my jumper...and although I had my finger through the handle, the body of the cup was all over the floor, in a zillion pieces.

If that was my reaction to a girlfriend proposal...I'd have probably jumped off the Bella heap if a lass asked me for a kiss and stuff.

I'd hurt my shoulder, so I lay still for a moment, then the face of an old lady...who must have been mam's age, appeared in front of me. "Are you all right young man...have you hurt yourself?"

No, of course not...I was just showing off with the chair juggling and cup smashing trick. That's what I fancied replying. I didn't of course.

"No, I'm alright. I don't know what happened." I could feel the tea soaking through to my skin. My jumper was wringing wet. "I'll be alright."

She turned to Milly, "And you, young lady, are you alright? there's no need to be crying; your brother's not hurt."

I was back on my feet by this time and putting the chair back. The guy from behind the counter had run over with a mop and a pan for the broken cup and squashed wagon wheel, and everyone in the café was taking an interest in the goings on.

I glanced over to Milly, she was still tearful, looking stressed and apprehensive, then our eyes met, and locked. I winked and smiled.

"It's not my sister missus...it's my girlfriend, and she's cryin' because her pet tortoise has run away."

I saw Milly turn away with a grin on her face as the lady, oblivious to the absurdity of my statement, continued.

"Oh dear, that's awful for her...and for you, too. Here, take this to replace your teas," she held a shilling in her hand, "and don't worry about the cup, I'll have a word with the man".

"It's alright"...I was shaking my head, "we don't need the money, but thank you for your kindness." I smiled at the concerned lady.

She put the shilling down on our table. "I insist young man. I know that you young folk won't have much to spare with Christmas coming." And with that, she walked away, to speak to the owner.

Ten minutes later we were standing at the bus stop, waiting for the 49. Not a single present had been bought. Our conversation was almost non-existent. Something huge had just happened. A seismic shift in our relationship...and it was difficult to talk about. We were two ten-year olds and both feeling somewhat self-conscious.

The bus pulled-in and we headed upstairs, sitting together halfway along the top-deck. The conductress came and I paid the fare for both of us. There was no conversation, and I stared at the back of the seat in front of me wondering what that silver thing was with 'stubber' printed on it...perhaps you had to press it if the bus crashed, or something...like one of those ejector seats in a fighter aircraft. Still not speaking, we were halfway down Cowpen Road before I felt Milly's hand sliding into mine and squeezing. Phew, that was a relief, I squeezed back.

"Were you just sayin' it Sid, for that woman...or did yer mean it...about me bein' your girlfriend?"

The moment of truth...and she didn't deserve a lie. "Aye, Milly, I meant it." I paused for a few seconds.

"If I've got to have a girlfriend...I might as well have the best one."

There were no more words spoken on the journey.

My life had just become more complex.

CHAPTER 11

A Christmas Tale

The rest of December was manic. Manic and magic.
This would turn out to be the best Christmas ever, for me at least.

Out of the nine previous, sadly, there was only one I remember, with mam and dad happy and smiling, and not shouting at each other.

I didn't know the details, but after that solitary happy Christmas, everything went pear-shaped and happiness went downhill.

The memories of Christmas morning after that are always of us three kids, opening presents, with mam on her own, subdued, trying to hold things together...pretending. Pitiful really.

New Year too was to be a time of hopefulness and new beginnings. When the old year departed...so would many of our worries. Our bad times and dark days, whilst not forgotten, would quickly fade into insignificance, and that in itself would make us grateful for our current circumstance.

But we had to get there first, and for now, it was a hectic and insane week that we faced before we could conjure up a Christmas that we'd all remember. Boy, was it a challenge?

And my brand-new girlfriend was a breath of fresh air. Any negativity had disappeared and she was so alive, a very happy, positive human being, like sunshine personified. We got on like a house on fire and talked non-stop when we were together, about hopes and dreams, about things we wanted to achieve, about the future...we were ditching the bleakness of the past and sending the bad stuff into oblivion...talking about it, chewing it over, then dumping it into the dustbin of life.

She told me about Titch's potential new girlfriend, Shona. Milly knew her - a snippet from her previous life, before things had gone wrong.

Shona's father, Mr Williamson, was a lecturer at Newcastle University, her mother a lecturer, too, and they'd lived in Whitley Bay before moving to Blyth, and Leeches estate. Milly had lived in Whitley Bay also...when life was better...before the bad stuff. She'd stopped at that point... but I had no doubt that there would be more to come. I felt quite honoured to be allowed into someone's inner struggles with a dismal past. I was sad for her, but happy-sad if that makes sense.

Up to that point, it was if we'd been trotting along, in a donkey derby, then after Charlie's windfall, suddenly, for all of us, everything changed dramatically, and we were involved in a Grand National, and our first big fence was Christmas...Beecher's Brook.

During those days, Milly and I didn't mention our girlfriend, boyfriend understanding; it just bubbled away beneath the surface, low key. We didn't talk about it, flaunt it, or act any differently towards each other. We were still, simply two close friends, who genuinely liked one another. It was just taken for granted, by ourselves, that we were now a pair.

I didn't realise anyone else knew...until mam asked me about it one evening when Milly had returned to her own house in Prince's Gardens. Mam and I were home alone, because Linda was at Milly's, too, wrapping presents, and staying over with her newly adopted sister and Olive. Wilf was still at Charlie's. He'd taken a liking to Bruno's old bed and didn't want to leave. That turned out to be a godsend, with mam and Olive working, and us kids shopping, Wilf staying at Charlie's meant he didn't have to be left on his own, and Charlie of course, was happy with the arrangement.

Mam was relaxing, and she was indulging herself...a glass of sherry, no less, and out of the blue she began with....

"A little bird tells me...that you have a girlfriend, Sid," she was smiling when I looked up from my book.

I have to say that I was unsure about the whole situation. I didn't even know what boyfriends were supposed to do... and I couldn't ask Titch or Batesy or anyone else...because I'd probably end up being laughed at.

I must have went red, before replying, "Would that little bird be about seven years old...and called Linda?"

"I can't divulge that information, Sid," she chuckled... almost a giggle. I think the glass of sherry had gone straight to her head...maybe it was more than one glass.

"Aye, it was that nightmare sister of yours."

I just shrugged. "I don't know mam...like...what I'm supposed to do and what-not. Milly asked me to be her boyfriend...an' I said okay 'cos I really like her, but nothin's changed. I don't know what to do next...she might want me to learn skippin' and hopscotch...an' I don't want to...'cos the lads would laugh their heads off."

Mam turned away and pretended to pick something up. She'd just made a noise like an owl...a distinct hoot... followed by a double hoot...and when she turned back she was attempting to not burst out laughing. She struggled, valiantly, but she couldn't quite manage it, and what began as hoots, quickly became a howl. I'd never heard mam laugh so long and so loudly in my entire life. She had tears...funny face tears, running down both cheeks, and I just sat back and watched as she struggled to regain control.

To be honest, I started off being really annoyed, but then I ended up giggling with my mam 'cos she couldn't stop... not for a long while, and even when she seemed to have got herself back on an even keel, the occasional sniggers would sneak out, like a little piglet noise...tiny snorts. I'm convinced that mam was more than a little bit tipsy"

Eventually though, she did compose herself. To be fair, I hadn't minded too much, 'cos it was brilliant to hear my mam having a proper laugh, a real, from the heart...without a worry in the world laugh. I waited for her to come down to earth and begin a conversation.

She began with a little grunt, then bit her lip, hands clasped in front of her...then an intake of breath, staring hard at the floor, composing herself, sorting out her chuckling. Then, control achieved, she sucked in another huge breath and, straightening up, shoulders back, she looked me full in the face, without a trace of flippancy.

"Sorry Sid, honestly, I'm an awful mother...laughing like that...it's unforgiveable...not something my mother would have done." Composure now regained, she was back to being responsible mam.

"What would Grandma have done...mam?"

No hint of mirth now, her face was calm. She'd found her sensible head. "Precisely what I'm going to do, and tell you, that at your age you just carry on being best friends and looking out for each other...nothing more, nothing less. Milly is lovely, and she's been through a rough time...you're lovely, too, and you've been through your own rough time, and you're both coming out the other side." She gave me a happy smile. "So, my advice as a mother...who loves you...and Milly, too. Just be kind to each other and see where that takes you. You may be boyfriend and girlfriend for weeks, for months, for years possibly...or even for life...who knows? It's all about trust and being true and honest. If you do that...then life will give you back what you've put in."

Wow...I remember thinking, I can't have been the only one listening to Charlie and Martha...it was just as if one of those two were speaking. And startlingly, mam had used the L word...'love'...to me...a lad.

"Can I say somethin,' mam."

"You'd be hard to stop, with that mouth." Mam grinned.

"Just...you know, lasses don't make any sense...with the stuff they like doing. But I don't want to do any of that kissy stuff...yuk," I pulled a disgusted face. "And Milly might want to and I don't know what to do."

Mam held up a hand, "Sid, you're overthinking again. You're really good friends with Titch. Do you do kissy stuff with him?"

"Ehhh?... that's daft mam...lads don't do that. Titch is me mate."

"Aye Sid, and so is Milly, she's your pal as well as your girlfriend. You and Milly are both ten...kissy stuff doesn't come for years yet. Stop worrying about it. Don't make it complicated. Just be happy that you have a really close friend...who happens to be a girl...okay?"

That made good sense. I felt much more confident now. Thanks mam.

It was the 23rd of December, and the night before Christmas Eve. It was to be Olive's last shift at the Red House, not just for this week, but for ever. She'd been making plans with mam, and something was afoot, because mam had informed us that she'd decided to drop her cleaning jobs. We would find out all the specific details when the holidays were over, we were told. But mam and Olive were going to talk to us tonight, to hear our thoughts on what was being planned, but for now we needed to make this Christmas a time for us all to remember and remember fondly.

The shopping had been successful, all the presents bought and wrapped. Milly and I had pooled resources, and she'd been absolutely fantastic, helping me to choose for the females in my life...mam, Olive, Linda, and Martha. She'd also wrapped all those presents for me...otherwise I'd have presented what would have looked like wrapped cabbages if I'd been left to my own devices. I was a rubbish wrapper... girls were certainly better than lads at some things, and not just skipping.

Kenny's present, too, was under the tree, along with a present for his girlfriend Jan. It turned out that he was on leave, and spending Christmas Day at his girlfriend's parents' house, and they were driving up to ours for Boxing Day. Jan was two years older than Kenny, and she had her own car. Her family must have been quite well off. I was pleased for Kenny. He seemed to be making the best fist he could of his life...and of course it had saved me having to post a parcel off to his army camp.

Once we'd discovered the news of Kenny coming home, mam and Olive set about planning a party. Boxing Day was to be a celebration with friends and family, a day of saying thank you for all the blessings...mam and Olive's words, not mine. Neighbours would be popping in, Charlie and Martha would be coming, too; a lift had been arranged, and any friends we three kids wanted to invite would be welcome also, but we were asked to keep the numbers small.

Milly, Olive, and Wilf were to spend Christmas Eve with us, so we three kids would be together on the big morning... and we had a new tree...not a real one, but it looked realistic enough and it was big...six foot. We had a fantastic time decorating it, and it stood in one corner of the living room, behind the couch, and it looked even taller, on top of an upside-down bucket, which we'd wrapped in crepe paper. We argued about the tree topping - angel, or star. Star won... and you could barely see any of the tree branches because we'd festooned them with so much tinsel, and ornaments, and cotton wool...as pretend snow. Our family tree that year was incredible...the best ever.

Everyone was sneaking around during that week, smuggling in gifts, wrapping gifts, hiding gifts. It was chaotic...and fantastic...a veritable maelstrom of activity... and somehow it worked. Underneath my bed must have resembled Fenwick's window.

171

The one dampener during that frenetic final week was a visit I paid to Charlie's to bring Wilf back one afternoon. He'd been staying at their house for the past three nights and when I arrived there was only Martha at home. Charlie had taken Wilf for a walk to somewhere called Monkey's Island, so Martha said. I'd never heard of it, but didn't want to ask, and show my ignorance, maybe she meant the Bella.

Martha was happy to see me. She was up and about and looking really well. If I hadn't known otherwise I would definitely have thought that she was in excellent health.

Martha had put a tree up, also. Not a big one like ours. Theirs stood on a side table. It wasn't one of the tiny trees... it was about half the height of ours. And she'd decorated it really nicely. There were a few decorations around the house, not many, just a few of the concertina decorations criss-crossing the ceiling from the corners to the central light, but what was most noticeable, on the long wall, was a big, framed picture of Jesus, with two children at his feet, a boy, and a girl. Across the top of the picture were the words 'Suffer the little children, to come unto me.'

We talked for a while. I said I'd popped in to see them both, and to check that they were both okay, but also to retrieve Wilf and take him home.

Martha's eyes dropped when I said that.

"Aahh, that's a shame...still, it is what it is. With Bruno gone, Charlie's been ten years younger with Wilf around. I think that's where they're going later...to Bruno's grave... just to say hi, and to let him know that we still miss him every day."

I didn't know what to say. What came out was unplanned. "Does it not get any easier...the missing Bruno thing?"

She stared at the floor and shook her head, slowly from side to side.

"Time moves on...the clock never stops...for us. But for Bruno, time is everlasting now. Not a single day goes by that I don't see Charlie, staring into nothing...remembering...his best pal. Not just Bruno, but others we knew, and who we'll never see again...at least on this side of heaven."

I think, in a strange way, she'd forgotten that I was there, and she was talking to herself.

"We lost so much...so much, those we would hug...and swear we would keep them safe...and friends...with dreams, and family. Their clock doesn't tick anymore...they live on, in our heads, always smiling...waving goodbye as we shut our memories down...ghosts, all of them ghosts...and our children, our blessed children...our future...standing in front of us, arms reaching out, for sanctuary...we let them go...let them go..."

She sat down in that big old horsehair armchair, her head in her hands, softly sobbing. I realised that she had been talking about the war years...and about her family...her children...her past life.

I was lost. I didn't have any tools for this situation. So, I did what British people do...I walked through into the kitchen and put the kettle on.

I stayed there, in the kitchen, hearing the muffled sobs, but unable to go through and give any comfort. I felt so impotent.

Five minutes later I handed Martha a cup of tea. I didn't ask how many sugars, I just guessed.

Martha had composed herself by now and she took the cup of tea without comment. She sipped at it and screwed her face up.

"Sorry Martha," I said, "too many sugars?"

"What did you put it in with...a shovel?"

We both grinned...well, I grinned, Martha gave a sad smile, her face was still tear-stained but she'd recovered.

"Sorry Sid...forgive me. Memory is something to be thankful for, and to be fearful of. It ambushes you sometimes."

"Now, let's change the subject...what have you been up to?"

I rambled on for a fair bit, and she was listening intently, as she always did. I was sitting opposite the Jesus picture, and there was just something about it that I couldn't put my finger on...until it suddenly struck me. The little girl at the feet of Jesus was the spit of Milly. I didn't say anything to Martha, in fact I didn't say anything to anyone but I was astonished, the likeness was extraordinary.

I continued talking, telling Martha about Vincent at Seghini's café, and how I hated him. I told her about his dad who was a psychologist and advised the police on human behaviour, and then about Batesy and how he'd faced Vincent down and made up a silly story about rump steak.

Martha laughed at the rump steak story and didn't even tell me off when I said about wiping a cow's arse.

She held up a hand to halt my flow.

"That fellow...who uses psychology to study human behaviour? That is absolute rubbish Sidney."

"No, Martha, honest I'm not telling lies...that's what Vincent said and some other people, too." I thought mistakenly that she didn't believe me.

"No Sidney, no, not you, I didn't mean that was rubbish, or that I thought you were lying to me. No-no, using psychology is rubbish is what I meant. Studying psychology to understand human behaviour is like studying ink to understand Shakespeare's plays. The man's a nincompoop."

I spent another hour with Martha, and we chatted about all manner of things, but when Charlie and Wilf hadn't returned, I took my leave, reluctantly, and headed home. Wilf had won a reprieve.

I talked the entire episode over with mam, and she gave it some serious thought, but left it there for the time being.

Wilf was back with us on that evening of the 23rd. He'd been with us the previous evening, too, and I was a little worried about him. He didn't snuffle or scratch, or whine, and ask to be up on my bed that night. He lay all night on his blanket pile. I was beginning to think he might be ill. He was happy enough to have his late evening walk, though, when we escorted Olive back to ours after completing her final shift. She brought two bottles of beer to celebrate her last night at the Red House, as well as the usual crisps and blackjacks, and Wilf's sneaky night-time treat.

That was the evening we had the full-on, in-depth family conference that had been promised by mam. Once we'd all settled down, and turned off the radio, mam and Olive poured some drinks, handed out the crisps and began, rather nervously to let us in to their thinking.

In a nutshell, mam and Olive had hatched a plan. By pooling their newfound resources, they reckoned they would be able to buy a pair of flats in one of the streets close to Morpeth Road School, and they'd also been toying with the idea of setting up their own little company and selling household products door to door, and possibly from a market stall, too. They'd even thought of a name, 'Homecare Hygiene'.

Their thinking was, that if they used one of the bedrooms in one of the flats for storage and as an office, then they wouldn't have to pay extra rent for business premises. Olive could do the deliveries, because she had a driving licence, and mam said they should be able to afford a decent second-hand van. Mam would do the typing and the accounts and the buying, and both mam and Olive would also do the selling. However...they would need consent from their three children, because it would mean, in all probability, that Linda and Milly would have to share a room, bunk beds possibly, because one bedroom in one of the flats would be full of the business stock and out of commission.

That then, was the general idea. The specifics would be a while in coming and take a lot of groundwork...but they wanted to know how we felt about the plan. It was plain to all three of us kids that it would only take one abstention from us, one demurral or veto, for them to ditch the idea... they were both so desperate to have the consent of their children.

We, of course, were cock-a-hoop. My mam...indeed, who'd have thought it?...with half of a business. Milly's mam with the other half....after all she'd been through, we were elated. For our mams it would mean no more drudging around cleaning up other folks' mess, no more serving drinks to inebriated blokes, no more scrimping and scraping to make ends meet. Mam and Olive were excited by the prospect...but we kids were overjoyed.

Milly's eyes, I remember were so wide open...she was on cloud nine, after all the days of darkness and doubt, this held out the prospect of...well...hope...a pipe dream with every chance of becoming reality.

We didn't just give the idea our blessing, we were euphoric...and they could see how enthused we were with just the discussion of such a possibility. We made two ladies very happy that evening. So much so that I, being the oldest, and obviously the wisest, was allowed a little glass of Amber ale. Was I pleased?...not in the slightest, it tasted like sweaty socks...I didn't say that though...I was showing off in front of Milly.

There was one other item on the agenda that evening. It was to give us all a bout of soul-searching. That one other item was something we all agreed would be tackled tomorrow...Christmas Eve, and we hoped that it would turn out successfully. We all had a lie in on that following morning. None of us getting up until about ten 'o clock. Last night's conference had gone on well into the wee hours, and amidst the excitement, I don't think any of us had realised just how late it was.

So, it was heading towards mid-day, Christmas Eve, and we three youngsters, were sitting on the floor in front of the telly, watching Elsa the Lioness, when mam and Olive brought our bacon sandwiches through into the sitting room, a late breakfast. Mugs of tea quickly followed, and all that could be heard for the next few minutes was the chomping sounds of hungry kids, coupled with the lion noises on the TV. Wilf of course had smelled the bacon and he hung around us three, waiting to be sneaked a morsel. He wasn't disappointed.

Then, mam and Olive, now both full of bacon butty and pumped up with coffee, went into bustling mode.

"Come on you lot, upstairs, clothes on....we've got a lot to do today." Olive was in control.

"Aahh, mam, man, there's a fantasy thing comin' on about Christmas, called the Twelfth Day or somethin'," cried Milly.

"Milly, Linda, Sid move your backsides upstairs," commanded a stern voiced Olive, "and out of those pyjamas, hurry it up...now! We've got presents to deliver, and baking to do and lots of other things to arrange...if you want your Christmas to be fantastic, then move it, move it, move it, chop-chop, the clock's ticking and Santa is getting anxious."

We moved it...they sounded serious.

Batesy's house was my first stop and Milly went with me. Mrs Bates answered the door and told me Jim wasn't in...he was at his cousin Irene's house in Dunston Place. I handed her a small parcel that Milly had wrapped for me.

"Can you just put that with his presents, Mrs Bates, and not say that it's from me. It's just to say thank you...cos he's helped me out a couple of times, but I don't want him to think I'm being girly."

Mrs Bates laughed, then asked, "And who's this young lady, is it your sister?"

"No, Mrs Bates, it's my girlfriend...Milly, and she wrapped the present. It's just a Biggles book...an old one, but I know he's been after a copy."

"Well, that's a nice thing for you to do Sidney...and I'm sure Jim will be pleased...and you have a good Christmas, both of you."

"Thanks Mrs Bates...Oh aye....me mam says would you like to pop into ours on Boxing Day...'cos there'll be neighbours comin' and goin' all day, and our Kenny's on leave from the army. Me mam and Milly's mam are havin' like a little Christmas party."

"Say thank you to your mam Sidney...and we'll try and pop in, but I can't promise... 'cos there's things goin' on here an' all. If I can't make it, then I'll get Jim to show his face... okay?"

"Okay Mrs Bates...Merry Christmas." And with that we left.

Next stop was to be Charlie's, but on our way back to Hallside, to pick up the bags of gifts and join up with mam and the others, we bumped into Milly's old acquaintance... Shona. It was bizarre the way it came about. A voice from nowhere took us both by surprise. She just seemed to appear out of thin air.

"Hi Milly...it is you; I saw you from along the street. I thought it was you last week...at the bus station, but I wasn't sure."

"Aye, thought I recognised you, Shona." Milly was immediately wrong-footed and looked like she'd rather be anywhere but there.

Their conversation was stilted, hesitant...some underlying tension. Minor pleasantries were awkwardly exchanged.

Then... "Sorry to hear what happened with you and your mam...I didn't believe it, you know? Nobody did when we heard about your dad...and him going to prison."

Milly didn't reply. Her head had dropped...and her eyes fixed on the pavement.

"We live here now...up at Leeches...in Bishopdale... you'll have to come and see us sometime. We've moved here because mother's going to have a baby, so she won't be working anymore, and she wants to be close to Gran." Then she smiled at me. "Who's your friend?"

Milly wasn't for answering, so I took over.

"Hi Shona, I'm Sid Brown, Milly's boyfriend...well, boyfriend and best friend and newly adopted brother, too. All of those things."

"Are you Alan Irving's friend...called Husky...or something."

"Aye that's me, but it's Hawky. Titch has obviously been talking."

She laughed, a friendly laugh. "Yes, he's a strange one, and he doesn't like it when anyone calls him Titch. I've only had two dances with him and he wants me to come to your house to pretend to be his girlfriend. He wanted to know if my father was really a teacher, and if I'd be interested in half a selection box. It's really weird, but he's a nice enough lad. He's okay, but I can't be his girlfriend 'cos I like lads to be taller than me, not smaller." She laughed again, then moved closer to Milly.

"Sorry Milly...I shouldn't have said anything. It's none of our business. It's just that me and mother were so worried when all that bad stuff happened and you and your mam just suddenly disappeared. People were saying that you'd been kidnapped or something."

Milly kept her eyes fixed on the ground, not responding.

"We've got to go Shona," I gave her a wide-eyed, raised eyebrows look...a signal to let it be, to leave well alone. "We'll be looking forward to seeing you round at ours, should be good..."

Thankfully she understood and gave me a knowing smile. I don't believe any of her words had been intended to wound or cause upset. She was just ten years old, same as us, and social skills weren't yet honed to perfection.

"Yeh-yeh, see you soon Milly. Hope you both have a lovely Christmas Day." And with that she turned on her heels and set off for wherever she'd been headed in the first place.

We continued our journey in silence, and we were almost back to the house before Milly spoke.

"You'll not be wantin' me for your girlfriend anymore." Her voice was raw.

I took hold of her hand and squeezed.

"Don't think you can get rid of me that easily," I responded. "Whatever happened with your dad isn't your fault...same as what happened with my mam and dad isn't my fault."

We'd reached the back door. I said, "If you ever really don't want me to be your boyfriend...just tell me. It won't stop me liking you or stop me from being your ordinary friend."

She turned, looked at me, and smiled. "Bend down a bit Sid, you've got somethin' in your hair." I bent down. She kissed my cheek, quick as lightning, and then disappeared into the house before I could react. To be fair, it wasn't as 'yuk' as expected.

Then, on to Charlie's. But, how come we had four bags of presents, and I got the two really heavy ones, and mam and Olive had one between them, taking a handle each, and the same for the two girls. Okay, Milly also had Wilf on a lead, but it was still nowhere near to being fair. By the time we reached Charlie's I was puffed out. My arms were aching and the parcels in boxes were bumping and knocking against my legs as I walked. Oh, how I wished that mam and Olive had invested in their new little van before Christmas.

Charlie and Martha were pleased as punch to see us all together, and before we'd even finished with the pleasantries a bottle of whisky and a bottle of sherry had appeared as if by magic. Chinking glasses swiftly followed, and a big silver plate materialized covered with little ball things in breadcrumbs and some triangle miniature pasties.....but they all smelled different to anything I'd ever known. Wilf, now off his lead, headed instantly for Bruno's old bed and snuggled down.

Mam and Olive both had a glass of sherry. Charlie and Martha both had whisky, and we kids had glasses of pop. They'd asked us young un's what we wanted to drink and I'd said, "No whisky for me Charlie...last time Martha gave me one we ended up dancing...it was embarrassing."

"Sidney Brown...you're a terrible young liar...you'll get me arrested," Martha laughed, and everyone joined in.

It was a good day...for all of us...a good time, without worry. And looking around the room...there wasn't a single gloomy face. It was smiles and laughter all round.

Linda, Milly, and I had been delegated with the present giving and Martha and Charlie were shocked when we emptied the bags and handed them over. There were seven presents each, and each one was meticulously wrapped and decorated with bows. Charlie looked excited, like a kid, and was about to get stuck into the first of his, but I stopped him.

"No Charlie...not until tomorrow morning. It isn't Jesus' birthday until then."

Charlie laughed. "Do you think he'll mind?"

I laughed back, I knew his sense of humour, and replied,

"Jesus won't mind, but we will, when you see what a pile of rubbish we've bought...and then you'll have to pretend to be pleased."

Charlie and Martha both laughed out loud.

"Best wait until we've gone...then you can make your disappointed faces in private."

"Okay young fella, your wish is our command." He neatly stacked the presents on the floor, beside the tree, sat back down beside Martha, and sipped at his whisky. But Charlie wasn't stupid, he could feel that there was something else, something unsaid. We were all a little edgy.

Mam and Olive stood up together. We three kids knew what was coming and we were anxious for them.

Mam cleared her throat...and swallowed, nervously.

She was having difficulty beginning. She seemed so apprehensive.

Charlie was aware...and held up his hand. "Marjorie... whatever it is, whatever you need...just say. I've heard about your plans...with Olive, for a business, and a house. If you need some more help, just say."

Mam looked to each of us in turn, and we attempted to give her a confident look, at least I did...and I'm sure the others would have also.

"It's nothing like that...Charlie....and Martha," mam began,

"I want to ask...no, we all want to ask...all five of us…" she paused and swallowed hard.

"After Christmas the kids will be back at school...and Olive and myself will be working so hard to build something for our future...our children's future, and we...were sort of wondering, but say no if it isn't going to be possible...we were hoping that you might fancy adopting Wilf."

I swear this next bit is true...even if you have doubts about other happenings.

At the very same time that mam was giving her nervous speech...Wilf left his comfy nest in Bruno's bed and trotted over from the far corner of the room. And at the very second that mam asked if Charlie and Martha would adopt Wilf he jumped up onto Charlie's lap, and snuggled in...honest.

To be truthful, there never was any doubt what the outcome would be. Charlie was ecstatic, and Martha had a beam on her face that could have lit up a small town. He had tears of joy in his eyes, and Martha had tears of thankfulness, we had made their Christmas Eve perfect. Tomorrow they would be at ours for dinner, and then back again on Boxing Day for our celebration...so it wasn't as if we'd be abandoning Wilf. We'd be able to see him any time we wanted. And to be perfectly honest, as much as we all loved Wilf, and he, in his inimitable doggy way loved us back...there was no question that when he was with Charlie, he'd found his dog paradise.

We stayed and laughed and ate...those spicy chicken ball things, and pasties that Martha had cooked herself and she said they were very much like samosas but she'd used her

Polish recipe. I just nodded, pretending that I knew who Samosa was.

And we also found out during that hour or so...well, we kids found out, that Karol, with a 'K' not a 'C', was Charlie's Christian name, and it was from the Ukraine. Charlie's father was Ukrainian, his mother Polish, his surname Demancjuk and he had been a professor in a Polish university. Martha had been a professor, too, and it was at university that they first met.

We left it there, not going any deeper, because I recalled what Martha told me about memories ambushing folk.

We said our goodbyes until tomorrow. And we left a very happy looking man and wife...and a dog with a waggy tail.

Mam had one more present to deliver. An old lady called Polly, who lived in the old folks' flats on the corner of Axwell Drive and Hortondale. Mam didn't make a big deal of it, she just said that the lady needed to know someone cared. She went alone, and wasn't away very long, but she seemed a little sad when she returned. We didn't ask any questions, if there was something to say, mam would say it in her own time.

Time was cracking on, it was around eight, knocking on for bedtime, and we kids were watching 77 Sunset Strip on the telly...and, truth is, I sort of fancied myself as a Cowpen version of Kookie...the young fellow in Sunset Strip who was constantly combing his hair, and Milly had a thing for the big star, Efrem Zimbalist Jr. – she said he looked like her dad. We were sharing a pre-Christmas selection stocking, with parental permission of course, and enjoying the programme.

Mam and Olive were slaving away in the kitchen and the smell was fantastic, just like walking past a baker's shop when they were doing fresh bread. There was already a table full of pies, flans, scones, and cakes, and they were finishing their last batch before cooking the turkey. To be honest the turkey looked way too big, and we wondered how they would manage to fit it in the oven. There was a mountain of vegetables to prepare and these were to be tackled by mam... because Olive was tearing her hair out, having messed up the trifle in mam's big glass Lalique bowl...the custard had been too hot and it had melted the jelly and the spongey bits, so that it now looked more like a Picasso painting than a trifle. Olive was not a happy bunny.

But we kids just kept out of the way. After Sunset Strip finished, the telly was really boring...okay for old people but it was rubbish for kids. We turned it over onto BBC...but that was rubbish too, the Billy Cotton Band Show.

At a loose end, and with the parents otherwise engaged, we decided it was time to bring down their presents and lay them out for the morning.

It took us a good half hour, but when we were finished the present pile for our mams looked fantastic. We'd placed them on either side of the telly and they had about ten presents each...and I have to say, the two girls had made a super job of the wrapping and decorating. They'd run out of gift tags, so Milly had even written out two signs, Olive, and Marjorie....just to ensure they wouldn't get mixed up.

When mam and Olive came through to the living room, about half an hour later with a cup of tea, and obviously tired out...they both looked at the piles of presents...and they were gobsmacked. Not a word was spoken; they looked at us, open-mouthed, then at each other, dumbstruck.

It was Olive who broke the silence. "Where...how, where have all those come from? You haven't been spending the Charlie money on us...have you?"

Then mam chipped in. "Ohhh, I hope not you three... because we haven't bought anything for you...so let's hope that Santa hasn't forgotten you."

Milly grinned at me, I grinned at Milly, and we both grinned at Linda. Our mams were pleased...and surprised... and happy...and that was better than any other Christmas present.

They ushered us off to bed, an hour earlier than my normal time, but I didn't mind. It went quiet for half an hour, then I could hear the pair of them sneaking up and down the stairs, the rustle of wrapping paper, the "Shhh" as they tried valiantly to make no noise in their secret Santa role. I knew the girls would be listening to the same noises in their bedroom...and I just knew for certain that they'd be smiling too.

A lad called Davy Preston once told me, that the only thing a person can never remember, is the exact moment they fall asleep. He was right, because next thing I knew it was morning, not yet light, but it must be near to getting up time...surely. I listened for sounds of movement, there weren't any...so I decided to go solo. I sneaked downstairs to have a look at the clock. It was five-fifteen, and the sitting room was awash with presents, the couch and the armchair were so full that they could hardly be seen. Time to wake the girls. Santa had played a blinder.

The rest of the day was incredible. We three youngsters had more presents than you could shake a stick at. The two girls were blitzed with new clothes and loads of girly things, while I had a pile of boy stuff, books mainly, but a tennis racquet and balls from Milly. Our mams had new skirts, jumpers, slippers, dressing gowns, pyjamas, wine, chocolates...and a new bracelet each, and when they opened their presents from each other they couldn't help but laugh, because they'd both bought the same dress, mam for Olive and vice versa, size being the only difference.

Milly was very tentative when she opened her presents from me. I'd bought her a jumper, a girl's jumper, chosen by mam, not me...and that made Milly smile with the memory of our first meeting. But she could barely speak when she opened the smaller present. I'd bought her a locket, in a heart shape, that you could put mini photographs in. I didn't have any that would fit, so inside I'd put two pieces of paper, one at either side, with an 'S' and an 'M'.

I immediately thought she was going to start with the tears and begin blubbing, but she fought it off and kissed me on the cheek again, before jumping up to show our mams.

Dinner was a huge success, if a little crowded. Even with the kitchen table extended it was a tight squeeze with the family five plus Charlie and Martha. The meal was perfect and a smashing time was had by all...apart from Wilf... who'd gorged on too much turkey and made himself sick... or perhaps it was the sprouts, 'cos they always made me feel like that an' all.

The grown-ups all had a little too much to drink and there was much laughing, giggling, telling of stories and a barrage of repetitive thank you speeches, for our newfound financial status, for our hospitality to Charlie and Martha, for adopting Wilf, for all mam's help. Four inebriated adults being watched by three delighted and jubilant children.

That then was our first Christmas day together. As it turned out it wasn't to be the last...but we weren't to know that.

Now we had to plan for tomorrow...Kenny and girlfriend, Charlie, and Martha again, friends and neighbours...our Boxing Day party.

CHAPTER 12

A New Year Dawning

———————————— ■ ————————————

Boxing Day went down a storm, too. Martha, Charlie, and Wilf arrived really early, just before lunchtime, and Charlie wasn't backward in coming forward at mealtimes. There was still so much turkey and pork left from yesterday... and that was basically our lunch, turkey and pork, and a fry up of the left-over vegetables, stuffing and yorkies, and Charlie did his utmost to clear the surplus. Watching him demolish a turkey leg was like watching a lion attacking an antelope.

An hour after lunch was over, the kitchen table, still extended, and freshly covered with paper Christmas tablecloths, was now chocker-block with pies, pasties, sausage rolls, tiny sausages on sticks with cheese and pineapple, bacon and egg flans...Picasso trifle...well, you name it and our table had it...Henry the eighth would have felt right at home if he'd dropped in on our banquet. All that was missing, from my perspective, was the head of Vincent, on a silver salver, with an apple stuffed in his mouth.

The main kitchen bench underneath the wall cupboards was bedecked with bottles of wine and spirits, and our little fridge was packed to capacity, honestly, you could barely shut the door. It was a frosty day outside, so mam had put lots of cans of beer out of sight in the back garden, and the bottled beer was on the pantry floor. Even the coalhouse, after a good cleanout, had been conscripted for storage duties - with a borrowed extending table holding the spare glasses, plates, and bottles of pop...all covered with tea towels. The fire was blazing away in the sitting room, with a full scuttle of coal and a pile of logs standing at the ready.

After lunch, and after the dishes were done, I overheard mam, Olive, Charlie and Martha talking, discussing the new business idea. Charlie was giving advice on how to set a new venture up, how to keep records, minimizing outgoings, how to do tax returns...hawker licences, and a dozen other things. Mam and Olive listened intently and they were expressing the sentiment, that if they worked really hard and the business was a success, then they would have found happiness.

This prompted another life observation from Martha. She'd overheard their comments on chasing happiness and she was very serious when she said, "Remember, you two ladies...that happiness is a shadow. If you chase it, it moves further away, always just out of reach. But if you turn around, and make others happy, it will follow you, and it will catch up with you. To make yourselves happy, make others happy."

I remember it sounding so profound, and mam and Olive being silent for minutes afterwards, letting the words soak in, absorbing the philosophy laid out in Martha's latest utterance.

Martha waited while they processed it, and when she thought they had understood she said,

"And don't set out to impress others. Do what is necessary to make the business flourish, listen to your instinct, and

ignore the outside noise. For you will come across those who
wish two women to fail, and they will wallow in it if you do...
and unfortunately, many of them will be women.

Some women talk about other people's failures with so
much pleasure that you would swear they are talking about
their own successes. So, play your cards close to your chest.
Those people I talk about, some will be known to you, friends
indeed, and jealous, and some will just be acquaintances
who glory in other folk's setbacks. But they will be there,
and they will surface at the first signs of a problem in your
business...so tread carefully."

Charlie nodded, but all he said was, "Martha's right...
take care."

Then people started turning up, and our house became
a hive of activity.

Charlie was made head barman, with myself as his
legs...handing out drinks, collecting empty glasses...ferrying
fresh supplies of beer from the back garden, and eventually
washing and drying the glasses as we began to run out of
clean ones.

Olive was in charge of food, with Milly as her waitress,
taking plates of nibbles around, washing and drying the
plates when empty, making up platters for the older folk,
and showing those more agile, to the kitchen table...which
was groaning with the weight of the banquet.

Linda was with mam, greeting and talking, offering
chocolates, hanging up coats, finding seats, putting 45s on
the Dansette record player, and generally just smiling and
being Linda. We kids had been asked to keep the numbers

down if we asked friends to come...but that same rule should have applied to mam and Olive, because at one point the house was full to bursting, like being at a football match. It was a cold day but there were a few times when folk were standing outside, drink in hand, just to have some personal space and not be jostled. But mam of course, looked as happy as a sandboy, and she grinned at everyone.

The Winters were first to arrive with their daughter, Linda, and she immediately made a beeline for my sister to help with the chocolates...help make them disappear, I hasten to add. Then came the Harris family from Axwell... then Sylvia...the blackie pie lady, then Harry and Mary-Jane Thompson from Axwell with their daughter.... then the Formans – Tommy and Lilla'...Roly and Lynn...and...well after that it was just a swarm...it was hectic, and crowded, with folk arriving and folk leaving. In hindsight we should have installed one of those revolving doors, and eventually, even though it was a chilly day, mam just left the front door open for folk to come and go as they pleased.

The food and drink were being depleted at an alarming rate, even though most of the guests brought a bottle of something with them...but then, all of a sudden, and as if by magic, folk began disappearing, the congestion abated and numbers in the house dwindled. Eventually, there was a period of half an hour or more with no guests whatsoever when we could all relax.

Charlie took the opportunity to ask if Martha was needing to go home. She'd been in the armchair since arriving... with Wilf up on her lap, and he was worried that she was overdoing it...was wilting.

"Not a chance Karol, I haven't had as much fun, watching people, in a long time." She gave him a re-assuring smile. "And our Wilfey is having a whale of a time, aren't you fella?" she said, scratching the back of his neck. "He's had more food sneaked to him than is good for him...he'll probably burst before we go home...no Karol, honestly, I'm enjoying the day. I promise I'll tell you if I get too tired."

That put Charlie's mind at rest and he wandered outside to roll a cigarette and have a little time to himself. Wilf jumped down from Martha's knee and followed him out.

Mam and Olive slumped down on the couch. Milly joined me in front of the fireplace and gave me a dig with her elbow. "Them two look happy enough," she said, pointing with her eyes to her mam and mine.

"Aye, it looks like it," I agreed.

Then miracle upon miracle, my sister Linda got the hoover out...without being asked, plugged it in and began running it over the carpet, now festooned with all manner of debris, crumbs and ground in food. Someone had even stubbed a cigarette out on the carpet and there was a distinct burn mark.

Wilf heard the hoover starting up and came running in from outside, barking at the nasty contraption, ready to give it a good old bite on the dust-bag. He'd never liked the hoover...and we'd never asked the hoover how it felt about Wilf. He jumped around it, yipping and yapping until Linda had completed the worst of the traffic area and shut the hoover down. Wilf wasn't convinced that it had finished making a noise, even after Linda removed the plug from the socket, and he followed her through to the passage and the vacuum's home under the stairs...ready to pounce if it growled at him again.

Then Kenny arrived.

Mam was so excited when we saw the Vauxhall Victor Estate pull up outside the house. We all crowded around the window. Kenny, in civvy clothes, emerged from the passenger side, and gave a big stretch, he saw us at the window, and waved, and we all waved back. He had a huge smile on his face.

Then his girlfriend emerged from the driver's side. Silence reigned; we were a tad shocked. She was Chinese... very, very, Chinese.

Charlie took control. "Wow...your brother has found a real beauty there Sid, she's absolutely stunning." He gave me a nudge...he'd felt the reaction in the room, "Be good, be sensible," he whispered, "she's going to be nervous...she'll need some friends...we'll be the first two...okay?"

I nodded...my brother's girlfriend was gorgeous...even I could see that. But I realised what others would think; Blyth was not a multicultural town, not so welcoming, and foreign faces stood out a mile.

When they walked through the door I could see that mam had her 'okay I accept your decision...but why?' face on. I was hoping that this would go okay, I was nervous for Kenny and his lass.

Charlie was the first to introduce himself. "Kenny...I'm Charlie, your mam has told us so much about you."

"Charlie who sent me twenty quid?" grinned Kenny.

Charlie seemed a little nonplussed. "It was nothing Kenny...just a gesture." He shook Kenny's outstretched hand.

Kenny was laughing, "Carry on gesturing for as long as you like Charlie, I appreciate it. But honestly...thank you for what you've done for my family, you've turned their lives around...seriously."

Kenny was just like an adult...and he wasn't seventeen for another few weeks. The army had grown him up...quickly.

Charlie looked embarrassed. Then he gave Kenny's girlfriend a hug.

"You must be Jan...pleased to meet you."

She smiled...a lovely smile. "My name is Shan...it means mild," she pointed,

Like that can of beer in your hand."

Charlie laughed...he'd been outdone on this occasion.

Mam was next up, then Linda, Olive, Millie, Martha... Wilf and finally me.

It went off okay. Nobody mentioned the Kam Tong restaurant, sweet and sour, or egg fried rice.

"Hello Shan? Is that right?"

"Yes...that's right Sid...I've heard a lot about you...the brains of the family." She gave me a big smile.

"Don't know about that...Kenny's just being kind. Where you from Shan?"

Her reply was unexpected. "Surrey," She said without making it an issue.

"Where are you from Sidney?" she asked quite innocently.

"Scotland...well, Fife...errrmm, Kirkcaldy." It was a question I hadn't expected.

"So...we're both trying to fit in...you and I." She winked, and I winked back.

We were now friends...without having to say it.

Presents were exchanged....and I genuinely think that Shan was surprised at the effort we'd all put into her gifts. She seemed genuinely touched. I can't remember what everyone else received, but I do remember that Kenny and Shan gifted me a Latin book. 'Teach yourself Latin grammar.' I really appreciated it, but I decided there and then, not to touch it until the eleven plus was done and dusted. Shan smiled when I opened it...and she said, "Do well at Latin Sidney...I mean it, everything we do is based on Latin...it will change your life."

Mam and Shan took themselves off into a corner and they had a heads down, frank, and candid discussion for a good twenty minutes...and they were only interrupted when the second tranche of guests began arriving. When they emerged, mam had her arm around Shan's shoulder, and Shan was smiling...it all looked promising.

I was back on beer duty, and Kenny had joined me to help out. Cans of beer needed to be opened with the budgie opener. A metal strip with a front end like a budgie's beak and a little hook thing for gripping the edge of the can, and the cans needed to be punctured at two points, preferably 180 degrees apart, or as opposite as possible. Just open one and the beer would only pour very slowly. Open two and you could have a full glass of beer in seconds. Charlie had been well prepared and had a stash of about half a dozen of these can puncture things....and they found plenty of use that day.

Then suddenly the house was full again. Batesy and his mam, together with Titch, his mam and his little sister, Sheila, arrived at the same time. Mrs Bates only stayed for a little while, accepting a glass of sherry, then had to return to her own household. Batesy gave me a punch on the shoulder to say thank you for the Biggles book and gave me a tin of toffees, and he'd even wrapped them, still with 'Merry Christmas Jim, from Aunty Mary' on the label...but at least he'd tried. The Winters returned for a second crack at the booze and food, and neighbours I only knew by sight, but not by name, filled the house, and filled it with a feeling... that we were maybe not outsiders anymore, we were just neighbours. The whole place was buzzing again.

Presently, Shan came through to the kitchen to see if we were okay, and to see if we needed any help. We didn't, but she sat down at the table, keeping out of the way...escaping from the living room. Something wasn't right. Kenny knew immediately....but Charlie and I picked up on it pretty quickly, too.

Olive came through and said to Shan.. "What was that about...was he rude to you or something?"

Kenny was up like a bantam cock. "Who? What's that all about?" He was ready for action.

"It's nothing...Kenny, honestly...nothing' said Shan, "just someone thinking they've cracked a funny joke...for the first time ever...about...you know, needing to tell all the neighbours to keep their cats indoors. Flied lice....sore finger, slanty eyes...jaundice...the usual."

Kenny was livid.

Mam came through into the kitchen too. "You okay Shan?"

"Yes...just having a breather."

"He's not a bad bloke really...just stupid. Mike Timmins, he's not the brightest."

Kenny was still up for it, "Then this Timmins or whoever it is needs the stupid knocking out of him."

"Pointless," said Charlie, making an observation, "knock the stupid out of him and there'd be nothing left for his wife to go home with".

Kenny smiled and cooled down a little.

"Here," said Charlie, shaking a can of Long Life vigorously, "Take that to him Kenny."

He handed the can of beer to Kenny along with the budgie opener. "Make sure you're nowhere near him when he opens it."

Kenny chuckled...he was seriously warming to Charlie.

He handed the can to me, "You take it Sid...please, I don't want to see the bloke's face...don't want to overreact and spoil things."

I did as I was asked. I went through into the sitting room, handed the can and opener over to Mr Timmins, with a smile, and retreated quickly.

Two minutes later we heard the shout from the living room, "Aahh.....shit, aahmm bliddy soaked...whee's done that? It'll be that little Scottish bugger that fetched it...shakin' it up. Howay, aahmm ready for gannin yem anyway...howay woman get yer coat. Me bliddy shirt's wringin."

And with that, the Timmins were gone, without a goodbye.

Charlie was grinning.

"Charlie, you are a very naughty man," laughed mam. "But to be fair he was drinking us out of house and home."

"Well, he's gone, and we managed to get rid without a scene. And let's be fair...if we didn't have stupid people like him...we'd have no-one to laugh at, would we?"

"Karol...what on earth's the matter with you?" Martha came through from the living room. "That's not like you... being a grouchy old man."

Charlie laughed, then there was a long pause... "Martha...I'm getting old...and some of us never have that privilege...as you know...anyway, there's no such thing as a grouchy old man. The truth is when you get old you stop being polite and start being honest." I saw the sense in that, but I think Charlie was more than a wee bit drunk.

"Would anyone mind if I change the records on the record player?" Shan jumped in...probably to help Charlie. "I've got all the latest hits in the car boot...my mum and dad play them in the restaurant, but I've borrowed them...honest, it'll go down a storm. Nobody wants to listen to Vera Lynn and Perry Como."

Nobody objected...five minutes later the entire living room was dancing, even me...with Milly...we were dancing, and I must say, rubbish dancing to 'Shakin' All Over, Runaway, Johnny Remember Me, Three Steps to Heaven, Will You Still Love Me Tomorrow...Shan was an incredible DJ, and from the way he looked at her, I think Kenny realised what a lucky lad he was.

That was also the first time any of us heard 'Let's Twist Again', the American version. And Shan showed us how the song should be danced, too. It looked amazing...and we all joined in...a roomful of folk bouncing around and looking as if they were stubbing out a cigarette with their foot or drying their back with a towel. Chubby Checker had a lot to answer for, but what an ice breaker, not that one was ever needed that Boxing Day.

The party had started...and it was amazing. Batesy even got to dance with Carol Thompson. Mam and Olive were dancing with another two women. Mr Cook was dancing on his own, head down, pretending to play a piano, and Mr Larkin accompanied him on the phantom guitar, pretending to play it behind his back like T-Bone Walker. They looked crazy...and we all had a great laugh, with them... not at them. Linda joined Milly and me, and so did Martha for a brief minute or two. The neighbours were having a whale of a time and the next half hour was manic.

Then, a turning point. Lonnie Donegan began belting out 'Does Your Chewing Gum Lose Its Flavour', and it wasn't something that could be danced to without looking silly. Everything slowed down, people took to seats, some sitting on the floor, everyone taking a breather from the dancing and the room fell quiet, just the hum of individual conversations creating a low buzz.

Lonnie Donegan was the catalyst for the party ending. Once again, neighbours began drifting away, gave their thanks, then peeled off to their own homes, and a successful Boxing Day steadily wound itself down to a triumphant close.

But not before the final record of the day dropped onto the turntable.

All of the remaining kids sat underneath the front window, myself, Milly, Linda, Batesy, Titch, Roly, Julie Harris and Carol Thompson.

We all burst into song as the record began...Big Bad John.

"Every morning at the mine, you could see him arrive,
He stood six foot six and weighed two-forty-five,

Kinda broad at the shoulder and narrow at the hip,
And everybody knew ya didn't give no lip...to Big John,
Big John...
Big Jo-o-ohn...
Big Bad John."

All the adults joined in with the chorus...Charlie, Mam, Shan, Olive Kenny...everybody. Nobody knew the second verse, except Martha, and she got up, as sprightly as you like, and stood in the centre of the room and sang it alone.

"Nobody seemed to know where John called home He just drifted into town and stayed all alone He didn't say much, kinda quiet and shy And if you spoke at all, you just said, "Hi" to Big John."

.... Then we all joined in the chorus once again....with gusto.

Martha sang us through the entire song, drowning out the record player and we discovered that day that what her voice lacked in quality, it certainly made up for in volume. Martha may have been incredibly intelligent...but she was also profoundly tone-deaf. Charlie even left the room, frowning, drink in hand, and stood outside smoking for several of the verses before returning.

At the end of the song, we had a roomful of happy adults and happy kids.

Martha however seemed a little annoyed when the record finished and she buttonholed Charlie and asked why on earth he'd left the room and gone outside while she was singing. Charlie looked her full in the face before replying,

"Just so the neighbours would know that it wasn't me hitting you". We all laughed at Charlie's cheeky comment, Martha included, she was under no illusions about the quality of her singing voice. Charlie was definitely the worse for wear from booze, though. Time for home.

Everyone had a great time and all with a smile on their faces. Even Titch, as he gave in gracefully and handed over a selection box to Batesy...his lass hadn't shown up, and he admitted defeat. He'd come prepared, so she must have told him beforehand. We all scored though, eight chocolate bars in the box, and eight kids. Titch took his downfall with good grace and we all had chocolate...the only bad bit being that I ended up with the Bounty...my least favourite. I gave it to Milly, and she swapped it for a Crunchie...everybody happy...

Christmas, however, was over for another year, only three hundred and sixty-four days to go.

CHAPTER 13

Dodging the Fame

___

A nd then the downhill run. In my head, I always used to picture the year like a clock face. Christmas was at twelve, then when it was over, down we'd go, clockwise past January - number 1, February – number 2 and so on right around the clock. Things began to get exciting come September – number 9, because by then we were climbing up the clock again, towards the next Christmas. Daft I know, but it worked for me.

New Year was a non-event for us kids. Mam and Olive were invited to several parties and decided, quite correctly, to take the sensible option and go to Charlie's. Charlie and Martha were having a small gathering and we kids were tasked with looking after Wilf at our house for the evening. Pop only, no glasses of sweaty socks.

It was Kenny and Shan's last evening before heading back to Surrey, and I think that mam was acutely aware of how cruel people could be, sometimes intentionally, sometimes not, with their clumsy attempts at racial humour. Boxing Day had been a close-run thing, and Kenny had been fairly calm and collected. But Mam knew how short a fuse Kenny had sometimes, and it wouldn't take much to light it. There would be no chance of a repeat performance at Charlie's.

Happily enough, Wilf enjoyed his holiday break and seemed really bouncing to be back with us again. So, New Year's Eve went off without a hitch and we kids, as instructed, were all in bed before the bells...honestly, we were as good as gold.

When we woke up, we were into our brand-new year, 1962, and little did we realise how much the world would change, and how quickly it would happen, especially for us young folk, as we trawled our way through a very special decade.

Just after New Year we were told that Mam and dad were to be divorced. Olive and Milly's dad were to be divorced too. Olive's divorce was to be easy. Her husband, in prison, had given her just cause, and he did the right thing, admitting blame and agreeing to give Olive her freedom. Olive would have been in her fifties before he came out. But now she would be a single woman again by the end of March.

I never once heard Olive bad-mouth her husband. And only once did I hear her question herself..."How on earth was I so stupid? to never ask where the money was coming from, just believing, just trusting...I didn't even have the sense to ask who he worked for. The police thought I was in on it because I was so gullible...never again." Sidney Brown had big ears and listened and remembered everything.

I never did discover fully, the story behind the jail sentence. Milly's dad had been caught up with a bad crowd involved with slot machines and gambling, and someone had lost their life. Then when the crunch came, and the police moved in, Olive and Milly lost everything - house, possessions, reputation, money - the lot. The house was locked up, so that they couldn't even retrieve their clothes or personal items, cast adrift...and Molly's dad, Olive's husband, ended up with a long prison sentence.

Mam's divorce was to be a little trickier. Dad had asked for the divorce, and she'd agreed, but they were haggling as to who would be the plaintiff and who would be the respondent. Dad wanted to marry again, but he didn't want to be named as the bad stick in the proceedings. Mam didn't see why she should accept any blame after dad's behaviour, and she wasn't for backing down. If he wanted to start a new life and disown his old one, then that had to come at a price...mam's price.

I wasn't given any further details other than being told that mam and Olive had put their house and business plans on hold until everything was finalized. They seemed concerned that my dad might find out about our stroke of luck, and decide he wanted a cut. From conversations I'd overheard, it would be just the kind of thing dad would do. None of us...myself, Linda or Kenny had received as much as a birthday card or a kind word in the past 12 months, and that was upsetting for us all. But to be fair, although I didn't have any time for my dad, and didn't want contact with him, his maintenance money arrived on time, and as regular as clockwork.

Mam was talking with Olive one evening and I heard the following comment. "Surely she can't be that thick...is she blind or what? If that new woman is so dumb, can't see what kind of a man he is, hasn't heard about his gambling, his handy hands, hasn't spoken with anyone, hasn't gone and asked around...then he must have taken up wit Helen Keller.

So, my mam wasn't daft...it was obvious to me that mam must have known the Keller family, but I couldn't remember anyone in my Kirkcaldy school with that name.

It would be several weeks later that I asked mam who the Keller woman was... and she threw me a rueful look and told me she'd been using sarcasm...and hadn't felt proud about the reference. Helen Keller was actually a famous author and disability rights activist who'd been born both deaf and blind. So, dad wasn't marrying her after all.

On the education front, the eleven plus exam was looming large. We knew we'd be sitting it sometime in March and from the first week back at school after the Christmas holidays, we had an exam test paper in front of us, at least once every week, but most weeks we would have two papers. One week would be arithmetic papers, the next would be English, and more often than not a problems paper thrown in. They came at us thick and fast, and it became quite hectic. The tension was mounting, and our nerves grew and grew as the exam itself drew ever closer.

Nerves seemed to filter out into the playground and those first few weeks back at school featured more fights than I'd seen in the previous four months. Raisbeck and Batesy went at it hammer and tongs, before Mona broke it up, then Raisbeck again with Fred Douglas and that was broken up, too. Ken Robinson, Andy Reid, a lad called Scone, and even some of the quiet kids. Titch even had a go...and to be honest he was quite impressive, holding his own with a lad much bigger than himself. But there were so many lads who you wouldn't have expected to be involved in bother, suddenly ending up in Tweddle's office. There seemed to be so many canings in those first weeks, it became quite disturbing.

I managed to give the fighting a body swerve...until the day came when I couldn't avoid it anymore. I didn't fight at school...I was ambushed at the Bella. I'd been at a bit of a loose end one weekend. I decided that I couldn't keep going around to Charlie's, because they were making life plans, and Martha was much more mobile now and enjoyed a little stroll around with Wilf and Charlie, even in the cold weather. Martha was in something called remission, and they were both so happy...with all the extra time, and each other. And, although I could have been mistaken, it sometimes felt as if I was being a bit of a nuisance. Perhaps not a nuisance, but I occasionally had the impression I was interrupting something.

Mam and Olive were back into the work routine, heads down, backsides up now that their plans were on hold. Olive had somehow managed to retrieve her shifts at the pubs... she must have been popular. Both of them had banked their newfound wealth, and they carried on working, but even harder and longer, and with new determination now that they had a common goal.

That particular Saturday, Linda was at Milly's house, with another couple of girls. Milly was popular now and accepted at school as just another lass...not as Raggedy Annie anymore, and having such a sunshiny personality, had garnered a small circle of good pals. Linda of course, clung like glue; my sister had acquired a big sister...and she loved it.

So, poor me, I was on my lonesome. Batesy, Titch, Willick, Stan, the Balmer twins, everyone, was somewhere else. I couldn't find anyone to knock about with, not even Roly, and I didn't fancy a trip down to Blyth by myself, so I decided to go adventuring.

My adventuring that day, took me through the fields to Newsham, and on the way I stopped to pay my respects to Bruno. I found his grave, with great difficulty. It was now overgrown, with just an indistinct hummock of newer growth to mark the spot. I hadn't planned the visit so I didn't have any flowers to put down, and I didn't have words to say or anything, because I hadn't known Bruno.

I was at a bit of a loss as to what to do. I bent down to give the mound a stroke, then stopped...thinking to myself, "how silly is that". So, I just emptied my head for a minute and thought of Charlie and Martha. Then after a decent period of time, I took my leave and moved on. The strange thing is, I made a sign of the cross like I'd seen them do on the telly, and like the kids at St Wilfred's school did, but I wasn't a Catholic.

I'd decided to hunt down the grammar school and have a look at the place that everyone was fixated on. I'd only ever heard it talked about and didn't know what on earth it looked like. All I knew was that it sat at the other side of town on Plessey Road. So, on reaching Newsham, and starting, as my reference point, from the little railway station, I began my trek by skirting the Willow Tree pub, then passing a little wool shop within a row of terraced houses which also housed a little general dealers. On the opposite side of the road stood a clutch of prefabs, and I carried on over the railway gates and past Cosimini's chip shop. Trundling leisurely on, with semi-detached houses on either side of the road, and the occasional car or wagon idling past, I finally came to the fabled, ivy-covered walls of the grammar School.

The gates were actually open, but I didn't dare go inside...I hadn't earned the right. A man wearing green overalls was painting at one of the window frames; he gave me a glance, but a glance isn't an invitation...it's just a glance. There was someone else pushing a wheelbarrow around. There was some sort of a house at the front of the school, and I surmised it must be for the caretaker or security or something. I just gawped from the roadside, but even from where I stood, the building looked mighty impressive. It reminded me of Greyfriars, even though I'd only seen pen drawings in the Frank Richards books, and it filled me with an inner awe. If only I could be lucky enough, or work hard enough, then maybe I'd be one of the chosen few.

I looked around me, and over the road were posh houses, not council ones, with neat gardens and pristine lawns, and a little further on towards Blyth, behind a tall fence, I could see the cricket club, where Batesy told me he sometimes went with his uncle Joe to watch a game, even though he disliked cricket. There was an unmistakable aura about the school and whole surrounding area...I was hooked.

Now that I'd satisfied my curiosity, and with my head full of mental pictures, I decided on a different route home. I was determined to explore more of Blyth and the surrounding area, because at that moment in time I was so naïve. I was still the little Scottish kid, from Kirkcaldy. I was just living in a house, on an estate, merely existing, without knowing anything about the locality. And because of that, I decided that I would always be considered a newcomer, unless I took decisive action to change that label.

So, I decided on a return route through the Avenues, an area I'd barely heard of, never mind set foot in. I headed for home down Twelfth avenue. Titch had talked me through the directions, 'cos Titch knew everywhere. Somewhere at the end of the avenue I should look for a railway bridge, just past Newlands School, and then up and over and onto Newsham Road, and then a choice...to turn left and head towards Newsham and return through the fields...or turn right and take the shortest route and brave the Bella.

I'd never been through the Bella, apart from that time with mam and Linda on the return from Newbiggin, but I reckoned I should be able to complete my journey unscathed. I popped into the little shop at the foot of the railway bridge for a couple of Bubbly-gums, before crossing over Newsham Road, then heading down Southend Ave. I honestly didn't have any sense of foreboding when I reached the Bella rows. It was a chilly day, really chilly, and it seemed quiet enough, so I thought I'd go down the central row, because it was the widest. Middle Row was very wide, but, as it turned out, a poor choice.

I was halfway down, on the left side of the Row, blowing bubbles, and feeling quite relaxed...when out of nowhere... or maybe out of backyard gates, two lads appeared in front of me, heads down, speaking quietly to each other, glancing, and pretending theatrically not to notice me as I approached. Their acting skills were non-existent, and my sixth sense was screaming at me... 'danger' – 'danger' – 'danger'.

I knew instinctively what was coming. I was about to be duffed up...their prey; and I needed to compose myself. So, I bent down and pretended to fasten my shoelace...spat out my gum, even though it was still juicy, glancing behind as I did so. There were another two lads standing guard behind me, twenty or so paces away, approaching slowly, and they looked primed for action. I realised that it was too late for flight, so I was stuck with fight. So be it!

Had this scenario materialized before Christmas, my trousers would have filled up rapidly. But not today, because I had a tennis ball in my pocket, and I knew what to do with it. As a matter of fact, I was full of calm confidence....a lad called Jim White, the hardest lad in our age group in Blyth, and from Cowpen Estate, had given me some crisis coaching. Well...if truth be told he had actually been talking with Batesy and a lad called Wally Anderson, and I'd just been eavesdropping, but, like a sponge, I'd soaked up some of the advice he'd been giving, especially a tip he gave about always carrying a tennis ball. And something else he'd said about BEBO...and I remembered...and that piece of information, critically, was about to stand me in good stead.

Laces now pretend fastened, I sucked in a breath, stood up and moved forward confidently, as if nowt was the matter. I pretended the two lads didn't even exist. But, at the same time, they moved deliberately across the pavement, to stand together, blocking my path. This was it then, the crunch. I knew I needed to act quickly because the other lads, who were being tail-end Charlies, would be alerted as soon as I sprang into action, and they weren't too far behind me.

I instantly picked out the toughest of the lads in front of me. Jim White's first lesson, leave the toadies until last. Wallop the biggest bugger first...and the others will think twice.

You know what? I even surprised myself that day, 'cos I wasn't a natural fighter. I wasn't nervous in the slightest, but the adrenalin was kicking in, and turning me into a monster. Nothing like a Bella monster, I have to say...I wasn't grunting and farting and biting horses or owt, I was just full of annoyance, who did these people think they were, confronting me? I wouldn't be confronting them...when they were out on the streets tonight, howling at the moon.

I didn't give the two lads a chance to ask the inevitable question, "Ye from Cowpen, like?" I just smiled broadly at the biggest lad as I took the tennis ball out of my pocket and walked towards him. "This what you're lookin' for?"

"Ehhh?" he was immediately confused. That didn't surprise me, he was from the Bella after all. Jim White had told us, "Chuck a ball to someone, and 99 times out of a hundred they'll go for it". It worked...I held the ball out to one side of my body, drawing in the big lad's eyes, then chucked it to him, quite high, so he had to jump up to catch it. When he did, and landed, legs apart...I jumped in swiftly and gave him an almighty hoof in the clems.

"Thhwwakk" it went..."Yarrggghhheeyaaa," he screamed, and doubled over and as he did so I followed up with a Winston, two fingers jabbed into the eyes...not gouging or anything, just a swift blinding jab so that he wouldn't be able to find his testicles for a while...if he had any of course,

213

although he looked about thirteen, and my foot had certainly squished something...perhaps his days of two-bally were over.

It was all done in two seconds. The lads behind were slow to react. His pal didn't even try to help, he just looked at me wide-eyed, and open-mouthed. He stepped back, and froze, hoping no doubt that I'd give his nether regions a wide berth. I obliged, pulled a face at him, and followed the BEBO acronym to the letter - Balls, Eyes, Bugger Off. I was out of there like a shot. The lads behind me were far too slow, carthorses chasing a thoroughbred, and I knew I could outrun them easily. Those two heavies came chasing past their downed comrade, who was now writhing around on the pavement, making monkey noises, and they tried to catch me for a few hundred yards, but they were falling further and further behind, and in a trice I was out of the Bella rows, onto the colliery railway line, and sprinting for the sanctuary of Cowpen.

The chasing posse gave up and shouted a few obscenities in my direction. So, full of bravado, I halted and waved, dropped my pants, and waggled my bum at them. They probably thought it was a mirror...then...pants pulled back up, and feeling on top of the world, I headed for home.

I didn't boast to anyone about my confrontation; that would have been a sure-fire way to set myself up for more fights. If today's event became common knowledge, the hard lads would be lining up to try themselves out against the new tough kid from the Bella saga. Honestly, I wasn't tough, and I didn't need the aggravation...but of course, I did need a new tennis ball.

Although I didn't mention it to anyone, a couple of days later news of it had leaked out, and Titch began telling me a complete fabrication of a tale, about one of his pals, whose name he didn't want to disclose 'cos he was sworn to secrecy. The lad had, apparently, been involved in a fight at the Bella and kicked one of the great unwashed in the willy. Titch proceeded to tell me how he'd been involved in the whole thing and helped the lad escape. He told me it would be best if I stayed clear of the Bella for a while, 'cos they'd be looking for revenge on anyone from Cowpen.... and I didn't say a word, not a single word...but I knew the rights of it...and I let Titch bask in the reflected glory of another fairy story.

The story circulated for weeks. There were many lads suspected to be the mighty Cowpen knacker-whacker, some of them making no comment, as if in tacit acknowledgement, happy to be associated with the exploit, and Titch refusing to give up the name of the lad who was to go down in Cowpen folklore. Not once, in all those weeks, did anyone ever point the finger at Hawky Brown, and for that I was thankful.

Things were happening in the big world too and they were quite scary. People were dying in Cardiff and in Bradford with a disease called smallpox. We'd been talking about it at school because we had two lads who wore irons on their legs from catching a disease called polio. Titch, and a lad called Mick Murphy told us that we were lucky in this country 'cos we just had smallpox. People in France were having it even worse with bigpox...and across the ocean in America they had hugepox.

215

Elsewhere, Helena's friend Lubbock, from the Liberal party was the favourite to win a bye-election in Orpington and bash the Tories, and to become an MP, news I picked up on one of my Charlie visits.

And Mr Hunter told us that, on one night in particular we'd be able to see all the planets, all the ones at least, that were visible to the naked eye, and they'd be in an almost straight line. I remember thinking to myself that if they were all in a straight line, then all you'd be able to see would be the first one. I forgot about looking out for it of course, and I don't remember any of the lads viewing the spectacle, but at the time it was a really big thing and they talked about it on the telly quite a bit.

So the weeks rolled on, and I just sailed through life. Our home routine was almost the same, with Milly and Olive staying at ours on Fridays and Saturdays. They were my favourite nights because I managed to spend some quality time with Milly and Linda, and it always gave us a warm and cosy feeling. I still walked to school with Milly most days, but she now had a following of friends, so we were rarely alone and able to discuss any family business.

Also, I now had a building society account, because mam didn't need any of my odd job money anymore, and she'd impressed on me the need to save for a rainy day. To be honest it rained quite a lot, but mam wouldn't let me take any money out.

Mam gave me half a crown pocket money every Saturday, and I would use this as spending money. My window cleaning and running messages money was invested in the building society at irregular intervals when mam had the time to pay it in for me. Some weeks I earned over ten bob and my little stash quickly began to mount up.

And, as a money-spinner, for several months, until I was stopped by the local policeman called Marnock, I would hang about outside the Red House, when Olive was working at the weekend. Food wasn't a big thing in pubs back then, only crisps and nuts, so I supplied a chip shop service. Olive would take clandestine orders until about 9.00pm and slip a list to me when I went into the off-licence at the pub front. The landlord knew what was happening but turned a blind eye...if punters were eating, they'd be drinking too. Mam turned a blind eye too, pretending not to know what was going on.

Sometimes I had a dozen or more bags of chips on order, with the occasional fish, fish cake or fritter on the list. My fee was 3d per order, a tanner if a fish or any extras were involved, and I'd shoot off up to the chippy on Swaledale with my string bag and I'd be back within half an hour with vittles for the hungry boozers. Most weekend nights I made as much as five bob in an hour, and occasionally, double that.

But as is the way in life, all good things come to an end and I was copped. Nothing bad happened, but I was warned by Marnock, after a slap on the head, a hard one, too, that I was doing something against the law. He said if I was caught again, my mam would go to prison, and I'd probably be sent to borstal, or even be birched. I was ten, I believed it, so I stopped.

My window cleaning had to stop for a few weeks, too. I'd been doing some bungalows at Leeches and somehow managed to plant my little ladders on an icy patch of flagstone. I was only three steps up, but the ladders slipped, I tumbled, and bashed my chin on the windowsill. It hurt, definitely, but it was wounded pride more than anything. The cut on my chin wasn't that big, or that deep, but there was blood everywhere...and I was blubbing like a little lass. Upshot was I needed two stitches...and getting them put in, hurt me twice as much as the accident.

To my eternal shame, I did a Titch, and my popularity at school soared. I said I'd been jumped by three lads from the Bella. I'd put up a good fight but one of them had hit me in the chin with a big stick. My junior school peers began to look at me in a different light...with a little more respect. I felt a little sheepish after the lie, but it did help me in another way. There was no chance now that anyone would think of linking me with the previous confrontation...so in a way it was a good lie; it didn't hurt anyone, and it took me completely out of the clem-kickin' equation.

The weeks were flashing by, and before we knew it, the exam was upon us.

When the big day arrived Mr Hunter walked around the classroom putting the exam papers face down on individual desks. The exam was to start at 10.00 a.m. and there was another man, a stranger, standing at the back of the class, watching. He was from the education authority or something, and he was there to ensure there was no cheating. There was another stranger, standing in the B. class across the corridor.

We were instructed to take our time, make sure we understood exactly what was being asked in each question. And when we'd finished the paper, to go through it again, checking and double checking our answers.

Ten o'clock came, and we began beavering away. Silence reigned, the occasional rustle of paper, scraping of chair, or frustrated sighing, being the only sounds. I whizzed through it. I'd found it easier than most of the practice papers we'd been working on for weeks. I went through it all again, as instructed, but I couldn't find a single mistake, which of course, didn't mean that there weren't any. Then it was just a case of having to sit, arms folded, paper turned face down, and wait until time was called. Looking around the room I could see that Willick was finished, as was Ken Robinson, Alan Lawton, Jack Jennings, and a few of the lasses.

And that was it, all over in two hours. Now we would begin the waiting game until early June and the results.

Outside, in the playground, little knots of pupils congregated. Some of those saying how hard it had been, some, how easy. We were comparing questions, comparing answers. Sometimes a "yes, knew it was right," but sometimes a disappointed groan..."Aahh flippin' heck, got that one wrong." I knew almost immediately that I had two of the questions incorrect. One of them had been – 'Write down words which describe a collection of – cows, fish, bees, sheep, crows. And I'd answered, herd, shoal, swarm, flock, flight. Apparently the collective noun for crows is 'murder'. Most of us agreed that we'd got that one wrong......but I decided that next time I bumped into a crow then I knew what I'd do to it.

Titch and Michael Lamb told me that I'd definitely cocked the second one up. It was – simplify $\frac{1}{2} + 1/3$ and I'd given the answer as 5/6ths. "Yer definitely got that un wrong." I was told in no uncertain terms..."It's three quarters". I thought I was right, but you know what...I couldn't be bothered to argue. I suddenly thought, there's no way I can go back and change my answers...so why even discuss it. It's over and done with. The discussions continued all that playtime, but I kept out of it as much as possible.

For the time being we were all in the same boat, but we were acutely aware that in the not-too-distant future we would all be splitting up, some to grammar, some to Newlands, some to PLR, and some to Bebside. It was a sad time in that respect, but also a happy time now that the exam was out of the way. Whatever the future held for us as individuals would be decided by those exam papers.

CHAPTER 14

Goodbye Morpeth Road

———————————◼———————————

Mam bought me a bike straight after the exam. I hadn't expected one unless I'd passed the eleven plus and I asked her why she'd bought it before the results. But she just smiled and said, "Do you think the only people riding around on bikes go to grammar school?" I didn't answer. "Sid, I know you've done your best and tried your hardest, so whatever the outcome of the exam then that's all I could have asked. The Balmer lads have had bikes for ages, and you'll be needing a bike whichever school you go to...so enjoy." She left it at that...and I was now mobile.

It wasn't a flash racer or anything, it was just a run of the mill, sit up and beg bike with five speed gears. It was second-hand, but in good nick and I found out later that Charlie had bought it from a friend in Devonworth, then sold it on to mam, no doubt at a loss.

My 'new' bike had a front light and a dynamo to charge it, a saddlebag, and full mudguards...I loved it. The problem was...I'd never been on a bike before and didn't know how to ride one. It stood in the coalhouse for two days before mam asked, "Is there something wrong with your new bike Sid? Because all I've seen you do is clean it."

I was embarrassed, even though it was my mother asking, but being my mam she seemed to realise.

"Why don't you take it on the track through the fields... you know, just to get the hang of it, 'cos new bikes can be a pain in the bum; they take some getting used to." Mam was magic, she knew I was struggling and didn't want to practice in the street and fall off in front of the neighbours... and tellingly, she'd said bum, not bottom.

So, my first bike ride, and a wobbly one at that, was in splendid seclusion, on the track leading through the fields to Newsham. How many times did I fall off? I can't remember, but it was more than a few. And after a while I was able to stay upright for minutes at a time. I was still shaky but building up confidence by the minute when I spotted two lasses approaching. There was no way I was going to take a dive in front of lasses, so I got off the bike, with difficulty, and started pushing it.

One of the lasses was from my class, Irene Cummings, and she was one of the nailed-on certainties for grammar school. I didn't recognise the other lass.

"Hi Hawky, what's up with your bike?" she asked, and smiled.

"Ehhh, oh just summat keeps catchin'...you know, it keeps on mekkin a clicky sound, aahh think it's one of the spokes or summat." I wasn't being convincing and needed to change the topic. "I see your brother scored for Aberdeen last week...third Lanark wasn't it?"

"Yes...I didn't know you supported Aberdeen." Her brother Bobby was a footballer, and quite a good one by all accounts.

"Well, I don't actually. I just look at all the Scottish footy results. Me and my brother used to follow Rangers, or Hearts sometimes."

"Sid's from Scotland," she informed her pal, as if this was somehow relevant, then cut the conversation short, "Got to go Sid...see you at school." She gave a grin, and without further ado the girls left.

I carried on pushing my bike until the lasses were out of sight, and as soon as they were, I mounted up, and rode all the way home, without mishap, and not a clicky sound to be heard.

During the following couple of weeks, as April matured, I rode everywhere, explored everywhere, sometimes with company, but usually alone. I cycled to Whitley Bay, North Shields, Tynemouth...mostly along the coast roads, but my longest journey took me an entire Sunday. With a saddlebag full of pop and sandwiches, I cycled inland to Stamfordham. Another weekend took me to Morpeth and all the places in-between, so now, at least I knew where Guide Post and Tranwell were. I was beginning to feel more at home in Northumberland and to feel comfortable in my own skin.

During that time I also found Monkey's Island. There were no monkeys, and it wasn't an island...just a claggy bit of land beside the river Blyth which was supposed to have had a fever hospital at some time in the past, and where folk used to go worm digging for their fishing. I met an old fellow there, who'd been digging bait and he told me that there had indeed been a scarlet fever hospital on the site but it had been bombed in the war. There was a little slipway and a few boats...but 'Monkey's Island?'...really!

Milly had also acquired a bike, but she was an expert. She'd had bikes from being five years old and one Sunday we set off together to discover Charlie's Garden. Not our Charlie, or his garden...but a pinnacle of rock which stood between Seaton Sluice and St Mary's Lighthouse. It had a flat, grassy top, and we were told that it had once been lived on by a hermit. That didn't seem plausible to us, but we found it and took photos on Milly's new Christmas Kodak camera. A good day was had, our first time alone for a while and we enjoyed it immensely. No questions asked, no doubts...we were still solid, and happy to be in each other's company.

Easter came and went as it usually does, but this year we three kids were bombarded by easter eggs. Last year I had two...one from mam, and one from grandad...but this year, eight. The girls also were awash with chocolate, and the three of us had pooled our resources to buy Easter gifts for mam and Olive, Charlie, and Martha.

We kids had also decided, to each give one of our eggs to a lad called Jumpin' George...a lad of about fourteen, with the supposed mental age of a five-year-old. I'd seen this lad on a few occasions at Spartans' matches. He'd usually be accompanied by his mother, and he'd spend most of the match just jumping up and down on the spot...shouting 'Howay Blyth' in a thick and guttural voice. Some of the older lads would have a good laugh at these antics and make fun of George, mimicking his actions. George of course thought this was great fun...with half a dozen lads jumping up and down on the spot and shouting 'Howay Blyth.' This would spur him on to higher jumping and louder shouting, and more outlandish behaviour, with a huge grin on his face... and it was sad, so sad to watch this human being become a figure of fun and appallingly humiliated. It must have been torture for his mother and she had a job controlling him at the best of times...because he was a big, big lad...with the body of a man.

Milly knew where they lived and told us that George went to a special school, more commonly known as the 'backward' school, and it was somewhere in the Northumberland countryside, out Hexham way, which was why he was only home at weekends. His mam was some sort of scientist and worked in Newcastle, at one of the university research departments. The father worked away from home, mostly in the United States, and was an executive in the chemical industry.

So, Saturday April 14th – Jumpin George, Blyth market, underpants...was my diary entry for the previous week.

Myself, Milly, and Linda were waiting beside the Central cinema as Olive helped to clear the fruit and veg stall at the end of the day. It wasn't yet four o'clock but most of the other stalls were also packing up. We'd been to the pictures earlier, then stopped off at Seghini's for a pop, after which we decided to hang about to cadge a lift home in the Bedford dormobile, which was now in the proud possession of Olive and mam.

They'd bought it the previous week and put it into Olive's name because her divorce was now finalized, but mam's wasn't. The vehicle was only three or four years old and was to double up as a work van for the new business and a holiday van for day trips, because it also had a little cooker and sink, fold down seats that could double as a bed and a strange roof contraption which could be opened up like a concertina.

But that day there was something of a commotion in the marketplace. It started off quite casually, with a few shouts and laughs...then the noise grew and grew. We could see from where we stood that people were hurrying to the central aisle of the market...and there were cheers going up, with women looking away, hands over mouths in surprise at the spectacle in front of them. We were intrigued and went rushing past the fruit stall and worked our way to the front of the gathered spectators. Across the road, folk were pouring out of the shops. Woolworths emptied in no time. A crowd of men tumbled out of the Market Tavern, and it was way past last orders.

And the voice at the centre of the commotion was as loud as I'd ever heard it. "Howay Blyth...howay Blyth...howay Blyth," as the big lad, with the huge voice, jumped and hopped his way down the market aisle wearing only a big grin and a pair of flapping white underpants...it was Jumpin' George... and he was loving the spotlight. Grinning and clapping and keeping up his football chant, and followed by a bunch of lads, all a good three or four years older than myself. Several of the lads I knew, and two of whom I recognised from the fishy episode at the changing huts. One of them was carrying George's clothes, while the others were in absolute hysterics with the spectacle playing out in front of them. It brought to mind a herd of donkeys, hee-hawing and having their jollies at someone else's expense. We spotted Batesy and Roly over the other side of the main drag and they gave us a swift hands up in recognition. They were as transfixed as we were with the happenings in front of us.

Suddenly, a lady...who we reckoned must have known George, or at least his circumstance, stepped out from the crowd, pluckily attempting to grab his arm and stop the shenanigans. George wasn't for stopping, intoxicated with being the centre of attention, and pushed the lady away with such force that for all the world, she appeared to be running backwards, before colliding with one of the stalls and banging her head. Seeing this, some of the men spectators became involved and three of them tried to bring George down. But George was a big powerful lad, and he began batting the men away, Henry Cooper style. Each time he connected with one of his roundhouse swings he'd cry... "Biff" ..."Crunch"..."Boosh"...followed by, "Howay Blyth... howay Blyth...howay Blyth". It would have been comical had it not been so pitiful.

The goons who had obviously set George up were shouting and laughing on the periphery of the battle... "Gan on George, give 'em a clag, boof-boof, howay Blyth...get stuck in Jumpy...ha-ha-ha."

"Sid are you gonna do summat?" that came from Linda. "Them lads are disgusting...and no-one's doin' anything."

Milly was looking at me, too. But those lads were fourteen at least, maybe fifteen, and there were half a dozen of them. My one moment of bravery had been that Bella incident... and I certainly didn't fancy being mashed up in front of my sister and girlfriend. But if I just hung back I think my respect level would have been greatly diminished in their eyes.

So, I began to remove my jacket...slowly...trying to make-on my arm was stuck. "Bliddy jacket, cannit get me arm oot...here Linda, pull this."

I was hoping beyond hope that Milly and Linda would grab my arms and hold me back... "Don't go Sid, please don't go, there's a whole passel of crazy injuns, they're after scalps, and you've only got one bullet left."...

Nothing!! It didn't happen. Now I had to do the courageous thing again...and I was ten years old, nearly eleven, and terrified.

Luckily for me, God must have been in a compassionate mood. The moment I stepped out of the press to go and die for Queen and country, the police whistles sounded. There I stood, fists up, facing death...and in rushed the cavalry. Two massive coppers, both at least eight foot tall, came thundering in...and the bad lads scattered when the shrill whistles sounded, bolting like rabbits with a fox in pursuit. George's clothes were chucked up into the air and strewn all around.

Then, as if on cue, and sensing the opportunity for a little fame, Roly jumped into the fray, making-on to chase the retreating lads, waving his fist around. "Come back here if yer dare," he shouted at their rapidly disappearing backs, "Ye'll get some more of this". He had a big grin on his face, standing alone like a victorious prize fighter. Batesy was laughing his head off, as were a few of the crowd, at Roly's antics.

One of the coppers subdued Jumpin' George, pulling up his underpants at the same time. George's bum had been on full display, his pants around his ankles.

The other copper chased after the lads and caught the one being held onto by the men out of the Market Tavern. I knew the captured lad by sight, it was Donald the dump picker...a lad famous for trawling the gutters for discarded cigarette butts.

As I stepped back from the kerfuffle, Milly took hold of my hand and gave me a look of admiration. "You're so brave Sid...you were really going to tackle them, weren't you? You're my hero."

Well, I wasn't going to turn that compliment down...was I? Yes, I realise it was more of an "Oliver Hardy...you're so slim," comment, but I didn't care. It was yet another notch on my bow, and not a bruise to show for it.

Diary entry...... Good Friday. Loads of Easter eggs. Jumpin' George's house, trip to Ingram Valley tomorrow.

It was Milly's idea to give George the eggs. She'd been really upset when she'd heard some of the girls at school laughing about the daft lad wi' no clothes on at the marketplace on Saturday. Milly remembered the times when she'd been laughed at, and ridiculed, and made to feel like dirt. She wasn't for listening to anyone else going through the same ordeal.

We turned up at George's house around mid-day on Good Friday...and we had eggs to give. George's mam answered the door. "Yes...can I help you?"

We immediately recognised her as the running backwards lady who'd tried to calm George down at the marketplace. Milly took the lead... "We've brought some Easter eggs for George."

"Why?" was the mam's response. Her face was unfriendly.

"Because we like him," was Milly's response.

The mother's face was impassive. George appeared from behind her shoulder, but for all the world he looked as if he had been drugged. His eyes were blank and he was so subdued.

I raised my hand to George and winked. George took a little while, but then smiled back...and mouthed "howay Blyth".

His mam took the eggs and looked at us quizzically. "Thank you," she said, unsmilingly, and without further comment, closed the door...leaving us standing, staring at a front door.

"Let's go," said Milly.

"Ehhh, is that all the thanks we get," said I, self-important and minus a 'Buttons' Easter egg.

"Leave it Sid," said Milly, "she'll be feelin' awful, an' she'll be out in a minute".

We walked away...and I think Linda was feeling the most upset. To give an Easter egg away at seven years old...well that was a sacrifice.

We hadn't gone a hundred yards when we heard the shout behind us. "'Scuse me, 'scuse me, can you wait a moment?"

We turned, and it was George's mam, as predicted by Milly.

"I'm so sorry for being rude," she said, apologetically. "Why are you giving my son Easter eggs? He doesn't have friends."

She had tears in her eyes and looked completely drained of everything...of life, of happiness...of hope. Milly again was the beacon of good sense. "We've all been through hard times missus...all three of us. We're not friends of George... you're right about that...but we care, that's all. Not everyone is an idiot...we just want George to know...that's all."

The lady stared at us, for what seemed minutes, but must have been a few seconds. The tears were real and rolled down her cheeks in a stream. She had no words for our gift... it had been a surprise.

"Thank you...thank you, she repeated...it means so much...I don't know what to say."

I chipped in at that point. "Have you tried... Howay Blyth?"

She actually attempted a smile, before turning away and heading for home.

I think we'd done a good thing that day.

CHAPTER 15

A Nod's as Good as a Wink

■

Then we were into June, and Titch's tumble.

Before we knew it, the day of the eleven plus exam results came and went. There were a few surprises, mainly of people whom we expected to pass and didn't, rather than someone passing who hadn't been expected to. There was only one of those, and she was as shocked as everyone else in the class.

We were allowed home to tell our parents the news, and then were expected to return to school within the hour. I didn't bother going home as I knew mam was working, so instead I made for Prince's Avenue and Olive's house. She wasn't in either...so I had no-one to be excited for me. Then I headed for Charlie's, because I knew he would be over the moon with my news. But Charlie, Martha, and Wilf were out, too. Inside I was ecstatic, but outside I was disappointed...my fantastic news, my dream now reality, but no-one to share the exhilaration.

I hung around, dawdling, trying to gauge the length of an hour, then headed back to school. Our first playtime after the results was really weird. My normal friends suddenly seemed to be keeping themselves at arm's length, and we began to congregate in our new groupings. Titch, Lamby, Jack Jennings, the Balmer twins, Decker Raisbeck...all of the usual crew kept their distance and I found myself with Willick, Batesy, Lawton, Robinson...it just seemed so natural, and unnatural at the same time.

To be fair that situation only lasted for one day. Mr Hunter gave a little speech to both classes, in which he said that this exam did not define our lives. Some people, he told us, were naturally good at exams, and some very smart people, unfortunately, were poor at exams. Then he said that most of the people who were going on to secondary modern schools would end up being more successful and earning more money than those who had qualified to enter grammar school. The speech had been so successful that next day at school, we exam passers actually felt like failures. We would be less successful and earn less money than those who'd failed the exam.

Whatever had been Mr Hunter's intention, it certainly worked. Not a single kid in our year at Morpeth Road felt like a winner or a loser...we were all on different paths and headed for different futures, and even I was unsure as to whether I'd been clever, or not so clever. I was back with all my regular pals, and we made a pact that we'd always be friends, no matter which school we ended up in. I couldn't imagine school without Titch.

Diary entry...Titch did the Shona thing. Charlie pleased I passed. Moving to Sussex. Wilf not well. Uniforms.

After the results of the eleven plus it was as if learning was off the agenda and enjoyment was the main business of school. Very little arithmetic, problems, English, comprehension or essays...now it was mainly fun and games...Foot running on the big field - although I don't know why Hunter called it that...what other kind of running could you possibly do? There were egg and spoon races, three legged races, drawing competitions, weaving, singing and all manner of fun. But one fateful day Mr Hunter and Miss Brown from 4b came up with the idea of teaching us dancing...and that was a terrible decision.

Dancing is not for ten- and eleven-year-old lads, definitely not. It wasn't Chubby Checker type dancing they were going to teach us...it was having to hold onto lasses type dancing, and apart from Titch, there wasn't a single lad at Morpeth Road School who had ever danced while holding on to a lass. The Bradford Barn was to be our manoeuvre of choice, and to do it correctly you needed a partner in a dress.

The groan that reverberated around the hall that day was heart-felt, we didn't want to be here, it was stupid, lads didn't dance with lasses...lasses danced with other lasses...and lads didn't dance...full stop.

Come the hour of the dance lesson and out of the thirty or so lads from 4a and 4b, at least ten developed serious limps. Two were caught hiding in the porch, one was nowhere to be found and didn't appear again until next day. Ken Robinson was makin' on to escape through one of the windows, with even more of us makin' on that we were feeling poorly. All to no avail. We were going to dance, whether we wanted to or not.

So, the girls were lined up against the long window wall, the boys lined up opposite, with much grumping and groaning, but we stayed standing. This was an ordeal for us, even worse than a fight in the playground or losing your pocket money. Whoever had invented dancing needed shooting. The ten-pace gap between the lines was our Somme, our no-man's land, and we were shortly to go over the top. From the looks on the lads' faces you'd have thought some of them were already wearing gas masks.

So, dancing it was to be, but not before we were taught the etiquette of the dancefloor by Mr Hunter and Miss Brown. Miss Brown had a chair against the long wall, and she sat down demurely. She motioned to the girls to sit on the floor, which they all did like little goody two-shoes, while Mr Hunter was to demonstrate the correct procedure for asking a lady up to dance.

He looked at all us wallflowers...and began, 'Boys...when you approach your lady...and your intended dance partner, it's important that you use the following introduction."

The lesson began. He walked over no-man's land to Miss Brown, halted, then casually extended his hand, and asked, "Miss Brown, may I have the pleasure of your company on the dancefloor?"

Miss Brown accepted Mr Hunter's hand and stood up slowly. "Why thank you, Mr Hunter, I would like that very much." And with that, she followed his lead to the centre of the hall. Then he turned to face us. "Next, we face each other...and the lady puts her right hand into the gentleman's left hand and the lady's left-hand rests on the gentleman's right shoulder. The gentleman...and by gentleman I mean you bunch of savages," he smiled as he said it, "then rests his right hand gently, above the lady's waist, in the small of her back, like so...any questions?" The teachers were now facing each other, locked in dance pose.

No questions surfaced...just a smattering of groans. Hunter disengaged from Miss Brown and turned to the line of lads.

"So, who's going to volunteer and give us a demonstration." He looked expectantly along the line. But all the lads' eyes had now hit the floor, attention anywhere but in the direction of Mr Hunter. There was much shuffling and attempting to shrink. I managed to hide myself behind Decka Raisbeck who was much bigger than me.

"Fred Douglas...would you do the demonstration for me please." Everyone who hadn't been picked breathed a huge sigh of relief...there would have been raucous cheers and much backslapping in normal circumstances. I emerged from behind Raisbeck, relieved.

Fred stepped forward a pace, and in a croaky whisper said, "Can't sir.... me voice," he clasped his hand to his throat to illustrate the point, "C'n hardly talk sir...had the mumps...still don't feel right." I don't know how he did it, he was a brilliant actor...because he'd been the loudest voice at playtime when we were doing Foreign Legion and Arabs on the field. Hunter fell for it though, hook, line, and sinker.

Another scapegoat was required. I didn't want it to be me, and I managed to hide myself behind Raisbeck again. Much repeat shuffling was going on. Invisibility cloaks were being donned frantically.

"Jim Bates...you always have plenty to say for yourself... would you step up here and demonstrate for us?"

There was an agonising silence, it seemed to last forever... then "Bliddy cacka," I heard Batesy mutter as he stepped out from the line. "Bliddy liar Fred Douglas." But he knew the game was up, no more excuses would work. He walked over and took up position, reluctantly, next to Hunter. Standing with his back to us and facing the girls I could see him making jabby two-finger signs behind his back.

"Good lad Jim," said Hunter, "can you remember how I did it?"

"Yes sir,"

"And how to ask the lady for a dance?"

"Yes sir, word for word."

"Good, good, good," smiled Hunter, then turned to face us. "Watch and learn boys because you'll be needing this in the future. So, no more silly behaviour; let's be sensible about it and pretend we're gentlemen. You'll all be seniors soon, nearly grown-ups. It's all perfectly normal, and nothing to be embarrassed about...Yes?"

"Yes sir," came the muted reply.

He turned to Batesy, "On you go Jim...take your time, don't rush it."

Batesy half-turned, face like thunder, to run his gaze along the line of lads, probably looking for Fred Douglas to knock him down with Superman eye blasts. His gaze came to rest on me, peering from behind Raisbeck, and he grinned and winked. I'd seen that look before. I could sense a Vincent moment coming.

Turning around to face the enemy, he took a big breath, pulled his shoulders back and walked slowly towards the line of girls. He stopped in front of a big, big lass, Dorothy Blenkinsopp, and that was weird...cos they were mortal enemies. Dorothy had spent the last few weeks spreading malicious rumours about Batesy, telling all who would listen that he used to go nicking stuff from Woolworths. This was all because he'd bashed her brother...so, perhaps asking her up to dance was just his way of trying to make amends, an attempt to put things right...aye, as if!

He extended his hand. His introduction wasn't the same as Hunter's but it wasn't picked up on.

"Fancy a dance?" he even smiled.

Dorothy looked dubious. She wasn't sure how to react. There was a long pause. You could see the question in her eyes... "Why have you picked me?" We were all wondering what would happen next, you could have heard a pin drop. But there was a long pause, and Batesy wasn't for waiting any longer, or for being rejected, so, patience exhausted, he reached down and roughly took hold of her hand, and in a really loud voice said, "Howay, off your wobbly arse, stinky pants".

Uproar...complete chaos. All the lads and lasses were in stitches...gales of laughter swept the room, and I'm sure I even saw Miss Brown turn away to hide a grin. Hunter went mental, his face a furious mask, and he marched over and took a bunch of Batesy's jumper and frog-marched him over to the corridor. Even above the giggling and snorting we heard Hunter in a terrifying voice shout, "Headmaster's office...now!...that was shocking, Jim Bates, shocking. You should be thoroughly ashamed."

We were all trying to look anywhere but at Hunter, attempting to keep our laugh in...no-one else wanted to be sent to Tweddle's office. Dorothy Blenkinsopp was the only kid who hadn't seen the funny side, and she was mewling. I felt sorry for her, but I was still sniggering. Things however were to get worse.

With Batesy gone for his caning, it all calmed down. After a minute or two of commotion, and menacing looks from the teachers to shut us up, Mr Hunter and Miss Brown decided to carry on as if nothing had happened. We kids were now more subdued, with the threat of Tweddle and his whipping stick giving us pause for thought.

Hunter decided on the easy option, and picked Titch for the demonstration, knowing that he was a regular Roxy attendee, used to the etiquette of dance.

What happened next was legend.

"Alan Irving," Mr Hunter smiled, equilibrium now regained, and pointing to Titch, "would you like to do the demonstration for us...show everyone how it's done?"

Titch wasn't best pleased, but stepped out of the line, and walked into no-man's land, looking around as he came to a halt, waited a few seconds then said, "Sorry, can't do it sir...I only dance wi' me proper girlfriend, and she goes to Bebside".

Hunter looked bemused; things weren't going to plan.

One of the girls piped up, "You're tellin' lies Titch Irving, 'cos Shona Williamson isn't your girlfriend.... she told us... so there".

"You're talkin' really stupid, Lynn Fawcus, that's not even me girlfriend's name, for your information."

"Aye it is...but she doesn't even like yer."

"No it's not...she's different, and you're still stupid, so there."

"Enough, enough...quiet all of you," said an obviously frustrated Mr Hunter. We've had just about enough of stupidity today.

"Quiet everyone.... quiet," he stared menacingly around the room and a hush descended. "What's this all about, this silly girlfriend stuff...who, Alan... who is your girlfriend?"

There was a brief pause, and complete silence.

"My girlfriend's Shona Winker, sir."

There was very little reaction from the kids. We had no clue. But Hunter and Miss Brown...their response was epic.

Hunter's face turned blood red and he sucked in his cheeks so that he looked like a horse with a moustache, his eyes bulging, his shoulders heaving. I distinctly heard "bugger me". He turned away from us and headed for the corridor... squeaks escaping through his hand, which was now pressed firmly over his mouth. Miss Brown didn't walk out with Mr Hunter, she trotted along behind him, and she couldn't hold back. She was oinking...that's really what it sounded like, oinks and honks...like we'd disturbed a pig stye or something.

We started giggling...at the teachers, not at Titch's announcement.

Titch was still standing alone, where Hunter had left him, and he was blank, a vacant expression written across his face. What on earth had just taken place...we were all a little confused, but lapping up the moment, this was more like kids' fun. From the corridor, just out of sight, we could hear all sorts of weird noises from our dance instructors, and they wouldn't have seemed out of place in a Tarzan movie. Grunts, screeches, and hee-haw's in abundance, and it went on for a good minute. Mrs Warner, a teacher from one of the younger classes came out to find out what the commotion was, and spotting Hunter and Miss Brown, she marched up the corridor to join them. Next moment there were three snorting teachers, and poor Titch just stood alone...a piece of flotsam, adrift in a sea of ridicule.

To cut it short, Miss Brown didn't come back to join us. Mrs Warner returned to her classroom, face averted and head down to mask the broad grin as she walked on by. Mr Hunter came back, stony faced, and let us all out for an extended playtime. I remember him being unable to look any of us in the eye, especially Titch, as he tried manfully to keep his laugh in. Dancing was now off the agenda and put on hold for the time being.

And Titch?... same as usual; next day he was back in school as if nowt was the matter. Water off a duck's back. To be fair none of us would realise the significance of the wording in the Shona episode for a few years, but those of us who did, I'm sure we remember it with glee.

And Batesy's trip to the headmaster's office didn't happen. He'd just picked his coat up from the porch, walked straight past Tweddle's office, and went home. It was never mentioned again.

Then, before we knew it, the school year was over and another round of summer holidays was upon us. We three kids were as busy as bees and all through that long, hot interlude we had a great time. Trips out in the dormobile were a regular treat. Ingram Valley, Eyemouth, Holy Island, Bamburgh...and once to Keswick for a day out on the boats and a tour around the Lake District. We were three intrepid explorers discovering a whole new world.

Mam and Olive finally began preparation for their new business. Mam's divorce came through, but we still had a wait of at least six weeks while it became absolute or something. They were now seriously house hunting and inspecting all manner of property all over Blyth and the surrounding area, and I realised that Cowpen would very soon become just another stop on my journey through life. But for now we just enjoyed the ride.

There was also the little matter of grammar school. Uniform to buy, sports kit to buy, new shoes and sandshoes, fountain pens and ink, pencils and maths kits with protractors, set square and a semi-circle thing with degrees on, rulers and notebooks. It was hectic...but fun and exciting.

Charlie and Martha were also making their plans for the future. Although we didn't know it then, they would still be with us for another Christmas before they finally moved to their new home in Sussex.

Kenny reached seventeen, I was now eleven, and Linda eight. Birthdays came and went and Mam often grumped about the big four zero looming large. Milly and I were rarely apart during that sunny summer, and we enjoyed many a bike ride or trip to the beach. She was my best pal and I was happy about that. She did express a little fear she had, about me finding a new girlfriend at my posh new school. I laughed and put her mind at rest. I told her she would always be my girlfriend until she decided otherwise...and with that I gave her a kiss on the cheek. She was happy with that.

Titch and I would be friends for a few years yet, but that summer was the last one in which we spent a lot of time together. Titch was bound for Princess Louise Road School, or PLR as it was known locally, while I was bound for grammar school but we decided it wasn't going to spoil our friendship. Then before we knew it summer was over, and September made its entrance. My junior years were winding down and coming to a close. It was time for growing up, time for putting childish things behind us. Time for a whole new life chapter.

CHAPTER 16

BGS Here I Come

■

The first day at a new school is always a nervy experience, and for most of the new first-formers it was exactly that, but it didn't bother me one iota. This would be the fourth school I'd attended in a little over eighteen months. I'd been working towards this day ever since we'd arrived in Blyth. Mam had been coaching and helping and I'd been lucky to have a good teacher in Mr Hunter at Morpeth Road...and of course all the assistance from Charlie, Martha and Helena had been invaluable. So, I was exactly where I wanted to be. Move over William Shakespeare.

I was as smart as a carrot that first morning, wearing my red blazer with school crest on the breast pocket, 'Steadfast and Faithful' in Latin of course, 'Tenax et Fidelis,' knife edge crease grey trousers, long ones...no more short trousers for me, a white shirt and my new school tie. I had new, sensible shoes, and I even had a cap, but that was stuffed into my haversack as soon as I was out of sight of mam...what had she been thinking about?...caps were for old men.

Four of us met up that morning at the 49-bus stop. Myself, Batesy, John Charlton and George Wilkinson. We had to change at Blyth bus station and take the Newsham bus from opposite the Roxy dance hall. Plessey Road...here we come.

And of course, we had to endure our first day initiation which was mild in comparison to some of the other senior schools. We were ducked in the porch handbasins, full to the brim, head pushed in for a few seconds, then out again, job done; unless you were unlucky enough to be captured by one of the psychos, and then your head went down the lav. I was caught twice, but it was all over in a short space of time. A nervous bevy of eleven-year-olds with wet hair and wounded pride, a small price to pay for our future.

We newbies began talking amongst ourselves after the ducking ordeal and I was astounded to discover that one of the other lads was from the Bella. Surprisingly, he had been washed, didn't grunt, wasn't carrying a granny stick, and he was canny. I wondered whether he'd been involved in our recent spat, but I didn't mention it. I also met up with lads we'd lost contact with. Alan Potter, Tom McDougal, Keith McNeil...and we were pleased to be joining up again.

There were many council house kids like me and Batesy, as well as kids from the posh houses around Broadway and Ridley Park; there was someone who lived on a farm, and a few nouveau posh from Leeches, someone whose dad was a copper, and a lad whose father worked at the Wellesley School...which was a sort of borstal. And significantly, there were lads from weird and wonderful places I'd never heard of – Annitsford, Dudley, Nelson Village, New Hartley, The Sluice, Seghill, Burradon, Shankhouse, Sleekburn....Oh my goodness, all these place names and most of them I'd never been to. Some I'd never heard of and didn't know where they were. There was even someone from a place called Bog Houses...honest. I thought it must be a made-up name. It wasn't.

To be fair, I had been to Whitley Bay and a few of the other places on the coast road, and with Milly just recently to Seaton Sluice, and of course I had visited Newbiggin on the train, but apart from those destinations I realised that I was still not up to speed when it came to local geography.

Then the bell went, and all the other age groups disappeared. They knew where they were going. We didn't, and eventually we were herded together, and two teachers in gowns, assisted by several class prefects, began to line us up in our allocated forms, North, South, East, and West.

North was for the youngest of the intake with birthdays in June, July, and August, and would be my class. South for the next youngest and so on. West being for the oldest, with birthdays in September, October, and November.

Then it was off to our classrooms.

The girls in my form appeared as if by magic, having their own entrance at the other end of the school, beside the tennis courts. None of the girls seemed to have wet hair, so, I surmised that their initiation must have taken a different form. Maybe they had to do skipping with a blindfold on, or something.

Then we all took our places, seated in alphabetic order for that first day.

Our first rollcall. Allsopp, Atkinson, Bates, Brown, Brownbridge, Charlton, Curry, Godfrey, Harrison, Hurford, Lough, McCluskey, Morey, Polwarth, Preston, Walker...and a lad called Wilkin, who had managed to attach himself to the wrong class. Then the girls...it was all exciting stuff.

My life had gone full circle in the last eighteen months. I'd achieved one of my aims...now it was time to make the most of it. No longer an outsider, or newcomer...but still lacking so much local knowledge, it was time to fully commit to the Blyth experience, lose the naivety, become a local lad, and make the next years memorable.

On that first morning we found out that Tony Morey had a cousin in the third form, Wilf Rees - funny that, he had the same name as our dog...well, Charlie and Martha's dog now. Wilf was like the big gripper. He told us in no uncertain terms who the bullies were, the prefects to avoid, which teachers to look out for...and all their nicknames. He was invaluable to us first formers...and made our initiation a lot less formidable. We would come face to face in the next few weeks with 'Fat Alec', 'Squeaky Reekie', 'Jack Plank', 'Porcus', 'The Maj', 'Gipper', 'The Taff', and the 'Chalk Chucker'.

I don't know if I'd slowed down or life had speeded up but the following weeks seemed to flash past at an alarming rate. I'd earned my cycling proficiency badge and cycled to school most days, sometimes with Batesy but usually alone as he preferred the shortest route, which was through the Bella rows, but I was still nervous about crossing enemy territory, convinced that I'd be recognised, caught...then pummelled into mincemeat. So, my preferred route took me through the fields, past Bruno's resting place, then into Newsham, most days calling into Greener's shop for sweets, then off down Plessey Road and on to school.

Routine had kicked in big style as one week blended into the next with little to tell them apart. Morning assembly, then into lessons whether good or bad, mini break, then back into lessons...lunchtime, back into lessons, mini break, back into lessons, then home time with homework. Weekends were usually spent window cleaning and doing odd jobs to supplement my pocket money which had now doubled to five bob.

Milly was still a big part of my life and turned eleven that September. We still had our weekends together but there was a distance emerging between us, and it went unsaid for a long while. Our divergent paths were leading us in different directions...and it was hard.

I was spending more and more time with Batesy...and the next few years would lead me into a completely different way of life, so alien to anything I'd experienced before...and who better to describe it, hopefully...than Batesy himself, if I can ever convince him to write it.

Batesy's Tale

CHAPTER 17

Who's Charlie Hurley?

———————————————◼———————————————

I liked grammar School immensely, and I also hated it with a vengeance, and therein lies a curious tale. Some weeks I'd be enthusiastic and wholeheartedly committed and everything was a doddle, life was nice and easy, a breeze. Fast forward several weeks, then the storm-clouds would gather, my head would fog up and life in general...not just schooldays, would become a nightmare, and my life seemed like a slog through quicksand. My very existence was like a seesaw, either down on the bottom or way up in the air and there didn't appear to be a midpoint...an equilibrium which all of my peers seemed able to maintain, whilst I yo-yoed through life either hanging on to the coat-tails of an upper or mired in the clarts of a downer.

There was no such thing as bi-polar in the early sixties unless you were aware of Peary and Amundsen, there were just difficult children who didn't fit into the accepted societal template. There was of course manic depression and Spike Milligan, but no self-respecting parent would stigmatise their offspring with such a label, and misfit was eminently more acceptable. My own misfit years began during my second year at grammar School...and Sid did convince me to write a few chapters, and this is my take on those years and some of my last enjoyable memories with my old mucker.

The first time Sid met Jesus was a bit of a non-event. I apologise to anyone of the religious ilk who may believe I'm being pagan...or a non-believer, which certainly isn't the case...it's mainly because Sid didn't believe it was him. For the man he met that day looked nothing like the Jesus in our school bible. He didn't have long hair, he wasn't wearing a white dress, there wasn't a gold circle thing hovering over his head, and he was wearing pit clothes and big steel toecap boots. And to top it all, of course, he didn't sound like Jesus was supposed to...he had a strange kind of Geordie accent.

It was Saturday morning, 12th September – 1962, and I'd completed my first full week at grammar School. I was pupil James Bates of 1 North, full of self-importance, and, having just delivered a bogie-load of coal to Charlie's house because he'd ran short; I was keen to show off and let Charlie know that I knew what an Isosceles triangle was, I could speak some French and Latin...and I'd been doing important sounding lessons like physics, biology and technical drawing.

It was a lovely early autumn day with the sun shining bright, the sky blue with only an occasional wisp of cloud and a kind of peaceful hush all around. It was so quiet that I could even hear sparrows chirping...on Cowpen Estate. We were sitting together on the long bench beneath the front window...myself, Charlie, Martha and the bloke from the timber yard at Bates' pit who everyone called Jesus. I'd shovelled the bogie load of coal into Charlie's coalhouse and joined the three of them after cleaning myself up.

Then, just as I was about to begin my boasting, Martha sat up straight and pointed and we all looked in the direction she was indicating. In the distance, peddling furiously past the Co-op and heading towards us was Hawky, on the trusty steed of a bike he'd nicknamed Trigger. I'd been half expecting to see him...he'd long ago adopted Charlie as a surrogate father figure, having no dad of his own to speak of, and he'd mentioned that he'd be visiting today...... and that bike of his was flying. Apart from anything else I knew with Sid's arrival that it would be myself taking a back seat whilst he became the centre of attention.

"Sidney...it's about time," I heard Charlie call out as Hawky pulled up with a squeal of brakes, dismounted, and carried his bike into the front garden. Devonworth wasn't somewhere to leave a bike unattended, even in the early sixties. Charlie and Martha had huge smiles on their faces as he approached and they shuffled along to make a space for him beside me on the bench.

"Hi Martha, hi Charlie, hi Batesy," said Sid as he stood his bike against the fence and walked over to join us. He gave Jesus a questioning glance.

"You're looking very grown-up Sidney," said Martha as he trundled over, "what a difference a week makes... this is our friend from Bates' Pit," she gestured with her hand towards Jesus.

The man smiled, stood up slowly and with a flourish offered his hand. "Pleased to meet you in the flesh Sidney. Karol and Marta have been singing your praises," he said as Hawky shook the proffered hand... "That was quite an introduction from Marta...our friend from Bates' Pit indeed'...he smiled, "my family name is Ben Joseph ...but you can call me Jesus."

Sid grinned, because he'd eventually managed during his first Blyth year, to lose a huge amount of the naivety which had plagued him when we'd first met, and his sense of humour had morphed into a Geordie wittiness instead of the dour Scots murk that had held him back.

"Pleased to meet you too Jesus," Sid shot back at him..."my family name is Brown...but you can call me Lord Snooty."

Jesus laughed. "Touché Sidney, I like your style," then shuffled to the end of the bench to leave him additional room. "Come park your hint-end young fella," he smiled, pointing to the vacant space. Sid did as told and sat down between the Jesus fellow and myself.

Without further ado, Sid's mouth went on the rampage. He had so much to tell them...a head full of information which made a mad rush to exit his mouth all at once, desperate to unleash all of his news before forgetting any of it. Ten minutes of blab followed as he told them about new friends, new teachers, new lessons...especially the important sounding ones, Latin, French and Chemistry...the very ones that I'd been eager to tell them about, but Sid was in the ascendancy and I was feeling a little put out. He told them about the dinnertime chess club organized by Mr Reekie, his first cross-country run, about having to wear an apron for woodwork that looked like his mam's pinny, and then told them about the air-raid shelters located behind the bike racks beside the woodwork shop, where the secret smokers congregated in the dark. He told them he couldn't take his bike to school before passing a cycling proficiency test, and about school dinners... which he didn't like in the slightest. Then the embarrassing bit about Mrs Simpson, the music teacher, who'd organized an audition for the first form choir...and when it came to Sid's turn to sing solo he'd sounded like a donkey with a sore throat, and then was laughed at by the other auditionees, myself included, before being politely informed that he hadn't made the cut. After that last piece of information he dried up.

Charlie had a big smile on his face, as had Martha, but it wasn't either of them who made comment. It was Jesus. He didn't look directly at Sid as he spoke, he seemed to be peering out into the distance, in a little world of his own, but his words were clear and piercing...and they rocked Hawky, more than a little.

"Forget the choir Sidney, it wouldn't work for you. It's not written for you. Singing won't be your forte. You'll grow up with the kind of voice suited to selling the Evening Chronicle," he smiled as he said it, "but carry on with your running...you did very well to finish fifth in the cross-country...with no practice."

Sid seemed a little miffed about the singing, as true as it was. As for the running, he was having none of it. "I finished fourth actually, and it could have been third, but I tripped up on the bridge. Anyway how would you know? I didn't see you watching."

Jesus took a second before replying, "No, that's true, I was at work...but I know that Danny McCluskey was first, Norman Hills second, your friend Batesy here was third...and young Allsopp fourth, if I'm not mistaken." There was silence for a few seconds, and Sid didn't know what to say. That statement really seemed to have startled him because it was spot on. Soppy had gone past him on the bridge when he'd fallen, but he must have forgotten, and apart from that...I could see the confusion in Sid's eyes...the question in his head...how did this bloke know?...How on earth? Unless of course he was a pal of our games teacher, Pete Butters. Then a look in my direction, he must have been wondering if I'd unintentionally blurted out the cross-country information. I hadn't. Sid fell silent, it was my turn to shine.

The trouble was, I had nothing left to shine with. Hawky took all the same lessons as me and he'd covered every blade of grass. Anything from me now would just be repetition. So, I went into clever-dick mode. But not before Charlie chirped up, attempting to involve me.

"What about you Jim?...You've been quiet. What interesting things have you been up to at school?'

I shrugged, "Nowt really Charlie, you know? We're in the same class, so just the same boring things that Hawky's been telling you about," I replied with a hint of petulance. "To be honest I'm much more interested in Jesus telling us some things that are going to happen...not stuff that's already happened...'cos anyone could know those things."

I got the distinct impression that Martha and Charlie were unhappy with my childish response, but Jesus himself turned to face me and looked me directly in the eye and it was scary. I was transfixed by his gaze...I felt like a butterfly must have felt...pinned to a display board, and time seemed to be suspended, as if I were inside a bubble. I had the weirdest ever feeling that someone was rummaging in my brain, opening drawers and filing cabinets...and the feeling lasted for many seconds. Then Jesus looked away.

"What do you want to know James?"

"Some things that haven't happened yet."

"How many?"

"Three," I replied, and I don't know why I picked that number. It actually felt as if there was a voice in my head, and the voice had picked three.

There was a distinct silence from the three adults and I felt Sid give me a dig in the side with his elbow. For whatever reason, the atmosphere on the bench had become uncomfortable and Martha stood up without comment, not even glancing in our direction, and headed into the house.

Then the Jesus fellow spoke, clearly and calmly. "First James, in October you will hear the opening sounds from some young insects, and it will change the direction of popular music forever." He paused for effect. "Secondly... towards the end of this month the heavyweight boxing champion will lose his crown by a knockout...in the first round." Then he turned back towards me and we locked eyes... "And finally, number three...your father may benefit from this information James...or maybe not, but a horse called Heathersett will win the St Leger this afternoon." Then very abruptly he said, "That is your three...and now I must be going...make sure you use the information wisely... goodbye".

And with that he was gone. He just left, without further comment. No more goodbyes or 'see you soon'...no 'thanks for the cuppa, Charlie,' or other small talk. The man just stood up and walked away, out through the open garden gate...and I was never to see him again.

Charlie stood up too, falteringly, shoulders hunched, then walked away a few paces before turning back and staring at us two kids. "You don't know what you've done," he muttered before lowering his gaze, turning, and walking into the house, closing the door behind him.

Twenty minutes later Sid and I were lying on the grass beside the rugby posts on Cowpen fields, with Sid's bike making up a threesome. Not much had been said, as we were both more than a tad surprised at the Charlie reaction. Something wasn't right about the whole situation. It wasn't as if I'd been really rude or obnoxious; I'd just asked a valid question, or so I reckoned.

"So," began Sid, "Do you reckon he was just being an idiot, that bloke? Or do you reckon he's got something wrong with his head and that's why Charlie's annoyed, 'cos you made him look daft?"

"Dunno," was my only response. Sid hadn't felt what I'd felt...when the Jesus bloke was browsing inside my brainbox.

"He can't be the proper Jesus...can he?" asked Sid.

"Dunno," again.

"Yeh...but he can't be, can he? I mean, he works at the pit. Proper Jesus would come back as a king or a prince wouldn't he? He wouldn't mess around at Bates' pit timberyard."

I thought about that for a moment. "Why not?...why wouldn't he come back at the pit, I mean. He wasn't a king or a prince when he was alive the first time was he? He used to go fishing and things like that...he did a bit of woodwork and that magic stuff an' all."

"Come on man, Jim, the pit? That can't be right. He would at least come back as a doctor or army colonel...or be a vicar or somethin'. Nah, he's just one of Charlie's friends and he guesses at stuff to look important. Anybody can do loads of guesses and if a couple of them are right then everybody forgets the wrong ones...like that Mother Shipton witch thingy...or that foreign bloke, Noseydormouse or somethin."

"Ehhh, what are you on about Sid?"

"That foreign bloke Noster Dum thingy, who used to write out what was going to happen in the future, in Quarter trains or summat. Mam told me about him, and said his predictions were written so vague that you could make them true or false both at the same time."

A silly thought flashed into my head. "D'yer fancy doing a bet on the horses? The one that Jesus said was going to win the big race today?"

"Ehhh...what you on about, Jim? We're only eleven man...there's no way they'll let us have a bet. Unless your dad would do it."

"Nah...not him, me mam would go daft if she found out, and me dad would get an earful. Anyway, dad wouldn't be betting on winners. He'll be sitting at home now picking four horses for his Yankee...and he'll be looking for the ones with three legs...or the ones with a twenty stone jockey. I don't think dad likes to win...if there was a one-horse race he'd back the loser."

"Who then?'

"Can't tell you Sid...honestly, but do you trust me?"

"Aye...course I do."

"Okay Sid, how much dosh have you got?"

"Only five bob on me...but I've got some more in the house."

"Five bob's good, same as me...ten bob then on that horse, Heathersett. What do you reckon?"

"I don't know Jim...what are we doin' it for?" Sid was treading water.

"'Cos we win either way. If it wins the race we get loads of dosh and you can come to one of the Sunderland matches with me...without worrying about not having enough for bus fare and pies and Bovril and stuff."

"Aye...but what if it loses...that's not winning is it?"

"'Course it is if you think about it. Charlie won't be annoyed with us anymore 'cos we'll have proved that his friend was just a big impostor...a fake. Then we won't be woggly about it either because I'm just not sure about the Jesus stuff. What about you?"

"Not really...I mean, well I don't think it can be proper Jesus, but I'm a bit worried about not believin', 'cos if it is him and we don't believe it then some really bad things could happen to us...couldn't they?"

"Aye Sid, I suppose. So are you in or out?"

"I'm in."

257

"Good...give us your five bob." I had a plan.

Seven o'clock that evening, and we're sitting in Sid's bedroom, myself, Sid and Milly with our winnings on the bed in front of us. Two pounds, two shillings and sixpence each. Betting tax had been deducted and my secret bookie had kept a little sweetener for himself. The Jesus horse had won as predicted, and not only that it had won at a big price.

Milly wasn't happy though...with me mainly, because I could tell that she thought I was leading Sid astray.

"You know what will happen If Sid's mam finds out? She'll go spare. You shouldn't be making Sid do betting and stuff Jim Bates...not after what happened with his proper dad."

She had a point, but there again it wasn't my fault... blame Jesus.

"It wasn't Batesy's idea Milly it was mine," said Sid, probably with fingers crossed. "I'll tell you all about it later, and about this man that we met who thinks he's Jesus."

"Ehhh?"

"Later Milly."

"Jesus?"

"It's a long story, I'll tell you all about it later."

Milly stood up and looked daggers at us both. "Don't even bother...it'll be another one of your daft ideas...you've changed Sidney Brown...and not for the better. It's like you're a different person now." And with that she turned and flounced out, full of hell.

Sid looked at me and shrugged. I half smiled and shrugged back. Then we put the Milly situation to the back of our minds and started making plans for our Sunderland match.

It would be another five weeks before we made it to the
match. Other things got in the way, like playing football for
the school team, Sid's mam setting up her business, a day out
at Ashington baths...Saturdays seemed full up for a little while.

There was also a day when Sid and I were completely
shocked.

Sid was around at my house one Saturday with another
new friend, Davey Preston, and my dad wasn't at work. We
were sitting on the coalhouse floor, chatting away, drinking
strong tea and chewing on Spanish root when dad opened
the door and joined us. That was a bit of a surprise, 'cos
dad usually just floated about in the background, sometimes
there, but never involved. But to be fair on that particular
day he began making a huge effort to do the bonding with
son and friends thing, which definitely wasn't his forte.

"There's some bread and jam in the kitchen lads, yer
don't need to be eating twigs," he joked, knowing full well
what Spanish root was, "Or I could go and sweep up some
leaves for yer".

Davey was new on the scene and didn't realise that dad
was attempting to be funny... "It's not proper twigs Mr Bates;
it's like liquorice in a root, and we got it from the shop...not
off a tree or anything."

Dad grinned at him, "Aye lad I know...I used to chew it
myself".

Then he went into full dad mode. He began asking all
the standard dad questions, about school, and lasses, friends
and fights, football and cricket...and the three of us listened
diligently, answering when required. Then he began giving
us the benefit of his sporting knowledge, telling us about

Stanley Matthews, Jackie Milburn, the Clown Prince - Len Shackleton...and Pele...the latest, greatest footballer in the world. Sid asked if Pele played for Sunderland, and dad looked at me, rolled his eyes and grinned. I did the eye rolling and grinning thing back at him...and Sid was none the wiser. Football wasn't his specialist subject.

Then came the crunch, the spooky thing...dad began telling us about Floyd Patterson, the heavyweight boxing champion of the world...who just last week had been knocked out in the first round by someone called Sonny Liston, and he was no longer the champion. I'm convinced neither Sid nor myself heard any more of my dad's conversation because we were flabbergasted. A miracle perhaps?...'cos another one of the Jesus predictions had come true. We didn't speak about it then; we said what had to be said with our wide-eyed stare at each other. It would be a long time before we got around to mulling it over.

Then came the day of the match. We were on our way to see Sunderland play Walsall. The bus we'd boarded at Blyth bus station was sparsely populated, maybe a dozen folk with red and white scarves dotted around inside an old thirty-six-seater which had seen better days. The Tyne tunnel in 1962 was still a pipe-dream so it was a boring old journey we were on, following the number six bus route to Newcastle, and stopping twice en-route to pick up supporters from High Pit and Burradon. Then on through the 'toon' and Gateshead before heading for the promised land.

Sid seemed more interested in the journey and kept asking about the different places we were passing. He'd only heard tales about Newcastle, and in his short Geordie existence he hadn't visited the city...not even once. He was fascinated and soaking up the whole experience as we crossed the Tyne Bridge and headed into Gateshead.

"Do people go swimming in the river, Jim?" he asked.

I had the gold standard answer to that question. "You can't swim in the Tyne Sid...you can only go through the motions." I laughed at my own response, even though I wasn't sure why it was funny, but I'd heard my dad say that when he'd been talking to one of his friends....and they'd both laughed, so it must have been hilarious...right?

Having left Gateshead it was ten minutes or so later that the bus began making a strange howl. Metal screeching against metal noises. Everyone in the bus sat up straight... and we noticed a big cloud of smoke coming out from under the engine cover at the front.

"Bugger," cursed the driver as he wrestled the bus onto the kerb and brought it to a shuddering halt. "Everybody off, quickly...quickly, mek sharp, just in case it gans on fire."

There was a rush to get off because there was only one exit, and we had to alight from the door at the front of the bus, and that was mighty close to the billowing cloud.

Disembarking safely and putting a decent distance between us and the smoking coach, we found that we were on the outskirts of somewhere called East Boldon and we all milled about at the side of the road, unsure as to what to do next. There were no mobile phones in those days and this old bus didn't have any communication system.

"That's it folks...I divvent knaa what to tell yer, this owld bugger isn't gannin any further," said the driver, kicking at the rear tyre. "Aahll hev ter gan and find a phone box... divvent think yer'll mek it ter the game, like."

"Can't we get a normal bus from here," piped up Sid to the driver.

"Divvent knaa son..... mevvys. Hev a look for the nearest bus stop...or ask somebody. Sorry aboot the game kid but aah've got ter stay wi the bus when aah've med me phone call. Those of yer what wants ter wait will get a lift yem and yer money back...I think, when they get a relief oot...but its gan ter be a while mind."

Sid wasn't impressed, down in the dumps. "That's another waste of money Jim...just like last bonfire night...a waste of money."

Sid was getting on my wick a bit and I was abrupt. "Shurrup man Sid, yer wouldn't even have had any money to waste if it wasn't for me and Jesus and the St Ledger...bliddy hell man, you're always moanin'...ner-ner-ner...poor me. It's happened man...it's naebody's fault wor bus has conked oot. Stop gannin on like a big bairn and find a proper bus stop; we've got plenty time afore kick-off."

Sid still had his pet lip on but ten minutes later we'd left the crowd around the broken bus and we'd found a bus stop.

"How do we know where it's goin" ...when it comes...if it comes?" Sid was still in depression mode.

"Ermmm...perhaps we could ask the driver...what do you think? Maybe he'll know where he's goin...if we're lucky."

Sid accepted the sarcasm and shut up.

We thought that buses around here might be infrequent, and we were both desperate to see the match...myself because I thought we might score a hatful today, with Cloughie playing, and Sid because he didn't want any more wasted money, so we decided to try and hitch-hike. Sid was a little hesitant at first because his mam had warned him about getting into cars with strangers, but I talked him round and said his mam would never find out. He agreed eventually.

So, I stuck my thumb out like I'd seen them do in a couple of films, and the few cars that came just sailed past...one of them even tooted...clever sod. The clock was ticking...four cars, and no luck. Then a car did pull up, a battered old estate, and it was to be one of the highlights of my life. It came to a halt perhaps twenty yards past the bus stop and the horn sounded our acceptance music. "Howay Sid, be quick," I shouted as I trotted up to the car. Sid followed on behind, lagging somewhat, still a little hesitant about strangers and motors.

I could see there were three men in the car as I approached, and the back window of the estate was basically blocked, with holdalls, footballs, kit bags and a whole bunch of other stuff. It couldn't have been remotely legal.

The passenger window wound down and a voice shouted, "You lads from the broken-down bus back there?"

"Aye mister," I replied as I turned back to hurry Sid up.

"Want a lift to Roker?" he'd seen my scarf.

Sid caught up and joined me as I turned around to reply, "Thanks very mu...u...ch"....then I stopped...stunned. The face of the bloke doing the talking from the passenger seat belonged to Charlie Hurley. My mouth dropped open...with such force that my bottom jaw almost smashed my kneecap. One of my heroes...probably the greatest of my heroes....and to add sauce to the pudding I looked at the rear seats...and who should be sitting in the back but Len Ashurst.

"Come on then lads jump in...use the other side door... the one on this side's a bit stiff. Hurry up lads we're in a bit of a rush."

I walked around to the rear door on the road side of the car...and felt Sid tugging at my arm, "Jim, are you sure it's safe...we can just..."

I cut him dead, "It's okay Sid, I know who they are man; it's alright."

We opened the back door and I climbed in to sit next to Len Ashurst and Sid shuffled in beside me. I hadn't a clue who was doing the driving, until he turned around and I realised it was Cec Irwin...I could have recognised any of the first team without a shadow of a doubt.

As the car pulled away Charlie turned around in the front passenger seat to look at us. "What happened with the bus?"

"Just loads of smoke coming out of the front, and crunching noises," Sid answered. I couldn't speak. I was in a state of shock. I was sitting in a car with King Charlie Hurley and he was talking to us like a regular human being...it was surreal. Sid hadn't a clue who he was talking with.

"Where you from?" Charlie asked.

"Kirkcaldy," replied Sid.

"Bloody hell...that's a long way to come for the game." Charlie was impressed.

"No...no, I didn't mean that. I come from Kirkcaldy originally is what I thought you meant. No, we've come from Blyth...I live there now."

Charlie smiled at Sid's misunderstanding. "So how are you lads getting back to Blyth?"

"Dunno," said Sid. "We'll probably have to walk, or hitch or something."

"Wait out front after the match...give Cec half an hour... he'll give you a lift back...won't you Cec?"

"Aye, nae problem...drop you off at Bebside. I live in Ellington."

"Thanks mister, that's really good of you," said Sid, still doing the talking.

"What's your names?" asked Len Ashurst.

"I'm Sid and this is my best pal, Jim."

"So who's your favourite player?" asked Charlie, butting in and looking directly at Sid. That was quite funny, because it was just like he was waiting for his name to pop up. It didn't.

"Don't really know," said Sid "I don't really like football that much...I like running and tennis the best, and me and my brother used to say we liked Rangers...but we didn't really. It's just that when you live in Scotland you have to either support Rangers or Celtic...and I don't like green very much...blue's much better. Anyway I just came with Jim today 'cos he's been going on about the greatest team in the world...and he just won me some money off the horses, so I had to come."

Charlie looked disappointed and Sid must have noticed, he carried on, "I suppose I like the same ones as Batesy... sorry...I mean Jim. The goalie bloke that he likes...errrmm with the same name as that famous field marshal...ooohh aye, Montgomery, and the other bloke he likes, 'cos he says he scores a goal every game...Barry Clough."

"It's Brian Clough" ...Charlie wasn't impressed..."What do you think about Charlie Hurley?"

Sid looked as if he was having a think...he wasn't, he didn't have a clue about football.

"Dunno, who's Charlie Hurley?"

I dropped my eyes to the floor....I could have crawled into a hole and died. Cec Irwin managed a snigger though.

Sunderland won that day, five-nowt. We watched it from the right of the goal at the Roker end. The penny dropped with Sid when he saw two of the men from the car in their red and white strip passing the ball to each other in the warm up...right in front of us.

"Jim," he pointed, "that's them blokes".

"Charlie Hurley and Len Ashurst...my heroes," I replied.

Sid seemed to shrink when the realisation kicked in. He was embarrassed.

I had a fantastic day....Sid, not so much. He wasn't into football in the same way as me. We joined a group of kids behind the goal and we cheered and waved scarves every time Sunderland scored. Sid joined in reluctantly, pretending enthusiasm, but it didn't sit right somehow. But he did come in handy when it came to pie and Bovril time, happily doing all the fetching and carrying. The bunch of lads we'd attached ourselves to went through their repertoire of songs.

"Brian Clough superstar...how many goals have you scored so far."

"If you support Newcastle snog my bot."

"Noel, Noel.... No-oh-ell, Noel...... Hurley is ki-ing of Fu-u-ulwell".

"Who's the greatest centre-half in all the world today...Charlie Hurley is his name...glory, glory hallelujah." Daft but good.

Then our day came to a most acceptable close. The lift from Cec Irwin and his pal materialised as promised although surprising. Cec had been very quiet on the way to the match, but on the return journey with no Charlie Hurley or Len Ashurst in the car he talked non-stop, and what a nice bloke he turned out to be. He hadn't played today because he was carrying an injury and Nelson had played in his place, but he told us he should be back for the next match. Not only that, he handed me a match programme when we were being dropped off.

"A little present for you son...enjoy." And with that he was gone.

It wasn't until I got home that I had a closer look at the programme...and it had the autographs of every one of that day's team...even Brian Clough. I was in heaven.

That was the one and only game that Sid and I attended together. I realised he wasn't a football kid and I gave him a half apology for having dragged him to a match. I promised that the next big thing we did together would be Sid's choice and whatever it turned out to be I wouldn't complain. That cheered Sid up no end, but it would turn out to be a promise that I'd regret.

CHAPTER 18

Runaway

—■—

That school year was bearable. Report time came around and I'd done okay. Not as well as Sid but I was quietly happy with my efforts. Top for history and geography, third for English literature...but not so great for English language, I couldn't understand box analysis. Okay, too, for Latin, French and General Science, poor for maths and terrible for Art and Woodwork. I was colour blind and sarcasm from a teacher because you've drawn a man with green hair does not instil you with a love for art. In woodwork we'd been making a pencil box...and mine was rubbish; I was just ham-fisted when it came to chisels and planes and things. Anyway I didn't see the point of carrying a wooden box around because I kept my pencils in my breast pocket. Games and P.E. were good up to a point. I loved football, cross country and athletics, but I hated gym. Malcolm Gaskin was brilliant at that whilst I needed a safety helmet and climbing ropes to get over the pommel horse. Also, I couldn't stand cricket... because that's all you seemed to do...stand about, waiting for something to come in your direction.

The first form Christmas party had been and gone and I'd spent the evening dancing with Marjorie Luke. Sid danced with loads of lasses but told Milly that he hadn't bothered and just messed about with the lads...and I backed him up 'cos I knew how jealous Milly was.

Christmas had been okay too. There was no party at Sid's house because they were packing up for their move to Salisbury Street, so Sid and his mam and Linda were at Olive's house for Christmas day, along with Charlie, Martha and Wilf, and Sid came to ours on Boxing Day for his tea, and it was fine.

The catalyst for our next adventure materialized because of an overheard conversation. It came about because of adults being secretive. And Sid was distressed about the whole thing.

Our new term had begun, our second year of grammar school...and we'd been informed that this was our final year in this building. Next summer we'd be moving to our new, purpose-built school in Cowpen, just across the field from Bebside school and nudged up next to the Leeches estate. Some folks were excited at the prospect, but for Sid and myself it was disappointing...a little upsetting. We'd been so proud to be attending a school with ivy-clad walls... like the posh schools you see on the telly or like some of those colleges in Oxford or Cambridge.

This led indirectly to the day that we went on the lam or were supposed to. The funny thing about plans is that they never go to plan. Sid had been unimpressed with our new school news and had been about to tell his mam all about it when he overheard a conversation in the kitchen. He wasn't one for sneakiness but he kept quiet and listened. Although they were talking in hushed voices he heard his mam telling Olive that his dad had been badly injured in an accident at the pit, a life-threatening injury...and was in a hospital in Kirkcaldy. Sid was more upset that his mam hadn't seen fit to tell him the news, rather than being upset about his dad's injuries.

So, it was on a Tuesday lunch time. Neither of us liked school dinners and we brought packed lunches....way before packed lunches became the norm. We would sit out on the field if the weather was nice and swap sandwiches and gabble away about everything and nothing while our schoolmates were locked away in an old dining hall, emerging after half an hour, smelling of mashed potato and cabbage.

"Fancy runnin' away?" asked Sid, in a matter-of-fact manner. "Up ter Scotland for a bit?" He just came out with it as he unzipped a banana.

I had to have a little chuckle at that. Sid often came out with a corker of a question or a daft idea. "What're you on about Sid?...runnin' away from home, honestly...from what?"

"It's not from somethin' man, it's to somethin" ....'cos me dad's in hospital and he might be dying for all I know."

"But you don't even like your dad, Sid. What do you want to run away to Scotland for...if you can't stand the bloke."

"See...see...Jim you just make promises and then break them. You said I could have the next pick of a big thing to do...and goin' ter Scotland's me pick. Kirkcaldy's where I used to live man."

Sometimes Sid was just a difficult lad to reason with, when he got something in his head it tended to stick, and stick like glue, so I ventured, "Sid, man, you're talkin' really daft...me mam won't let me bunk off school and go ter Scotland with you."

"Aahh know that man...my mam wouldn't let me go either. She doesn't even know that I've heard about me dad. So I'll need to run away...not forever or nowt, but just for a bit...a few days, or a week or summat."

It struck me at that moment that he was serious, "Sid, man...I've never heard you say one good thing about your dad."

"So what Jim?...That's easy for you 'cos you've got a dad, and a good one, but just 'cos my dad isn't as good as yours... he's still my dad, and I can't pretend he isn't just 'cos he's a bad'un...can I?...Anyway forget it I'll go by myself... I knew you wouldn't anyway."

"When do you want to go, like?"

"The morra."

"The morra? Bliddy hell man, Sid, that's ower sharp... we'd need to do plans and stuff and look at maps... and make disguises like moustaches and hats and loads of other things...and we'll need money for food and that. How much money have yer got?"

"Five bob."

"Ehhh, five bob? that's not enough man, Sid...that's not even enough to run away to Ashington...yer'll need more than that...loads more, yer'll need to save up...or nick some money from somewhere."

Sid wasn't impressed, he just shrugged and gave me a snidey look. I had no option and I knew it. Your word is your word...but it was with great reluctance that I said, "Okay Sid, fair do's, a promise is a promise...so I'm in. The morra it is."

I didn't sleep at all that night. I had too much rubbish floating around in my head... making plans, thinking out routes, preparing excuses and apologies. We would need food...and money, and a good cover story for any driver who gave us a lift. I left the house the following morning with a big black cloud looming over my head. I had a quid and a half in ten-bob notes, and another quid or so in silver. One of the ten-bob notes had been nicked from my mam's purse to top up Sid's stash, and in my haversack were two filched tins of beans, a tin of peas, a tin opener...and a toilet roll. I had an old pen-knife nestling in my pocket...just in case we got into bother...'cos I'd heard about the Glasgow gangs, and I'd also included my school atlas for directions. I even had a plastic compass that had come as a free gift with Sugar Puffs.

I'd told mam that we were doing a school biology trip to Seaton Sluice; we were going to be down on the beach, making notes about rock-pools and seaweed, so we didn't need to wear uniforms. She believed it and even gave me a half-crown. That compounded my guilt, and I remember standing with fingers, toes and eyes crossed, hoping she wouldn't look in the other bit of her purse and notice the missing ten-bob. She didn't.

So that morning I turned up at our meeting place, the bus stop at North Farm. We needed to head north, so our first destination would be Morpeth, and I was feeling nervous, but a touch excited...we were heading off for an adventure, not of my doing, but I had butterflies nevertheless. I was wearing jeans, with a windcheater jacket over a thick jumper, and my bulging haversack slung over my back.

Five minutes later, a dormobile drew up at the bus-stop. Olive was the driver, and after a few seconds Sid alighted from the passenger seat...and he was wearing his school uniform. He couldn't bring himself to look at me, completely embarrassed and conscience-stricken.

"Sorry Batesy," he said, with his eyes down on the pavement.

I was stunned. I wasn't thick, I recognised what was coming and what it would mean for me. He wasn't riding about with Olive because he was up for our running away adventure. He'd probably blabbed to his mam and now the ratbag was about to throw me under the bus.

"Sid man...what...?" I couldn't say any more, I had a brain-freeze.

He was crying. Not the squawky out-loud crying, more of a whimper, but the tears were real, and copious. "Et tu Brute" would have been a perfect response to the situation but I didn't have the words. I was facing the depressing realisation that Sid had fired me up and then doused the flames with a bucket of cold water.

"It's not my fault Batesy...it's me mam; she's takin' us to see me dad at the week-end...aahh didn't know."

Dismay had kicked in big-time. My stomach was churning and felt as if it was down around my knees. I was hopping mad, "Shut ya stinkin' gob ye skinny fat pig...if Olive wasn't watchin' I'd smash yer ugly face in."

Then Olive got out of the dormobile and came to stand beside Sid. She'd heard the shout and sensed the tension.

She was doing the bodyguard thing. "Do you want a lift to school, Jim, there's still plenty of time...we know about... well, what's supposed to be happening." Sid kept his gaze on the floor.

That day was to be the beginning of my misfit years...I just didn't realise it at the time.

In response to Olive's question I looked her full in the face and held my arms out to my sides. It was Olive who looked away, knowing the truth of the situation. Inside I was seething. "Aye Olive...I'm dressed for school, aren't I?" I was being really obnoxious, but I didn't care. "You're as stupid as that little worm...and if he ever talks to me again he'll get a bliddy wedging...you stinkin' rat Sid....squeak back into your sewer. Aahh even nicked ten bob out of me mam's purse to give to you so you would have some proper dosh." And with that I turned and walked away, fists clenched. Twenty paces on, and behind me I could hear Sid blubbing and van doors slamming. Now I had a problem to face, and this one wasn't my fault.

Although that day was the beginning of my misfit era it was also one of the few times during the following five years that I made a balanced, correct decision, and doing so pulled me out of a situation that could have caused me a whole world of pain. My head, understandably, was all over the place after Sid's stab in the back. I didn't know what to do, or where to go. Every possibility seemed to be fraught with danger and disappointment. Every avenue I explored ended up with me getting a good hiding, or expelled from school, starving to death in an abandoned building...or captured by the school board man. My head was completely scrambled after the first half hour of my storming off in a hissy fit and my addled brain was functioning like a huge marshmallow. I was twelve years old and frightened.

That was the first day I'd ever bought cigarettes and matches. I wasn't a smoker, although I'd had a couple of puffs now and again to make myself fit in with a few of the popular lads. But today was different. I was a young lad with a huge problem and buying five woodbines from Carlo's shop instantly made me feel older, and more mature. I coughed and spluttered my way through the first woodbine, wandering aimlessly around the estate, keeping away from the main roads where the school board man often lurked. I was feeling so desolate and found myself on the verge of tears several times. There was nothing I could think of that would end in an acceptable outcome. What to do?

It must have been two hours or more before I landed up at Charlie's front door. It wasn't part of a plan...I just found myself there. I stood at Charlie's front door for a good minute, frightened to knock. Then the door opened as if by magic and Charlie loomed in front of me.

"Come in Jim.... we've been expecting you."

"What...?" I asked as I followed him through to the sitting room.

Martha gave me a smile from the armchair as I entered. The room was full of cardboard boxes and carrier bags. She noticed my stare.

"We're moving out on Friday Jim...to our new house in Sussex."

"Ohh, that's a shame," was all I could manage.

She continued, "Marjorie and Olive are out in the van looking for you, and your mam is walking around the estate, too. Marjorie has told us the whole story...and how it's all Sid's fault...not yours."

My head dropped. Now I was in for it.

"I'll make a cup of tea," said Martha as she stood up shakily and wandered off into the kitchen to brew up.

I was still lost...I needed help...some guidance, "Charlie man, me mam's gannin ter kill us. I nicked ten bob out of her purse to give to Sid...cos he hardly had any money to run away with...what am I gonna do?"

Charlie put his hand on my shoulder. "I think you'll find that you didn't nick ten bob from your mam Jim, she found the missing money sticking out from under the clock on the sideboard."

"Ehhh...but..."

"Olive and Marjorie went around to your house to explain the whole situation to your mam...and she miraculously found the missing ten bob just after they left," Charlie raised his eyebrows and smiled. "It seems she must have forgotten that she'd put it there for the insurance man."

"So... what now?" I said, "I did nick ten bob Charlie. Even if Sid's mam sneaked it back under the clock."

"No Jim...you didn't. It never happened."

"But that's just lying."

"Aye, it is...but...and you'll have heard this before. Sometimes a lie is the best way to save someone from hurt. It's not good...and it's not right, but it saves your mam from being disappointed, and it saves you from being branded a thief. At the minute your mam is just worried 'cos you're missing...and she knows you've been hung out to dry by your friend. As far as I know you're not in any trouble...well, only a little." Charlie dug me in the shoulder.

"So?"

"So, go home Jim...and when your mam asks about your escapade, apologise and tell her the truth, about everything that happened...except for that one thing. Then get on with your life and don't do anything so stupid ever again...even if you feel obliged... okay? And don't be too hard on Sid... he's not as streetwise as you and the other lads...don't do the revenge thing...just give each other some space for a while... until things calm down."

"Okay Charlie, thank you."

Charlie shook his head, "Don't thank me, thank Marjorie...Oh and by the way, you owe her ten bob," Charlie allowed himself a chuckle. Then Martha came through from the kitchen with mugs of tea on a tray. The sense of relief I was feeling at that moment was enormous. I left their house that day feeling a thousand times better than when I'd arrived, but on the downside...I was never to see them together again.

I was back at school the next day with a note for the teacher saying I'd had an upset stomach. No-one was any the wiser and life and school just motored along as normal. It would be another two years before I ran away from home for real and the best part of a year before I spoke to Sid again, but those events are for a future telling, a tale to cover a period when life for both of us became difficult and cloudy. Funnily enough I never did return the ten bob to Marjorie.

For Fans of Mining Stories

Two books from another North-East author which vividly recapture the lives, the blood, sweat, tears and humour of ex coal-miners. In 'Tales From the Deep' - chapters include "The Corpse on the Pit Bus" - "The Ghost of Bobby Baxter" - "The Delinquent Pit Pony" - "A Village Consumed by Disaster" - "Pit Canteen capers" - "A Picket's Life" - "The Pit Brow Girls" and many more. The second book (Presence in the Pit) in which miners recall eerie tales of events they just couldn't explain, with some even refusing to return to the pit because they were so unnerved. Both books are available from source (Brian Long) on bwlong53@yahoo. com or alternatively both books, Tales From the Deep and Presence in the Pit are available on eBay.

PRESENCE

Compiled By
Brian Long

IN THE PIT

Stories from miners that DIDN'T feel ALONE

TALES FROM THE DEEP

COAL MINING MEMORIES, RECOLLECTIONS & STORIES
FROM THE LAST OF THE MINERS

COMPILED BY
BRIAN LONG

Printed in Great Britain
by Amazon